Is Christ Divided?

Is Christ Divided?

Approaching Our Conflicts In Christ

Richard C. Carroll

© 2008 by Richard C. Carroll. All rights reserved.

WinePress Publishing (PO Box 428, Enumclaw, WA 98022) functions only as book publisher. As such, the ultimate design, content, editorial accuracy, and views expressed or implied in this work are those of the author.

No part of this publication may be reproduced, stored in a retrieval system, or transmitted in any way by any means—electronic, mechanical, photocopy, recording, or otherwise—without the prior permission of the copyright holder, except as provided by USA copyright law.

Unless otherwise noted, all Scriptures are taken from the *Holy Bible, New International Version*®, *NIV*®. Copyright © 1973, 1978, 1984 by the International Bible Society. Used by permission of Zondervan. All rights reserved.

ISBN 13: 978-1-57921-924-6
ISBN 10: 1-57921-924-1
Library of Congress Catalog Card Number: 2007932944

To my wife Launda,
faithful follower of Jesus and love of my life.

CONTENTS

Acknowledgments

I want to take this opportunity to thank those who have played instrumental roles in the creation and development of this book. Let me begin by thanking my Savior and Lord, Jesus Christ. I thank Him for allowing me the blessing of sharing in His fellowship with our Heavenly Father and including me in His living body, the Church. It is my hope this book will bring glory to Him.

Beyond the precious gift of eternal life in Him, the Lord also gave me my wife, Launda. Those who know her also know she is more than my "better half." She would have to qualify as my "better three-quarters," or more. Her unwavering faith in the Lord, and her constant encouragement led me to take the plunge to fulfill the lifelong dream of becoming an author. The lessons shared in this book were learned side by side in life and ministry, and I will be forever grateful to the Lord for having experienced all of this with her.

I also want to thank our twelve children and their spouses: Danielle, Alyson (and her husband, Jeff), Aaron (and his wife, Linde), Aricka (and her husband, Casey), Adam, Andrew,

Jonathon (and his fiancé, Rachelle), David (and his fiancé, Angela), Micah, Angela, Kaylhee, and Ben, and our nine grandchildren: Hannah, Kyle, Ethan, Alexis, Nicolas, Annelise, Christian, Sofia, Landon, and Alexandra for their continued love and support. You are by far our greatest achievement and joy in this life.

I also owe so much to my parents, Robert and Beryl Carroll, and Launda's parents, Carl and Donna Gustafson. My parents offered me a wonderful life filled with love, and they inspired my love for reading and learning. Launda's parents introduced me to a personal relationship with Jesus Christ. And Carl went on to encourage my passion for the Church.

Our Lake Shore Community Church family is our extended family, to which I owe so much. They truly are brothers and sisters in every meaning of the word. In this very special local expression of the living body of Jesus Christ, the Lord revealed the content of this book over the last twenty-seven years. They have supported this project, as well as Peace Connections Ministries, with unwavering commitment. I am truly blessed to be included among them. I must also thank Dan Jensen and Tom Bulkley, who have volunteered numerous hours working side by side with me as we have ministered to churches struggling with unresolved conflict.

There is also a group from the Lake Shore Community family—Sharell Martin, Launda Carroll, Scott and Debbie Grove, and John Milem—who volunteered to go the second mile and more in this project. They met each Wednesday night for weeks to read and re-read each chapter, offering corrections to grammar, as well as making sense of my rambling thoughts. Amazingly, they all have expressed a desire to do it again.

Special thanks to the many people who have played important roles in the creation and development of Peace Connections Ministries, as well as my development as a Christian mediator. Greg Abel, of Sound Options Group in Bainbridge Island,

Washington, was the facilitator of the first training I received on my journey to become a mediator. He is a dear brother in the Lord, mentor, and good friend. Many of the materials in our trainings, as well as in this book, came from him. Through Greg, I met another brother in the Lord, good friend and fellow mediator, Conrad Green of the Western Center for Conflict Resolution in Poulsbo, Washington. I have been blessed by Conrad's wisdom and insights on numerous occasions.

It was Conrad who introduced me to the wonderful folks at Peacemaker Ministries, Inc., of Billings, Montana. Special thanks go to Ken Sande, Peacemaker Ministries founder and President, and to Dave Edling, whose wonderful spirit and biblical understanding greatly enriched the training I received from Peacemakers, and to Rev. Bruce Zagel, who so graciously guided me through Peacemakers' two-year process to become a certified Christian mediator.

Another group who played a major role in my initial training as a mediator is the staff at Community Mediation Services (CMS), Vancouver, Washington. What a great staff, providing neighborhood and small-claims-court mediation services to the citizens of Clark County, as well as the city of Vancouver. Special thanks to Nancy Pionk, director of CMS, for her professional leadership; and a very special thank you to lead trainer Debbie Nelson, one of the most *peace-full* people I know, a wonderful teacher, and a good friend.

Of course, a project like this is not possible without the diligent oversight of editors and publishers. I am blessed to have a good friend who is also an excellent editor. I'm not sure how, but Jerry Gramckow and I have known for over a decade that we were eventually going to work together on a book. Fortunately for readers, there are talented people like Jerry, who can take my feeble thoughts and transform them into readable sentences and paragraphs. I also want to thank the staff at WinePress Publishing Group, who helped bring this message to printed form. Thank you all, very much.

Introduction

This book is to the Church, about the Church, and for the Church. While the principles shared here can and should be applied in every relationship, my primary focus is on brothers and sisters in Christ, and our relationships in the living body of Christ.

What is the first word that comes to your mind when you think of conflict?

I ask that question when beginning the seminar titled, "Approaching Our Conflicts in Christ." I write the word "CONFLICT" in the center of a flip chart. As people respond, I record their words. Quickly the paper fills with words such as fear, avoid, painful, sin, inevitable, hard, compete, win, lose, and many more. I then draw a large circle, being careful to include all of the responses within it. At the top of the circle I draw a cross to symbolize the fact that our conflicts, including our reactions to them, all take place "in Christ."

Perhaps your reaction to that last sentence is similar to those who attend our seminar. Their initial reactions often range from surprise to rejection. Those who register surprise often admit they never considered this possibility. It's a reality some are unwilling to accept.

The apostle Paul often used a two-word phrase to describe our relationship with Jesus. That phrase is "in Christ." In Ephesians 2:6, Paul wrote: "And God raised us up with Christ and seated us with him in the heavenly realms in Christ Jesus. . . ."

This is but one of the dozens of references Paul makes to this powerful truth: The Christian life is lived "in Christ." When we give our lives to Jesus Christ, God places us "in Christ." From that day forward, every aspect of our life, including our conflicts, takes place "in Christ."

In Ephesians 4:1–6, Paul continued the application of the truth he declared earlier in his letter.

> As a prisoner for the Lord, then, I urge you to live a life worthy of the calling you have received. Be completely humble and gentle; be patient, bearing with one another in love. Make every effort to keep the unity of the Spirit through the bond of peace. There is one body and one Spirit—just as you were called to one hope when you were called—one Lord, one faith, one baptism; one God and Father of all, who is over all and through all and in all.

Peace among the parts of His body reflects the life and character of Jesus Christ. As Christians, we are placed together in His body. What takes place within us and between us takes place in Jesus Christ, for we are "in Christ" together.

I did a word study on the word "all" Paul used at the conclusion of the text above. Guess what? It means "all," as in absolutely everything, no exclusions. This means God is "over all" of our conflict, "through all" of our conflict, and "in all" of our conflict. It is not like we can check the Lord at the door once we enter the conflicted zone with other Christians.

This is not a part of our life that takes place apart from Christ. He is in the midst of it with us. Thus, we need to recognize our need to approach our conflicts in Christ. More importantly, we need to recognize that the path of approaching our conflicts in Christ is much different from the reactionary path established by the world. Rather than reacting to conflict out of ourselves, Christians have been given the opportunity to respond in Christ. They are two different paths, originating from two different sources, and producing two different results. It is the attempt of this book to identify these paths, their sources, and their results. I hope those who read this book will choose the path that originates in Jesus, flows in Jesus, and produces the life of Jesus.

1 Conformed to the World or Transformed by Christ?

Jack sat in his car a few moments before turning the ignition key, attempting to quiet a raging storm of emotions before starting for home. His wife, Kathy, sat in the passenger seat, staring out the side window, her normally warm and pleasant personality replaced with a cold glaze. Anger and resentment swept through him like a powerful tsunami, creating chaos in his normally ordered and controlled life. How could such a simple suggestion generate the level of criticism he had just experienced? He had simply suggested they consider adjusting the support the church provided two missionaries, in order to increase support for the new youth mission that was expanding beyond anyone's expectations. How had that led to Alice accusing Jack of never being supportive of these missionaries (whom, she tearfully reminded everyone, the church had been sponsoring for more than fifteen years)? Then, when he attempted to defend himself from this unfair accusation, he was blindsided by Bill's defense of Alice—including an additional dig that Jack was always pushing his own agendas on the group.

Jack was dumbfounded; over the last five years he'd given hours of his life each month to work and worship with these folks, sacrificing time with his family, and time for himself. Hadn't they had opportunities to express these concerns to him privately? How could they possibly say they felt too intimidated to discuss these matters with him? How could they assume it wouldn't do any good; that it would "put him over the edge"? His growing frustration gave way to the anger building within him, and he went on the attack. Before he realized it he was lashing out at Alice, Bill, and anyone who dared to try quieting his escalating anger. That was when he jerked his arm out of the hand that grabbed his elbow—Kathy's hand—and stormed out of the meeting, slamming the door behind him, unaware of Kathy trying to catch up. On the drive home, Kathy sat beside Jack in ice-cold silence.

Jack's ringing cell phone breeched the cold barrier between them and disrupted his smoldering storm of thoughts and emotions. Mike, a friend and fellow committee member, was calling. "Jack, I can't believe what just happened. I wanted to say something, but it all happened so fast I didn't know what to say. But we've definitely got problems; know what I mean? What Alice and the others said in there was way off base. I just want you to know they're a minority. In fact, if anyone's causing issues in the church, they're at the front of the line. So, I just wanted you to know I'm on your side in this; and I know I'm not the only one. In fact, I think it's about time the rest of us do something about it. I'm going to make some calls and see if we can get a meeting of some like-minded people, and decide what we can do about this. What do you think?"

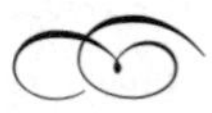

What do you think? How would you respond to Mike's query if you were Jack? How do you respond to situations like the one described above, when you suddenly find yourself in the midst of conflict? Do you become swept away by your emotions, as Jack was? Or is your reaction more like Kathy's silence? Or perhaps, like Mike, do you prepare for war? What about Alice and Bill? Have you ever been guilty of suppressing your personal opinions and feelings toward another person on numerous occasions, only to let it all burst forth at once? Instead of approaching relationship issues directly and privately, as Jesus instructs us in Matthew 5:23 and Matthew 18:15, have you reacted as Alice and Bill did? Or, as we will see as their story develops, have you "shared" your feelings and opinions with others, rather than dealing with the involved individual directly?

Here are two of the most important questions of all, and the ones most often overlooked in situations like this: *How would Jesus express Himself? How does He desire to be expressed in and through you?*

Years of experience in conflict resolution have shown us how overlooked these last two questions are. After listening to conflicted parties describe their views and perspectives, we have seen the confused, and often embarrassed, look on their faces when asked what they thought the Lord's perspective might be, and how He may desire to be expressed. More than a few times people have told us they never considered His perspective; nor had they entertained the idea He would have a position in their conflict, unless it was in agreement with them.

The World Pattern—or Christ?

Romans 12:1–3 says, "Therefore, I urge you brothers, in view of God's mercy, to offer your bodies as living sacrifices, holy and pleasing to God—this is your spiritual act of worship. Do not conform any longer to the pattern of this world, but be transformed by the renewing of your mind. Then you will be able to test and approve what God's will is—his good, pleasing and perfect will."

It appears the church in Rome was conforming to the world pattern, and nothing short of a transformation was going to change their behavior. Creating a church life that revealed God's will was not possible through the familiar world pattern. The church in Rome needed to perceive, understand, and experience things in a whole new way: ". . . to be able to test and approve what God's will is—his good, pleasing and perfect will."

The Church today needs an equally profound transformation, especially in dealing with relational conflicts. Over the years we have often encountered the same pattern of perception, understanding, and experience that is commonly encountered in the world. These include, but are certainly not limited to the following:

- Seeing conflict fundamentally in competitive terms of win or lose and right or wrong
- Seeing conflict primarily in negative, threatening terms
- Seeing conflict as wrong, or sin
- Reacting to conflict by fighting or fleeing
- Initial conflict quickly spreading to include others beyond those originally involved
- Insisting that *my perspective* is accurate, truthful, and right, while the perspective of others is inaccurate, untruthful, and wrong
- Experiencing conflict as a relational disconnection between the conflicted parties, often leading to an increase in the conflict and a greater sense of disconnection
- Believing that one can get over, past or beyond conflict without directly resolving it

- Believing that a negotiated, mutually satisfying solution created by the parties is the primary goal of the process of conflict resolution
- Believing that the resolution of the conflict does not necessarily include the reconciliation of the relationship(s) of the involved parties
- Due to all the above, perceiving conflict as something to be avoided whenever possible

Note: We have chosen to use the term *world pattern* not only as a noun, but also as a compound modifier, because it so clearly conveys Paul's message about two different lifestyles

These are the most common elements we have encountered in congregations that reflect the world pattern of perceiving, understanding, and experiencing conflict. I would strongly suggest that these elements do not reflect Jesus Christ, or who we are in Him. But they do reveal the very areas where the Church needs to be transformed in dealing with our conflicts with one another.

In our opening scenario, Jack felt Alice and Bill opposed him. Each saw his or her individual view as "right," and those opposing as "wrong." As the conversation continued, Jack felt more than his views being judged and attacked; he felt himself in the crosshairs. First he reacted defensively, but when that didn't work he began attacking his "attackers." Eventually, overwhelmed with anger, he stormed across the room to leave, and slammed the door behind him. Alice was reduced to tears. Bill was angry, flushed, and shaking. Others in the room felt shocked by what took place. Some moved to console Alice. Others sat shaking their heads and looking at one another in disbelief. None of them had a clue what divisive forces were released in their midst at that moment. They would all be shocked by the degree to which it eventually would divide them and numerous others in the church.

Though these were people who had worked together closely for years, and called each other "brother" or "sister," their sense of relational connection was damaged in a matter of minutes by their "right or wrong" differences, their fear of "losing," and their strong urge to "win." Encouraged by Mike's phone call, Jack's relational connection with Alice and Bill was on a bubble. He could avoid dealing with them, try to work things out with them, or align with Mike and others opposed to them.

As with most situations like this, Alice and Bill will have their supporters as well. As soon as they hear Alice and Bill's stories, and of Mike's attempt to gather support for Jack, these folks will move into high gear, again out of the competitive "right or wrong" and "win or lose" pattern of the world. If allowed to continue, before long much of the church will be divided into warring camps, their sense of disconnection growing with each new phone call and e-mail passed between them.

Following the world pattern, some members will react to the conflict and what "it is doing to the church" by leaving, and either aligning with another gathering in the local area, or perhaps by taking a break from church involvement to tend to their wounds. This exodus experience is unique to each situation, but there are a number of similarities.

Those who stay likely will view those who depart as ". . . those whom God has removed to solve the problem." Meanwhile, many of those who leave will report their decision as obedience to God, who led them away from the conflict and the people creating it. By taking this action, they will profess they have, in effect, ". . . put it all behind us and moved on." Oh, how I wish such a "simple" solution were possible.

Many of those remaining in the church—whether or not they experienced conflict with those who left—will also see the departure of these folks as "God's solution." Those who did experience conflict with them before they departed will often describe their departure as an act of "God pruning the dead wood from among us." I can't even begin to count the numbers of times we have heard that view expressed.

Among those who stay, there will be those who dig in and "fight for what is right." Of course, whatever side they find themselves on is the "right" side, which automatically makes everyone on the other side "wrong." If it continues, eventually this division will give new meaning to the lyrics of the familiar camp song "Deep and Wide."

This development will be a shock to those who thought God had solved the whole thing by "pruning the deadwood" in the church. Once they begin to realize there may be more "pruning" to do, they tend to move in one of two very different directions, either silence or violence. Those who move toward silence often throw in the towel, and join the silent majority in the church—those who have decided to just wait things out. Those who move to violence, figuratively speaking, pick up the biggest pruner they can find and start whacking away, for the good of the church of course. This is often the time someone decides the church needs outside help, and folks like us get a call. A little late, but as my Grandma used to say, "Better late than never."

Continuing with the world's conflict pattern, we often find other similarities having to do with a reduction in attendance, financial support, and involvement. For some, this is a passive means of voicing their disagreement with "the other side." For many, it is a way to avoid further conflict, and simply a symptom of the drain that is placed on the entire ministry due to the unresolved conflict among them.

While all of this is going on, there is also a fair amount of the world pattern of denial present in the church. You can detect its presence in those who, in the midst of all we have described thus far, will declare, "Problem? What problem? I didn't know there was a problem." When asked, they will readily admit to having noticed the declining attendance, along with a host of other "trouble signs." But to listen to them, they have remained apart from it all; thus, it is none of their concern or responsibility.

New Patterns, Perceptions, Understandings, and Experiences

So let me ask you, does any of this sound familiar? Would you agree that these reactions to conflict reflect common patterns found in the world? Would you be interested if I told you it doesn't have to be like this for those who are in Christ? Oh, I don't mean we can live lives immune from conflict simply because we are Christians. Conflict is a normal part of this life, whether we're Christians or not. What I am referring to is the way we deal with conflict. Unlike the rest of the world, Christians do not have to conform to the pattern of the world; we've been given a new pattern in the life of Jesus Christ.

New patterns offer new perceptions, understandings, and experiences, which renew our mind and transform our life. And just as the world pattern of dealing with conflict contains a number of elements, so does the pattern that flows from Jesus' life. These elements include, but certainly are not limited to:

- Seeing conflict as a cooperative, collaborative experience together with Jesus
- Seeing conflict in terms of the unique opportunity to know who Jesus is, and who we are, together in Him
- Seeing conflict as normal, beneficial, and even necessary at times

- Experiencing conflict by responding in Him
- Limiting the spread and impact of our conflict
- Understanding there is only one truth; His name is Jesus
- Recognizing we are always one, together in Him
- Experiencing the full resolution of conflict, together in Him
- Understanding a primary goal of the process of conflict resolution is discovering His solutions together
- Understanding the resolution of the conflict begins and ends in our oneness in Him
- Due to all the above, perceiving conflict as our mutual friend to approach together in Christ

Throughout the book, we are going to be following the experiences of Jack, Alice, Bill, and others. As we do, I encourage you to observe closely how each of them handles conflict. What perceptions and understandings of conflict do their experiences reflect?

You might also reflect on those that are familiar to you. Which of these two lists most characterizes your experiences with conflict?

Finally, you may ponder what it might look like if the elements of their experience, and ours, reflected Jesus Christ rather than the world? When encountering conflict with one another, what would it look like if, rather than reacting out of ourselves, we responded in Him?

It is my prayer that Christ will use the content of this book to renew minds, transform lives, and allow us together "to test and approve what God's will is—his good, pleasing and perfect will," even in the midst of conflict.

2 Back to the Future

As soon as Pastor Tim walked through the front door, his wife, Hannah, knew something was wrong. He looked as though the weight of the entire world was on his shoulders.

"Honey, what's wrong?" she asked. She put down the book she had been reading and approached him with concern and fear sweeping through her. As she neared him, she saw tears welling in his eyes, and her arms instinctively went out to embrace him.

Pastor Tim had remained strong and controlled during the entire episode at the church. He had concluded the meeting with prayer, and asked everyone present to return home and continue praying for those involved, as well as for the entire church. He then busied himself with making sure all the lights were off and doors were locked, before heading home. During this entire time, he had felt rather detached from the experience, almost numb. Then he walked into the living room and saw Hannah look up from her chair, and the tears began to build. By the time she reached him near the door, extending her arms toward him, he felt the dam break, and the flood of emotions came pouring forth.

They stood there for some time; Hannah with her arms wrapped around her husband, trying to hug away his pain as her own feelings of concern and fear threatened to overtake her. Tim pressed his face into Hannah's neck, his body heaving with sobs of grief.

Eventually, Tim was able to regain enough control to lift his head. "I'm sorry," he said, as tears continued to flow down his face.

Hannah wiped each of his cheeks. "Oh, honey, what do you have to be sorry about? What happened? Did something happen at the meeting?" Taking his hand, Hannah led Tim into the living room toward the couch, where they could sit and talk. Once seated, she waited for him to speak.

Tim took a deep breath. "There was a big blow-up in the midst of the meeting. And in a matter of minutes, I watched three of our key leaders turn on one another like they were the worst of enemies. I still can't believe it happened. Where did it all come from?"

His tears began to flow once again, and Hannah got up to retrieve a box of tissues, as much for her as for him.

As Christians, we can choose how we deal with conflict. We can either react out of ourselves, or we can respond in Jesus Christ. The former reflects the world pattern; the latter reflects who we really are in Christ. Unfortunately, we find Christian brothers and sisters conforming to the world pattern far more often than being transformed by the reality of who they are *together in Christ.*

One of the most pervasive and destructive elements from the world pattern we have found in churches is reflected in the conflicted parties' perceived relational disconnection. On many occasions we have interviewed brothers and sisters in the Lord who, prior to the conflict, were best friends, but who now no longer speak to one another—or worse. I'll never forget the brother who broke down in sobs during one interview as he related how former friends now used a side door on the Sundays he was a greeter at the front door. Or there was the pastor's wife who tearfully described church members crossing the street to avoid encountering her in their community. Talk about feeling disconnected.

We have read volumes of letters and e-mails between church members, and we have come to recognize a different perspective of Paul's observation that "the letter kills." We once heard the recorded messages left on a home phone, and then listened to a mother's pain and anger as she described the shock and fear experienced by her young children when they listened to these angry and threatening messages, and recognized the familiar voices of a church elder and a Sunday school teacher.

We have also interviewed some of those who have said or done many of these things. They're never the monsters one would like to picture responsible for escalating the conflict and producing so much pain. They don't have horns growing out of their heads, beady eyes, or forked tongues. You would never be able to pick them out of a crowd. They look just like us. All too often *they are us*. Often the same person can be both victim and victimizer. That, too, is part of the world pattern of conflict.

So how can they (we) do such things? During our interviews, they have often had a difficult time understanding and explaining it themselves. Sometimes they deny the severity or seriousness of their actions, or try to justify them in some way. Many have explained their behavior as "an overreaction" to the conflict. "It wasn't personal" is an excuse we hear often. There are those who come to a place of regret, desiring to "make it up somehow." But foundational to all their experiences has been this sense of being disconnected relationally.

For some, this perceived disconnectedness has been of little surprise, as they have admitted to not having much sense of a relational connection with one another prior to the conflict. They have often defined their connections in terms of attending the same church, and sharing a number of social and religious experiences and values.

For others, the conflict has been a painful experience in which they have suffered deeply. In some cases, long, personal friendships have been broken as people take different sides in the conflict. Their reactions have often included a profound shock and disbelief that the conflicted situation could get to this point.

Although the experiences of their relational disconnections have varied from indifference to brokenness, the constant has been this element of a perceived separation in their relationship. That is probably no surprise to anyone who has experienced conflict with another. Feeling disconnected from someone is often experienced as a natural result of the conflict. Generally, the greater the level of conflict, the greater this void between us appears. This is a foundational element in the world pattern of conflict. Whether at home, work, school, in the neighborhood, or among the church, we often feel relationally disconnected from those with whom we experience conflict. But it does not have to be this way for those in Jesus Christ.

The Chicken or the Egg?

You are no doubt familiar with the riddle regarding which came first, the chicken or the egg. In conflict and relational disconnections, we are often faced with the same type of question. It is hard to know for sure which came first in each situation.

Is the conflict a result of the perceived disconnection between the parties? Or is the relational disconnection the result of the conflict?

I believe it is the perceived relational disconnection that eventually leads to unresolved conflict among Christians, which in turn increases the void experienced between the parties, often leading to further expressions of conflict between them. In other words, we bring this perceived disconnection into our relationships with us. When we do, we introduce a fundamental element of the world pattern into our relationships, and into the church.

A Group of Individuals—Independent and Separate

We have found this fundamental element of the world pattern evidenced in people's relationships with the Lord, and with one another. When we have asked individuals to describe their relationship with Jesus Christ, many have described an individual and private relationship, independent of and separate from the individual and private relationships others have with Him. We have also found this same element of separation in their relationships with other church members.

Because of this world pattern of perceiving, understanding, and then experiencing life as individuals, independent of and separate from one another, church folks have substituted cooperation for unity. As long as this group of independent, separate individuals is able to cooperate with one another, they perceive themselves to be united in Christ. But as soon as there is a disagreement between any two of them, then elements of the world pattern of conflict flow into the perceived void between them. Very quickly, cooperation of individuals is replaced with competition, and all sense of unity appears lost.

Because of this perceived disconnection between individual relationships with Jesus—and with one another—it is not uncommon for Christians to stand together one Sunday, singing about being one in the bond of love, and the following Sunday to no longer be speaking to one another—and the entire time to believe their individual relationships with the Lord to be unaffected.

These elements of the world's pattern of conflict characterized the perceptions, understandings, and experiences of Alice, Jack, Bill, and most of the others in their congregation. Because of this, their church experience was based more on individuals and groups influencing the congregation than on the entire body experiencing the Lord and responding to Him together. Because each person operated from his or her individual perceptions, understandings, positions, visions, values, passions, and more, when confronted with conflict, they reacted out of themselves. Because they operated as a group of independent, separate individuals, in due course, disagreement and competition between their individual views and positions arose. Eventually, this competition got personal. Actually, it always was, but now it was out in the open for all to see.

Alice perceived any action that threatened the continued support of the missionaries and programs, so dear to her heart, as a personal threat to her passion, her vision, her very self. Jack was just as passionate about the mission of the church, and just as self-focused as Alice. This is why he grew so frustrated and angry by what he perceived to be the older members' lack of support for the local teen ministry.

For years they all faked peace by being nice, while suppressing their growing frustration and anger with one another. Of course, they didn't conceal all of it. They each shared a fair amount of it with spouses and close friends, who in turn shared it with others. That's why, though this particular situation occurred within the confines of a committee meeting, news of it spread like wildfire. Lines were drawn, and positions were taken throughout the entire congregation in a very short time.

In a matter of days, friendly communication was replaced with gossip and slander. Just a few phone calls, e-mails, and private conversations mustered the troops for action. Pentagon planners would have been proud.

At some point in the future, when talking about this period, many members will share their shock and dismay at just how quickly their "nice, peaceful, little church" suddenly became a civil war battlefield, flowing with the emotional and relational blood of brothers and sisters in Christ. Many will be shaken by how quickly church members turned on one another. Some of them had been friends for decades, raising their families together, sharing in life's seasons and experiences, even taking vacations together. They served on boards and committees together, sharing the same visions and goals. And it all seemed to blow up before their eyes.

Many will ask, "What is wrong with us? How could something like this happen?" Much time and energy will be spent trying to figure out who is right, who is wrong, and where to lay the blame.

Those with strong needs to get things back to the "peace and unity" they enjoyed before will pressure the conflicted parties to resolve the issues between them, or to "simply get over it," so the church can move on. Without recognizing they are conforming to the world pattern of reacting out of themselves, they will often contribute to the conflict by pressing for their self-focused need to have things as they were, or at least to have this conflict settled.

While many of us may question how something like this can happen, we might wonder instead what else we would expect from a church-life experience built on the world pattern of a group of separate, independent individuals. No wonder pastoring a church has been likened to herding cats!

In the Beginning There Were Two Trees

Where did this self-focused, independent, separate world pattern come from? And why is it so foundational and prevalent in the conflicts experienced in churches today? To find the answer, we have to go all the way back to the beginning; way, way, way back—all the way back to Genesis 1–3. Today, the well-worn path flowing from this pattern is as broad as the world itself. But if you were to trace it to its source, you would eventually find yourself stepping into the very footprints of two trailblazers named Adam and Eve. Their trail would lead to the base of one particular tree at the center of the Garden of Eden.

In Genesis 2:9 we read that the Lord God created all kinds of trees in the Garden of Eden, with two trees receiving special recognition. In the center of the Garden were the "tree of life and the tree of the knowledge of good and evil." Connected with these two trees was this command from the Lord: "You are free to eat from any tree in the garden; but you must not eat from the tree of the knowledge of good and evil, for when you eat of it you will surely die."

Volumes have been written about these two trees, and what they represent. I believe each of these trees represents a way of life; a pattern containing perceptions and understandings that produce experiences conformed to each tree. The "Tree of Life" is a pattern containing perceptions and understandings that produce experiences conformed to "life." It appears eating from this tree was a part of God's original plan, as He did not place any restrictions on it, not at first anyhow.

The other tree represents a pattern containing perceptions and understandings that produce experiences conformed to "the knowledge of good and evil." It is clear, Adam and Eve were not free to eat of this tree. Instead, God told them they ". . . must not eat from the tree of the knowledge of good and evil, for when you eat of it you will surely die."

One tree conforms to life. The other tree conforms to death. Two patterns, leading to two different paths of perceiving, understanding, and experiencing.

"Good and Evil," by Any Other Name . . .

Guess which of those patterns we find most often in the conflicted situations we work with. It isn't the pattern flowing from the Tree of Life. Admittedly, we don't often hear people proclaiming themselves good and others evil, though we have encountered that a time or two. Instead, people tend to invest a great deal of time and energy trying to determine who and what is right and wrong.

Interestingly, the meaning of the Hebrew word for "good" in this Genesis text includes the concept of being "right." And the meaning of the Hebrew word for "evil" in this text includes the concept of being "disagreeable" or "wrong." Good and evil may be different words from right and wrong, but they are fruit from the same tree. Because they come from the same tree, when we conform our lives to their pattern, we end up with the same results God declared: death.

Oneness and the Image of God

Right after God informed Adam about the two trees, God declared, "It is not good for the man to be alone." Beyond referring to Adam as the "only" human, "alone" also carries the concept of being in a state of "separation" and/or "isolation."

God declared Adam's state of being separated or isolated to be "not good." Why? Because this state of being a lone, separate, isolated individual was not a full reflection of the "image of God" in which Adam was created. Genesis 1:26–27 says, "Then God said, 'Let us make man in our image, in our likeness. . . .'

So God created man in his own image, in the image of God he created him; male and female he created them."

God's image reflects the Father, Son, and Holy Spirit in the relational intimacy of being "one" *together.* God's image is an image of community—three in one. There are not three, alone, separate, isolated individuals, with each one being a god unto himself. He is three in one. So God created Adam and Eve in His community image of three in one, and placed them in a relationship with Himself. The relationship between Adam and Eve He called "one flesh," an image of community, reflecting God's image.

Then in Genesis 2:25, we read, "The man and his wife were both naked, and they felt no shame." Huh?

It's as simple as this: God created man and woman for relational intimacy with one another. Their original life experience was of community. That was the form of their life; for that was the image they were created to reflect. The description and experience of this relationship was "one flesh"; "naked" and experiencing "no shame."

Adam and Eve were two distinct individuals, expressing their God-created individuality, but for an unknown time period we find no evidence of them experiencing life as individuals, independent of or separate from one another or Him. In the two being "one flesh" together, they reflected the image in which they were created—His image of oneness. There was an openness and freedom in their relationship, symbolized in their shame-free nakedness. We find no expressions of self as independent of, different from, separate from, or opposed to the other. There was no cover-up, competition, hiding, playing games, and no personal or self-centered agenda. Their intimacy of oneness was an authentic, open, and free relationship. Adam and Eve's oneness was the human expression of the essence of oneness experienced by God the Father, Son, and Holy Spirit.

It's hard for our minds—shaped by a world pattern with a highly developed sense of self, separate from and independent of all others—to grasp this experience of oneness and community shared by Adam, Eve, and their Creator God. It still shows up when a calamity like September 11 occurs, or a tornado blows through town, or some other life-impacting event takes place on a large scale, and people forget themselves and become a community of one. And there are still cultures that experience daily life from this perspective of the communal whole, rather than separate, individualistic selves, though they are few and far between.

It appears to me this is how God desired our relationships with one another to be in Him: open, free, authentic, and filled with His life. Being one in Him is the "oneness" of being individuals with distinct, God-created and God-purposed individuality, but not conforming to the world pattern of being independent of and separate from each other. He created us to be interdependent on Him and one another. Paul described it in terms of many parts forming one body, and each part "belonging" to all the others. We will delve into all of that later, but for now, let me simply shout, "Hallelujah, and thank you God!"

The Choice of Life or Death

In the Genesis account we read that after the two became one flesh and experienced the intimacy of their oneness together, the serpent came to tempt them to act individually, independently, and separately of one another and of God. Surprise! Surprise!

Since Eve's creation, Adam and Eve had never experienced life independent of or separate from one another, or God. Their perception, understanding, and experience of life was that of the "interdependent-interconnected us," not the "independent-separate me" and the "independent-separate you." The serpent, who was already slithering down this path of individualistic, independent, separateness apart from God, engaged Eve individually, and she responded in like fashion. Adam, who was present, remained individually detached from the encounter. For the first time, Adam and Eve acted independent of and separate from one another. In so doing, they acted outside of the God-image in which they were created, the very image God described as "one flesh." For the first time they acted as "two individuals: independent, *separate flesh*," rather than one.

Another new element was introduced when the serpent suggested God held something back from them regarding this Tree of the Knowledge of Good and Evil. You notice he wasn't interested in enticing them to eat of the Tree of Life. But more than introducing doubt into Eve's heart, his comments raised within her a self-focused desire: an expression of self, independent of and separate from her oneness with Adam and her Creator God. Acting independently of them, she responded to her desire by reaching forth her hand to take the fruit for herself. James describes it this way: ". . . but each one is tempted when, by his own evil desire, he is dragged away and enticed. Then, after desire has conceived, it gives birth to sin; and sin, when it is full-grown, gives birth to death" (James 1:14–15). God described it this way: ". . . for when you eat of it, you shall surely die" (Genesis 2:17).

By the way, before the guys start empathizing with poor, innocent Adam, let us not lose sight of his contribution to the scene—or his lack of contribution, as the case may be. At any point in his "one flesh" relationship with Eve, Adam could have stepped in and placed his arm around her, and refocused the situation on their oneness with one another and God. It is apparent that at some point prior to this moment, Adam had shared God's word with Eve regarding this tree. By her response to the serpent, either Adam had already edited what God had first spoken to him, or Eve had placed her own spin on God's warning. But the point is this: Adam did not step up when the serpent showed up. Instead, he stood back and let the scenario play out before him. He can't even use the excuse he was distracted by a game on TV.

Was Adam an innocent victim in all this? Hardly. At best, his self-focus kept him from intervening in the situation. At worst, he also selfishly desired what the serpent was offering, and simply let Eve take all the initial risk. She may have come to doubt God's warning, but Adam wasn't taking any chances. Let her eat first and see what happens. From this moment forward, their life experience changed dramatically.

Prior to this moment, Adam and Eve's relationship had been described as "one flesh." Their relationship had mirrored the image of oneness of the Father, Son, and Holy Spirit. Now, as Eve acted independently and separate of Adam, and Adam stood aside separate and independent of Eve, they both acted independent of and separate from their Creator. The community-interdependent-intimate image of being one was broken. Everything looked different to them.

From Our Oneness Together to Our Individual Differences

After eating of the Tree of the Knowledge of Good and Evil, for the first time in their lives, Adam and Eve realized they were naked. That must have made for an interesting scene, but I'll leave the imagining of that to you. As independent, separate, individuals, they now saw one another as *different*. And their first act was to cover up.

They not only saw differences between them, they each began to see *themselves* differently as well. No longer did they see themselves as expressions of the oneness of their community together with God. Now they each saw themselves individually, independently, and separate from the other. This is such a natural reaction for us today we are not often consciously aware of it. But prior to seeing things through the filters of good and evil or right and wrong, such differences were not the focus at all; they weren't even on the radar. Prior to this, they had perceived, understood, and experienced life corporately, communally, interdependently, and interconnected together *as one flesh*. Now Adam and Eve each saw themselves independent of and separate from one another. They began to experience all of life from this new perspective.

This new perspective impacted their relationship with God as well. With this new perception and understanding of life in terms of good and evil or right and wrong, they also saw themselves as independent of and separate from God. For the first time, they saw themselves as naked before Him. No longer did they see themselves as reflections or extensions of Him and His image of oneness; now they saw themselves as different from Him.

Sensing this new *different-ness* and the disconnection it created, when they heard Him walking through the garden, they experienced a new emotion: fear. So powerful was this feeling, they reacted by doing something they had never done before; they "hid" from Him. In this very moment, the "flee response" was introduced into the human experience, and the "fight response" would soon follow. The world pattern of reacting individually within ourselves was taking root.

Imagine the revolutionary change from what God first intended for them, for us, and for our relationship with Him and one another. From the openness and freedom of living in oneness with Him, they were now living in fear, hiding from Him, and covering up from one another. Rather than seeing things in the life of their oneness (His life), they were now seeing things through the differences between themselves. Seeing things from such a self-focused perspective changed everything.

Every relationship was changed dramatically. That which was created to be open and free was now covered up, protected, and filled with fear. That which was created to be intimate was now disconnected. They were no longer "naked and felt no shame." Now they were covered and experiencing shame and fear before one another and God. The experiencing of God's *community image* in them was beginning to die, just as He had warned: ". . . but you must not eat from the tree of the knowledge of good and evil, for when you eat of it you will surely die."

As their perceptions and understandings began to conform to the pattern of this tree, their life experiences began to conform as well. Their former community of oneness was now filled with shame, cover-up, disconnection, fear, hiding, and guilt. They began to defend themselves by "blaming" each other for their situation. The "flee response" was already giving way to the "fight response" in their relationship with God and one another. In the span of one generation, this path would lead to the first experience of jealousy, rage, and murder, as one brother would slay another.

The "fight or flight response" became hard-wired in all mankind, and another element of the world pattern was revealed. In the distance we can still hear His warning: ". . . but you must not eat from the tree of the knowledge of good and evil, for when you eat of it you will surely die."

Every time we make relationships about good and evil or right and wrong, we become self-centered and conform to the world pattern, venturing down this same path to death. I am not speaking of the death from which Jesus Christ saves us. I am speaking of the death our Peace Connections staff has encountered in numerous churches: the death of ministries, relationships, visions, trust, faith, emotional and relational safety, and so much more. It all can be traced back to that moment when two individuals, whose reality was the community of oneness, acted individually, independently, and separately from one another and from God, and stepped on the path of perceiving, understanding, and experiencing life in terms of good and evil or right and wrong. It's a well-worn path now, made wide and easy by millions upon millions who have walked it before us. And it pains me to say I've left my footprints there more times than I care to admit. Perhaps you have, too.

A New Life to Live

As Paul declares in Romans 6:4, "We were therefore buried with him through baptism into death in order that, just as Christ was raised from the dead through the glory of the Father, we too may live a new life." Hallelujah! A new life, brothers and sisters! Not the old life, which we inherited from the old Adam back in the Garden of Eden; but the new life of the new Adam, Jesus Christ. We aren't talking about a cleaned-up version of the old life. We're talking about a whole new life—His life—the life that flows from the Tree of Life in the garden!

We do not have to conform our lives to the world pattern any longer, including how we deal with conflict. Because of Him who dwells within us, our minds can be renewed, and our lives can be transformed. Together, we can "test and approve what God's will is—his good, pleasing and perfect will" (Romans 12:2b). And all God's people said, "Amen!"

3 From Death to Life . . . and Back to One

Moments after the parking lot meetings broke up among the three committee members who left first—and among those who lingered together long afterward—the cell-phone towers in the area were buzzing with calls to family and friends, most of which began with, "You're not going to believe what just happened at the church meeting." Moments after those calls ended, other connections began to relay a new set of calls, as those who just learned of the events that had taken place at the church, were now relaying the news to others.

Our Heavenly Father created us (plural) for a purpose: for a relationship (singular). He created us (plural) for a relationship (singular) that would share in and reflect His image (plural) of intimate community (singular), of the "oneness" shared by the Father, Son, and Holy Spirit. He created us for an inter-dependent community relationship of openness, freedom, and intimacy with one another and with Him. This community (singular) is what the Bible calls the Church (singular).

He never desired these relationships be built on the perceptions, understandings, and experiences of the pattern that flows from the Tree of the Knowledge of Good and Evil. It was never His intention that our relationships would be about what is different between us, or what separates and disconnects us. It was never supposed to be about who is right and who is wrong, and where to place the blame. He originally intended that our relationships would be about the life of being one together, His life; you know, that other tree in the garden.

Originally, we were invited to eat of this tree freely. Because of God's love for us, He sent this "Tree of Life" to earth once again. Our lives were always supposed to be about the life and pattern that flows from this tree. He who declares Himself to be "the life," this One who claims to be "the way"—this very same One who invites us to eat of Him in order to experience the fullness of life in Him and through Him (see John 6)—this One came to a place of "shame," to die on a tree, "naked" before God and all others. He came to this place of shame called Golgotha, and instead of being covered with leaves or clothes, He was covered with our sin, our shame, our self-focus, our individualistic, independent separateness. He was covered with our world-pattern need to make life about good and evil and right and wrong, and all that disconnects us from God and one another. In this place the "Tree of Life" was crucified on a tree of death.

As Paul declared of Jesus in 2 Corinthians 5:21, "God made him who had no sin to be sin for us, so that in him we might become the righteousness of God." In other words, God made Him who never expressed Himself individualistically, independently, or separately from His Father, to be the fullness of our individualistic, independent, separate selves. God made Him whose focus was never independent of or separate from His Father, to be our focus, so that in Him our self-focus would die, and we would once again live life in the oneness that reflects the community image of our creator God.

In that place of shame—naked and yet covered in our sin—He did not defend, He did not blame, He did not flee, He did not fight, He did not claim His "right" and condemn our "wrong." Instead, He cried out, "Father, forgive them, for they do not know what they are doing." Today, we are the ones who don't know what we are doing when we make relationships about our *selves*, and about what is good and evil or right and wrong between us. Our lives are not supposed to be about such things, not us individually, or our differences. It's supposed to be about Him, who is life itself.

On that cross, the Righteous One tasted the bitter fruit of the Tree of the Knowledge of Good and Evil for the very first time. He tasted of this fruit that changes everything from oneness, openness, freedom, and intimacy, to "individual-ness," cover-ups, fear, and relational disconnection. In the midst of His physical suffering, the emotional pain of being disconnected from the community of God overwhelmed Him, and He cried out, "My God, my God, why have you forsaken me?" I don't know about you, but the power of that moment impacts me to my core.

Eventually our self-focus (our sin) had its full course in Him, and He gave up His Spirit and died. He took upon Himself the full harvest of the bitter fruit of the Tree of the Knowledge of Good and Evil; this self-focused, right and wrong, pattern of the world. He took it all to the cross, and there it died along with Him. For the Father had once said, so long, long ago, ". . . but you must not eat from the tree of the knowledge of good and evil, for when you eat of it you will surely die."

Choosing Paths: The Broad Path of Right and Wrong, or the Narrow Path of Life?

Conforming to the world pattern—and perceiving, understanding, and experiencing life by the knowledge of good and evil—places us on the all-too-familiar path of seeing ourselves independent of and separate from all others. It's a well-worn path trod by innumerable generations.

I've left my own footprints on that trail far more times than I care to admit. I have wandered down this path when dealing with my family. It has happened in my dealings with other brothers and sisters in Christ, as well. Each time I do, the Lord reminds me this is not His desire, nor is it my reality in Him. Life in Christ is not about our differences. It's not about who or what is right or wrong. It's actually not about us at all. It's all about Him. This reality is a pattern, a path leading to a much different experience than the path that flows from the world pattern.

In their dealings with one another, Jack, Alice, Bill, Mike, and all the others in our continuing story have left their footprints on this path of good and evil and right and wrong. Each time they have looked at one another through this relational pattern of the world, they have set out on this path that leads to disconnection and death. Each time they have acted out of their independent, separate *selves*, they have put one foot in front of the other along this way. It is a relational path that expresses less of Christ and more of themselves.

Good News! There is Another Way!

It sounds dark and depressing, doesn't it? But as I've said, we have good news! The Lord has come to reveal, offer, and share with us a new way, His way. He who is "the way" has come to offer us Himself. "Enter through the narrow gate," He said, "For wide is the gate and broad is the road that leads to destruction, and many enter through it. But small is the gate and narrow the road that leads to life, and only a few find it" (Matthew 7:13–14).

In dealing with conflict, many enter the wide gate and travel the broad (and easy) road that leads to destruction. The entry is wide. The pathway is as broad as relating to one another individualistically, independently, and separately and making relationships about our differences, and who's right or wrong. As we have seen in dozens of churches, when brothers and sisters tread down this path in their dealings with one another, it leads to the destruction of relationships, ministries, and sometimes even the local church.

But there is another way. Its gate is small, and its path is narrow—His name is Jesus. Remember, Jesus claims: "I am the way and the truth and the life. No one comes to the Father except through me" (John 14:6).

There is one way. His name is Jesus. He is the way. He leads to life, not destruction. He leads to connection, not disconnection. He leads to interdependence, not independence. He leads to reconciliation and wholeness, not church splits and unresolved conflict.

There is one truth. His name is Jesus. He is the truth. The importance is not that we each have our individual truth, but that the Truth has us. He does not have us individually. He has us corporately, communally, and together as one.

There is one life. His name is Jesus. He is the life. The life of Jesus in each of us is a shared life, for there is but one Christian life. To share in His life He has made us one together, thus restoring God's community image in us.

So when and how did that happen? You did wonder that, didn't you? I believe it began with a prayer in the upper room. Actually, it began long before that. I suspect it began before

Genesis 1:1. But we first hear about it in a prayer recorded in John 17.

A Prayer Offered

During the stressful evening He was betrayed, and hours before His crucifixion, Jesus shared the Passover with His disciples in the upper room. At the conclusion of this time with them, Jesus prayed the prayer recorded for us in John 17. Reflecting His awareness of the impending end of His human life, and His return to His Father at the completion of His work on earth, Jesus also prayed the following:

> My prayer is not for them alone. I pray also for those who will believe in me through their message, that all of them may be one, Father, just as you are in me and I am in you. May they also be in us so that the world may believe that you have sent me. I have given them the glory that you gave me, that they may be one as we are one: I in them and you in me. May they be brought to complete unity to let the world know that you sent me and have loved them even as you have loved me.
>
> (John 17:20–23)

Initially His thoughts and concerns were for His disciples gathered near Him. But soon He included all those who would come to believe in Him by means of the apostle's words. Included in those numbers are people like Jack, Alice, Bill, Mike, you, and me. From His heart to His Father's heart, Jesus prayed that we would all be one, just as He and His Father were one: ". . . just as you are in me and I am in you."

Ponder this request for a moment. What exactly was Jesus asking of His Father when He requested that all Christians would be "one" with one another, just as the Father is in Jesus, and Jesus is in Him? Did He have any idea what He was asking of His Father? Did He have any idea what He was asking of us? Did He have any idea what He was asking for us? I have my suspicions. What do you think?

For our purposes here, we won't consider the world pattern existing in the greater Church within our local communities, where differing beliefs and practices serve to disconnect one part of His body from another. Nor will we reflect on the magnified disconnections experienced in the multitudes of divisions of the Church throughout the world. Sadly, we have lifted this good-and-evil-right-and-wrong world pattern of perceiving, understanding, and experiencing life to an art form. But what about the local gatherings of brothers and sisters in Christ we find ourselves in today? We usually have no difficulty accepting and actually enjoying a sense of "oneness" with those Christian brothers and sisters we like. Sometimes we just "click" with other people and enjoy them and being around them. We tend to agree on a lot of things, seeing, understanding, and experiencing life in much the same way. But what about those whose personalities rub us the wrong way, or those who don't share the same views and positions we do? Did Jesus really desire us to experience the very same oneness with these disagreeable people as He shared with our Heavenly Father? He could not have imagined some of the folks in our gatherings when He made this request, could He? Did He? I believe so. What do you think?

That the World Might Know

While you ponder the questions above, what about the two connections Jesus made in His prayer about our being one together in Him and the impact this is to have on the world and on us? Again, speaking of us, Jesus prayed, "May they be brought to complete unity to let the world know that you sent me and have loved them even as you have loved me" (John 17:23).

Did you get that? He requested we be one, together in Him; first, so the world would know the Father sent Him to the world, and second, so the world would know the Father loves the Church with the same love He has for His Son.

You might want to set the book down for a moment, and just reflect on the request Jesus voiced to His Father in this prayer. Go ahead; I'll be here when you get back.

I'd love to hear what you thought as you reflected on the content of His prayer thus far. But, as we are unable to do that at the moment, let me share with you my thoughts, and see if we're on the same page. My initial reaction was, "What?! You gotta be nuts! This is crazy! You want to risk all this on how the Church lives out our reality of being one in You? Please, Lord Jesus, have mercy!"

Eventually I settled down a bit, and my thoughts turned more practical: "What is this all about? How would it work today? What would it look like being lived out with my Christian brothers and sisters? Lord, didn't You realize we would have our differences, disagreements, and conflicts, and sometimes they would get really messy, and the world would see all that? Of course you did. So why would You risk linking our living out this reality of oneness in You with things as profoundly important as the world believing the Father sent You to the world, or giving witness of His love for us?"

I still don't have a clear understanding of the full purpose of His request. It just doesn't seem like a plan that would pass any risk analysis. But this I am very sure of: It is what He requested of His Father, hours before His appointed date with the cross.

From Glory unto Glory

In verse 22 Jesus prays, "I have given them the glory that you gave me, that they may be one as we are one. . . ." He spoke this, not just in reference to the disciples gathered near Him at the time, but He included ". . . those who will believe in me through their message. . . ." He was praying about you and me! Isn't that awesome? Aren't you relieved He didn't expect us to pull this off ourselves? He had a plan. He gave us the glory our Father gave Him, so that we "may be one," together, as He and His Father are one. We already have what we need to live as one, together, in Him.

He has given us the glory our Father gave Him. This gift of glory from the Father to the Son, and now to us, is the source for the life of being one together in Him; it is the pattern taken from the Tree of Life in the garden. This gift is the pattern from which all that is life freely flows. By means of this glory, we can now live together as one in Christ in such a way that when the world sees His life in us together, it will know that the Father sent the Son to the world, and He loves us as He loves His Son. Now that is one approach to evangelizing the world I haven't heard much about, have you?

Entire books have been written on the subject of this glory given to us, so I won't even attempt to go into it here. But the short version is this: He gave us Himself, His essence, His nature, His life. Jesus is the Tree of Life in the garden. It is as Peter proclaimed in 2 Peter 1:3–4:

> His divine power has given us everything we need for life and godliness through our knowledge *(intimate experience)* of him who called us by his own glory and goodness. Through these he has given us his very great and precious promises, so that through them you may participate in the divine nature and escape the corruption in the world caused by evil

desires. *(note in italics added to give clarification to the use of the word "knowledge" included in the text).*

Amen and hallelujah! He has already given us, *together*, everything we need for living His life in the world. Everything we need for living out the reality of our oneness in Him, He has already given us, *together*. Everything we need for living out the reality of our oneness in Him—which will lead the world to know and believe the Father sent His Son to the world—He has already given us, *together*. Everything we need for living out the reality of our oneness in Him—which will show the world the Father's love for Jesus and us—Jesus has already given us. He has given us Himself, that we may be one *together* as He and His Father are one, *together*. Again I shout, "Amen and hallelujah!"

Only One "Oneness"

I'm not sure if you've wondered this yet—it didn't come to me right away. It took me a while to get over my initial shock, before I began to realize what Jesus was praying for during His last hours before the cross. But eventually I started wondering what being one together in Jesus meant. It wasn't exactly a foreign idea to me; after all, I had memorized the song that proclaims we are one in the spirit and one in the Lord. I had read John 17 hundreds of times, and had encountered other passages about our unity and oneness in Christ. But for the first time, I started wondering just what being one in Christ was, and what it would look like when lived out by Christians like you and me.

I'm always amazed how the Lord uses little things to make big impacts in our lives. In this case, it was the two-letter word "as." In John 17:22 Jesus prayed, "I have given them the glory that you gave me, that they may be one *as* we are one" (italics added). The word "as" is such a little word; only two letters. Lest we forget, when the Lord prayed these words, He was referring to us. He requested that we experience the same connection of being one together that He and His Father experienced.

Based on the scriptural references we will be looking at in just a moment, there is something else profound about this request. Jesus is not just asking that we experience the same kind of oneness He and His Father experience, though that would be awesome enough. His request goes far beyond that. What Jesus is requesting of His Father is that we be allowed to experience *their fellowship* of being one. Do you need to set the book down again for a while, and just let your mind soak in this request from our Lord's heart?

If we can begin to grasp the "oneness" shared by our Heavenly Father and His Son, we can begin to grasp the "oneness" Jesus desired all of us to share with them together. Can you imagine? You really should set the book down and either close your eyes, or go for a walk (but not both at the same time, please) and reflect on Jesus' incredible prayer.

Welcome back. Do you have some sense of the oneness between the Father and Son? If so, then go the next step and begin to picture the brothers and sisters He's connected you with these days. Do you see some good friends and smiling faces? It's not too hard to feel connected with these folks, is it? Now picture the people who don't exactly fill you with all kinds of warm fuzzies when you're in their company. Perhaps you've had some run-ins with them in the past; maybe there is some unresolved conflict between you and them, and at some point you decided to "put it behind you" and just "move on." Do you feel the void or distance in the relationship between you and these brothers and sisters, as compared to the others?

Now ponder this: Hours before He was to die on the cross, Jesus thought of you and all these folks you just pictured in your mind, and He requested of His Father:

> I pray . . . that all of them may be one, Father, just as you are in me and I am in you. May they also be in us so that the world may believe that you have sent me. I have given them the glory that you gave me, that they may be one as we are one: I in them and you in me. May they be brought to complete unity to let the world know that you sent me and have loved them even as you have loved me.
>
> (John 17:20–23)

A Prayer Answered

Can you imagine the Father not answering a prayer from Jesus? Neither can I. In John 8:28, Jesus said He did nothing on His own, but He spoke only that which the Father first taught Him. Therefore, I'm led to believe Jesus prayed this prayer because He first received these expressions from His Father. For the Father to have denied His Son's request, He would have had to deny Himself.

Another reason I believe God the Father affirmatively answered His Son's request is because of the abundance of references revealing the content of this prayer lived out in the life of the apostles, as well as those who came to believe in Jesus because of their words.

The book of Acts describes the manifestation of this "oneness" in many forms. Acts 2:42–47 says,

> They *devoted* themselves to the apostles' teaching and to *the fellowship*, to the breaking of bread and to prayer. Everyone was filled with awe, and many wonders and miraculous signs were done by the apostles. *All the believers were together and had everything in common.* Selling their possessions and goods, they gave to anyone as he had need. Every day they continued to meet *together* in the temple

> courts. They broke bread in their homes and ate *together* with glad and sincere hearts, praising God and *enjoying the favor of all the people. And the Lord added to their number daily those who were being saved* (italics added).

From this brief description of the beginnings of the Church, we find that everything about the early believers' lifestyle reflected the oneness Jesus prayed for in John 17. Just as Jesus had prayed, we find their being one together in Him having a favorable impact on all the people, resulting in others being saved and added to their number on a daily basis. Apparently, the world saw in the oneness of the Church what Jesus said they would, and a great many of them wanted in. I suspect people still do.

Acts 4:32–33 says,

> *All the believers were one in heart and mind. No one claimed that any of his possessions was his own, but they shared everything they had.* With great power the apostles continued to *testify* to the resurrection of the Lord Jesus, and *much grace was upon them all* (italics added).

Mind you, the church was in excess of 3,000 members by this time, as new members were being added daily. They came from various parts of the Middle East and beyond, bringing with them their different cultures, values, perspectives, and even languages. And yet, Luke described them all being of "one heart and mind." What a powerful testimony of the Lord's prayer (in John 17) being answered in the life of the Church.

Many today see this story as simply describing the socio-economic reality facing the Church in those early years; they don't believe it established the norm or pattern for the Church. On the other hand, others believe this narrative did establish the norm, and they pattern their lifestyles accordingly. I'm not convinced it matters, as it isn't about how they lived, but why they lived as they did. They did so because they were living life every day in the flow of the relationship of the Father and the Son.

When we see the life lived by the early Church, it makes me wonder if there was a direct tie between their experience and Jesus' prayer. Which reflects the "oneness" of the Father and Son: the early Church life described in Acts, or the Church life we are the most familiar with today?

Called into the Fellowship of the Father and the Son

Years after the events described in Acts 2, Paul wrote a letter to the church in Corinth, the letter we call First Corinthians. In 1 Corinthians 1:9, Paul writes, "God, who has called you into fellowship with his Son Jesus Christ our Lord, is faithful." Paul wrote to folks like us. We often read this and other similar passages as though Paul is referring to each of us individually; that God has called each of us, apart from every other believer, to an individual fellowship with Jesus Christ. But that is not what Paul is writing or declaring here. The "you" Paul is writing to here is plural; it refers to all those to whom he is writing the letter. Too bad the interpreters of Paul's letters weren't Texans; they would have had Paul refer to "ya'll or y'all" when using the plural "you." All in the Corinthian church *together* had been called to this fellowship with Jesus Christ. The good news is that we are included in that fellowship. This fellowship to which we have been called is a group experience. You could even say we are "one" in Christ, just as Jesus prayed.

But, there is more to this seemingly simple declaration in 1 Corinthians 1:9. The Greek text has an important definite article attached to this "fellowship" that often is left out of most English translations. If it were included, verse 9 would read, "God, who has called you into (the) fellowship with his Son

Jesus Christ our Lord, is faithful." The significance is this: Paul is referring to the fellowship shared between God the Father and Jesus Christ His Son. This is the very same fellowship of "one" Jesus referred to in His prayer to His Father, recorded in John 17:20–21:

> My prayer is not for them alone, I pray also for those who will believe in me through their message, that all of them may be one, Father, just as you are in me and I am in you. May they also be in us so that the world may believe that you have sent me.

Paul is saying God the Father answered yes to His Son's prayer. The Father has joined us to the fellowship He shares with His Son, Jesus Christ. And remember, it's a group experience. Together we are called to this fellowship of the Father and Son. Together is how we experience this fellowship with them, for there is only one fellowship, the fellowship of the Father, the Son, and the Holy Spirit. *Together* is how we experience this fellowship, for we are "one" *together* in Christ. As Christians this is our reality, this is our life; we are one in Him.

Another Perspective of "Us"

Now just in case you think I'm reaching, referring to some dropped definite article in the English translation of the Greek text above, look at John's first letter. John reflected on this same reality of oneness in Christ in 1 John 1:3–4, when he wrote, "We proclaim to you what we have seen and heard, so that you also may have fellowship with us. And our fellowship is with the Father and with his Son, Jesus Christ. We write this to make our joy complete."

John begins with the fellowship enjoyed by the Father and His Son, Jesus. This is at the very core of life, as John understands it. John and all of the other believers have been included in this fellowship between the Father and the Son. Thus, when John speaks of "our fellowship," he is referring to the fellowship of the Father and the Son and all those who believe in Jesus Christ. There is one fellowship, the fellowship of the Father and the Son, and all those who believe in Him—*together*.

John does not write from the singular first-person perspective, but rather from the plural. Rather than "I," he writes from the perspective of "we" and "us." While he certainly would have had some personal and individual experiences with the "Word of Life," he nonetheless writes from the corporate experience of the fellowship of the body of Christ. John appears to have seen life in Christ as being a "we-us" experience, rather than "me-you." Rather than being conformed to the self-centered pattern of the world, John revealed the transformed community life of being one, *together in Christ*.

From Many to One

More than a group of separate and independent individuals sharing individually held views and positions, the Church is the living body of the living Jesus Christ. As Christians, our reality is that we are *one in Christ*. This is our only position, whether at peace or in conflict with one another. Once we are in Christ, there is never a point at which we are disconnected from one another. We are one in Him. Our life is His life. Our fellowship is His fellowship. Our conflicts are in Him. And they need to be approached and dealt with in Him.

No matter our feelings, views, positions, decisions, actions, or circumstances, as Christians our reality is this: *We are one in Christ*. We can choose to live out our reality in Christ with one another, or we can choose to follow the self-focused, disconnecting pattern of the world. But our reality remains the same: we are one in Christ. This is so because our reality is about Him, and not about us; it's in Him, and not in ourselves. It is so because our life is His, and not our own. We share in His life together, and not independently and separately.

There is the world pattern, and there is Jesus Christ.

4 Avoidance by any Other Name is Still Avoiding

"So, who are you calling?" Bill had returned to the kitchen to pour another cup of coffee and grab another freshly baked cookie. He and June had talked for quite some time after he returned home from the meeting. After he told her about Jack "going off" at the meeting, she wanted to hear every little detail, and spent a considerable amount of time venting her own feelings toward Jack and a number of other people in the church. When Bill went to the kitchen he expected to find June busy with her cookies, but instead found her with the receiver in one hand, and dialing with the other.

Hesitating a moment, she lowered the receiver and turned to face Bill: "I'm calling Mary," she said.

"Mary?" Bill quizzed. "What are you calling her for? You're not going to tell her what I told you, are you? She's the biggest gossip in town!"

June hung up the receiver. "And she happens to be on the church council. And she needs to know what's going on in this church!"

Bill slumped into a nearby chair. "Oh, June, please, can't you just let this go? He didn't yell at you, after all."

June flushed with anger. "He might as well have! I've got to live with the results, just as if he did yell at me. You come home all upset, just like you do after most of these meetings. And who has to live with the results? I do, that's who! And do you ever do anything about it? No! You just come home all upset until the next time it happens, and then it's the same old thing. Well, this time it's gone too far. Something needs to be done. And if you aren't going to do anything about it, I will. I'm going to call Mary and make sure the council knows about Jack's behavior today. And then I'm going to make sure they take the necessary steps to get him off of that committee . . . and maybe out of the church, if necessary!"

Bill looked up at her. "June, please. . . ."

"Don't 'please' me. I've had it! I'm going to do what you should have done a long time ago." With that, she turned back to the phone, lifted the receiver and began to dial Mary's number once again.

Bill shook his head, gathered up his cookies and cup of coffee, and retreated back into the living room to his favorite chair.

In identifying the elements of the world pattern of reacting to conflict, we have discovered the foundational, self-focused element of being independent of and separate from others in our relationships. And we have traced the roots of this world pattern back to its source, the Tree of the Knowledge of Good and Evil, located in the center of the Garden of Eden.

We have all experienced this disconnected feeling when in conflict with someone else. We often believe this disconnection is a result of our conflict. I have observed that we actually bring this worldly element into our relationship with Christ, and with one another, thus creating relational experiences in the Church that are no different than the relational experiences in the unbelieving world. As in the world, many Christians see themselves, and their relationships, independent of and separate from all other individuals. But, as shown in the previous chapter, this view does not square with the New Testament description of our reality in Christ.

I believe this perceived relational void quickly fills with elements of the world pattern of reacting out of ourselves, especially when experiencing conflict. Among the many reactions found within the world pattern of dealing with conflict, we have encountered two with great frequency. I have, therefore, chosen to use three chapters to focus on these two elements: (1) *avoiding conflict* and (2) *perceiving truth as a personal possession.*

When Avoiding is Appropriate—for a Time

Before we focus on the ways in which avoidance reflects the world pattern of reacting to conflict, we first need to recognize there are times when the Lord will lead us to avoid a particular situation. There are situations in which it is best if the warring parties go to their respective corners until they have cooled down, and are properly prepared to approach their conflict in response to Jesus, rather than reacting out of themselves. This is especially true any time there is the risk of emotional or physical abuse.

There are times when the Lord will lead us to overlook an offense. Proverbs 12:16 says, "A fool shows his annoyance at once, but a prudent man overlooks an insult." Proverbs 17:14 states, "Starting a quarrel is like breaching a dam; so drop the matter before a dispute breaks out." Proverbs 19:11 declares, "A man's wisdom gives him patience; it is to his glory to overlook an offense."

While there may be incidents when it's more beneficial to avoid a conflict than to approach the person as the Lord instructs in Matthew 5:21–24 and Matthew 18:15–17 (see full text below), I do not believe avoidance automatically renders the situations resolved and no longer needing to be approached in Him. In many cases, these situations serve more as delays in approaching the conflict than permanently avoiding it.

Even when we feel led to overlook a particular incident, there are other important considerations to evaluate. As pointed out in material produced by Peacemaker Ministries, we need to ask ourselves if the offense is dishonoring God, seriously damaging our relationship, or hurting others[1]. If we can answer yes to any of these questions, then we will need to prayerfully seek the Lord's guidance in how He will have us deal with the situation.

The #1 Reaction to Conflict in the Church

In working with dozens of conflicted churches, we have observed that the most common world pattern reaction to conflict within the church is avoidance. Certainly there are numerous reactions, from "fight to flight," and everything in between. But Christians tend to use all of them to avoid dealing with the conflict "in Christ." In our experience, avoiding conflict when it is but a spark allows it to become a major blaze. Allowing conflict to grow, while continuing to avoid approaching it in Christ, is like pouring gas on the fire.

Three Types of Avoiders

Avoiders come in both genders and in all sizes, colors, and ages. It is commonly thought that people have a natural tendency to react to conflict in one of two different and opposing

[1] Ken Sande, The Peacemaker (Grand Rapids: Baker Books, Second Edition, 1997) p. 73.

ways, by either fighting or fleeing. It is my opinion they are simply two different expressions of the world pattern of avoiding the conflict. A third expression combines the first two.

1. *The Passive Avoider (flee)*
2. *The Aggressive Avoider (fight)*
3. *The Passive/Aggressive Avoider (flee . . . flee . . . fight)*

1. ***Passive Avoiders***

Among the *Passive Avoiders*, who conform to the world pattern of reacting to conflict by fleeing it, we find at least three sub-groups:

- *The Leavers*
- *The Silent Majority*
- *The Deniers*

The Leavers

We have observed that an overwhelming majority of Christians avoid conflict, and most do so by fleeing it in one form or another. During our trainings offered by Peace Connections Ministries we have an exercise in which the students identify their natural reaction to conflict. We then ask them to group with those who share their major reaction to conflict. Without exception, the vast majority of the attendees gravitate to the avoiders group. I remember in one particular church more than 90 percent of those at the training identified with this group. It was an eye-opening moment for everyone.

During our work with conflicted churches, we often encounter many members who have reacted to the conflict by physically leaving the congregation. Though many do not want to meet with us, most of those we have interviewed have professed that God led them to leave. Perhaps He did. But if He did, then how do we explain the wholesale disconnection we encounter in conflicted churches, if there is but one body and all parts belong to Him and to one another? And how do we explain it if we all belong to each other prior to, during, and following the conflict? Do you really think the Father is responsible for all of this disconnection in the living body of His Son? Do you think Jesus is?

How is it the Lord seems to be leading so many to disconnect from one another, without also attending to His clear commands to deal with these conflicts in a direct, person-to-person manner? Does He actually countermand, on an individual or situational basis, His own commands given in Matthew 5 and Matthew 18?

In the midst of His sermon on the mount, in Matthew 5:22–24, Jesus said,

> You have heard that it was said to the people long ago, 'Do not murder, and anyone who murders will be subject to judgment.' But I tell you that anyone who is angry with his brother will be subject to judgment. Again, anyone who says to his brother, 'Raca,' is answerable to the Sanhedrin. But anyone who says, 'You fool!' will be in danger of the fire of hell. Therefore, if you are offering your gift at the altar and there remember that your brother has something against you, leave your gift there in front of the altar. *First go* and be reconciled to your brother; then come and offer your gift (italics added).

And later, in Matthew 18:12–15, He said,

> What do you think? If a man owns a hundred sheep, and one of them wanders away, will he not leave the ninety-nine on the hills and go to look for the one that wandered off? And if he finds it, I tell you

> the truth, he is happier about that one sheep than about the ninety-nine that did not wander off. In the same way your Father in heaven is not willing that any of these little ones should be lost. If your brother sins against you, *go* and show him his fault, just between the two of you. If he listens to you, you have won your brother over (italics added).

In both of these references, the Lord elevates the value of our human relationships. In the first reference, He instructs us to resolve our conflicts before we worship. How well attended would our worship gatherings be if we seriously applied this teaching? In the second reference, the Lord speaks of His heart when even one part of His body disconnects from the others. Perhaps we might think of this the next time we feel the departures of our brothers and sisters are "God's solution to the conflict."

The Silent Majority

Another expression of the *Passive Avoider* is represented in those we call "The Silent Majority." This group is made up of those who were present during the conflict and remain in the church following the initial blow-up. They don't physically pack up and leave, but they don't resolve the conflict either. Their number usually exceeds the number of *Passive Avoiders* who react to conflict by leaving. They have told us they learned from the pain of the fight and relational disconnections that it was better to keep their views and opinions to themselves than to risk starting a fight that might lead to a repetition of what they just experienced. Some build walls of self-protection, and never allow themselves to get emotionally and relationally connected with others again.

The Deniers

Others protect themselves with a good case of world pattern denial. When we interview them during our conflict intervention process they often say, "Conflict? What conflict?" They eventually admit to noticing more empty places each Sunday, and a list of other "trouble signs." But, they assure us, they haven't been involved in "any of that." They simply "tend to their own business." Of course this also means they have not involved themselves in offering any solutions to the situation either.

We have observed another interesting dynamic in connection with *The Silent Majority*, and *The Deniers*: others often misinterpret their silence. Some folks assume they have no opinion or position in the conflict, which is rarely the case. The *Aggressive Avoiders* often interpret *The Silent Majority*'s and *The Deniers'* silence as agreement with, or approval of, the *Aggressive Avoider*'s views and positions in the conflict. This is a big mistake that often leads to more conflict down the road.

2. ***The Aggressive Avoiders***

I mentioned earlier that *The Leavers* rarely sense being "one in Christ" with those they leave behind. Likewise, there is not often much of a spirit of being "one in Christ" among those who choose to remain. This is especially true among the *Aggressive Avoiders* who react as fighters.

While the *Aggressive Avoiders* are fewer, they make up for their small numbers by their aggressive reactions. As you might expect, we often find the fighters at the center of the storm, stirring things up. They are often the ones championing a particular position, and are ready to go to war with any perceived threat to their cause. Because of this, they are often seen as being the major, or only, source for the conflict impacting the entire congregation. But there are far more contributors to the conflict than just this handful of folks in each congregation.

AVOIDANCE BY ANY OTHER NAME IS STILL AVOIDING

Following a conflict—such as the blow-up among Jack, Alice, and Bill—*Aggressive Avoiders* often pick sides and expand the conflict beyond those originally involved. Even if those on the "other side" leave the church, conflicting views and positions often remain within the gathering. *Aggressive Avoiders* tend to press the fight to get those folks to agree, give in and quiet their opposition, or join the others who have chosen to leave. Once this is accomplished, the *Aggressive Avoiders* often initiate changes in the organizational structures and/or policies of the church. These changes are often said to be for the purpose of protecting the church from similar conflicts in the future. When we dig a little deeper, we often discover these changes also strengthen the views and positions held by the *Aggressive Avoiders*. Surprise!

3. ***Passive/Aggressive Avoiders***

Another expression of the world pattern of avoiding conflict is the *Passive/Aggressive Avoider*. I suspect some of these folks are *Aggressive Avoiders* at heart, but in the spirit of "being nice," or "being a good Christian," they avoid dealing with a conflicted situation until they can't suppress their feelings any further. Then they blow up.

In our story, Alice and Bill are this type of avoider. As we have already learned, there was a long history of conflicted moments in their relationships with Jack, and yet they both reacted by avoiding him, rather than responding to the Lord's commands in Matthew 5 and Matthew 18. In their case, this pattern continued for years, until the line between passive and aggressive avoiding was crossed. Their approach changed, but the results were the same. They still were not approaching their conflict with Jack *in Christ.*

Imagine trying to hold a beach ball under water. Depending on the size of the ball and how deeply it is shoved down, most folks can hold it under for a while. But if the ball grows (escalating conflict) and/or we try to push it down further (burying our feelings), then the task of keeping it down grows more difficult. Eventually, life (Jesus) has a way of tipping us off balance. When it (He) does, the ball pops loose. The bigger the ball, and the deeper it is held, the bigger the splash. We have dealt with the results of some mighty big splashes.

I remember one situation involving an associate pastor who was a *Passive/Aggressive Avoider*. His conflict was with the elder board, and specifically the head elder, who was an *Aggressive Avoider*. For a number of years, the men kept this conflict below the surface, but it grew larger so they pushed it down, further and further, until one particular meeting. Once again, the associate and elder began to disagree, but this time, before anyone knew what happened, the associate exploded at all of them. Issues from years earlier began to flow forth like some great flood. While the others sat there stunned, the associate spewed years of unresolved issues. He finished his outburst by storming out of the room.

Some of the elders, led by the *Aggressive Avoider,* wanted to fire the associate pastor on the spot. Fortunately, a couple of calmer board members helped the group process what had just occurred. The elders eventually contacted Peace Connections Ministries, and our team began an intervention and reconciliation process with them. I am happy to say that, at this writing, the associate is still on staff, and a great deal of the Lord's peacemaking work has been accomplished in and through those who committed themselves to the process. Unfortunately, the head elder was unwilling to be involved in the process, and has since left this congregation. Those who remained continue to pray for the Lord's guidance in reaching out to their brother in the Lord. And, as I've told them, the end of this story has yet to be revealed.

Creating *Third-Person Warriors*

One of the most unhealthy and destructive elements of the world pattern of avoiding conflict we encounter is the creation of *Third-Person Warriors*. Conrad Green, a Christian mediator and wonderful brother in the Lord, first coined this name to describe an activity we are probably all guilty of performing.

When involved in a conflict with person A, have you ever avoided approaching person A, but instead shared your story about the conflict with person B? Sometimes we call this *venting our feelings*. Most of the time it qualifies as gossip, as we share personal information with person B about person A, without person A's knowledge or permission. For sure, it is the first step in the process of creating a *Third-Person Warrior*.

Have you ever shared your conflict story about person A with person B, and person B has reacted to your story by joining "your side" in the conflict? Perhaps it is because of person B's loyalty to you, or their own experiences and feelings toward person A, but after hearing your story, they are now upset with person A as well. Congratulations; you just helped create a *Third-Person Warrior*, formerly known as person B.

In the field of mediation, the mediator is called a *Third Person/Party Neutral*. In other words, the third person does not hold to any side, but remains neutral. The purpose of this neutral third person is to help facilitate the process of resolving the conflict. *Third-Person Warriors* are not neutral, nor do they help facilitate any resolution of the conflict. If anything, they expand it.

Person A has no idea you spoke to person B about him, until he encounters person B and gets a cold shoulder, or something a bit more aggressive than that. So now, rather than just a conflict between you and Person A, we have an additional conflict between Person A and Person B.

If, rather than approaching you, person A talks about your conflict to persons D, H, and T, then they may become

Third-Person Warriors on person A's side. So now, rather than approaching the conflict between you and person A, you both have now contributed to creating additional conflicts between yourselves, and persons B, D, H, and T.

I hope you don't assume that persons B, D, H, and T are going to keep to themselves all that you and person A have told them. Oh, I know, when you talked to person B you told him to keep everything confidential. Person A told persons D, H, and T the same thing. Some of them may even honor that commitment. Others will not. And it won't be because they forgot your request. As they prepare to pass on the gossip burning a hole in their mouth, they will often say, "I probably shouldn't tell you this, but. . . ." And the process of making another *Third-Person Warrior* will begin anew.

The Lord does allow for us to involve third parties to our unresolved conflicts, in the role of helping to facilitate a process of resolution and reconciliation. Only those who are willing and able to serve in such a capacity should hear about our conflicts with others.

The Baggage of Unresolved Conflict

When we avoid a conflict, it remains unresolved. It also remains with us. So we are never able to put an unresolved conflict "behind us." Most of the elements of our conflicts are internal. So when they remain unresolved between us, we take them along with us.

I have seen evidence of this reality many times when interviewing brothers and sisters who begin to recount a particular situation. As they tell their story, it is as though it occurred just moments before. Emotional responses are heightened, and sometimes they cry or grow angry.

During one such interview, a sister in the Lord was recounting an incident that had obviously been very painful and upsetting to her. I noticed she was using names and describing a situation I had not heard of in two prior days of interviewing church members. I eventually asked her when and where this incident took place. It had occurred eight years earlier, in a different church, in a different town. This conflict had never been resolved. Instead, it was as much alive in her during our interview as it had been the day it actually occurred.

We not only take our unresolved conflicts with us wherever we go, but their impact and results go with us as well. It became very obvious to us that the reaction to the conflict this sister was having in her present church was directly fueled by the elements of this painful, unresolved experience she had been carrying with her for eight years. It had not only impacted her life for the past eight years, it was continuing to impact her relationships in her new church, and helping to fuel the conflict occurring there.

The Unwelcome Gift that Keeps on Giving

As the elements of unresolved conflicts accumulate within us, we become the walking wounded, often unaware of the wound we carry, or the infection it is spreading wherever we go among the body of Christ.

How many times have you been excited to have a new family show up in your midst, and in visiting with them discover they have recently left another local expression of Christ's body? You listen with compassion as they unfold their story of how poorly they were treated by "that other church." You listen to them describe the sinful attitudes and actions rampant in "those people," and you begin to share their view of "that other church." So you wrap your arms around these new folks, and assure them of better treatment in your church. And the whole time no one realizes the infection being shared, much less the fact you are one in Christ with "those people" you now feel so disconnected from, often without ever meeting them.

We have found epidemic proportions of this world pattern of avoiding conflict and seeking relief by fighting or fleeing. Often, at the center of the storm will be folks who arrived bearing the wounds suffered by the "hurtful people" at their previous church. Then, after they disconnect from you and connect with another gathering of Christ in the community, you get to become the new "other people" who treated them so poorly, as they describe you to the next congregation to welcome them with open arms. And the infection of unresolved conflict continues its spread through the body of Christ and the local community.

By the way, pastors are not immune from carrying the wounds and infection of unresolved conflict from one congregation to another. A common solution in conflicted churches is either for the pastor to resign "for the good of the church," or for the congregation to fire him for the same reason. Rarely does the congregation or pastor work on resolving the conflict(s) and reconciling the relationship(s), whether or not the pastor moves on to a new assignment. In a recent online newsletter article, Ken Sande of Peacemaker Ministries shared a number of shocking statistics about the high cost of conflict among Christians. Sande reported that 23 percent of the current pastors in the United States had been fired or forced to resign in their ministry experience. It was also reported that 34 percent of all pastors presently served churches that forced their previous pastor to resign.[2] Where do you think all that unresolved conflict went?

When you realize the degree to which this cycle of avoidance and unresolved conflict takes place in the daily experiences of the Church today, you begin to see the impact of not

[2] Ken Sande, Peacemaker Ministries, "The High Cost of Conflict Among Christians," 26, Aug. 2005 <http:www.peacemaker.net/html/artic57.htm>.

recognizing the reality of our oneness in Christ and living it in our relationships with one another. When you realize that Jesus connected our being one with Him to the world knowing the Father sent His Son to the world, and recognizing His love for the Church is the same as His love for His Son, then the impact takes on drastic proportions indeed.

A Personal Fantasy

If I could, I would invent a conflict detector, something along the lines of the security machines at the airports. I would place one of these detectors at every point of entry where Christian brothers and sisters gather. When you passed through, if you were clear of all unresolved conflict, you would be allowed to continue. If the machine detected any unresolved conflict within you, the sensor would go off to alert you and your brothers and sisters of this present danger. In addition, a printout would soon appear, with a listing of each of those with whom you have unresolved conflict. Then, according to Galatians 6:1, and in view of your oneness in Christ, those "who are spiritual" would come along side you to begin the process of "gently" restoring you in your relationship in Christ with these brothers and sisters.

Had this detector been located at the doorway where Jack, Alice, Bill, and the others gathered, it would have gone off years ago when Alice stepped through, following the first time Jack had questioned the level of support for the missionaries so dear to her heart, and she reacted to it so personally. For sure it would have gone off when she attended the most recent meeting. What flowed out of her that day had been building for a long time.

A few weeks earlier, she had listened with interest as Jack described an opportunity for beginning a new work with teens in the community. It seemed like a great idea—until someone raised the funding issue. Alice perceived Jack's suggestion of reviewing the present mission support as a personal attack. She wanted to say something right then, but she held her tongue. She found Jack rather intimidating, so she feared being seen as opposing him and his ideas. It wasn't that she was opposed to ministering to the teenagers, but she kept her views and feelings to herself, at least until she was having coffee later that week with June, Bill's wife. That was when she poured out her fears of what Jack was planning to do, and the tragic impact it would have on "our poor missionaries who have come to depend on our support all these years." The seeds of disconnection were growing, not only in Alice, but now also in June. Of course, they were growing in the hearts of Jack, Mike, and others as well.

My Conflict; Your Conflict

But our reality is this: He has made us all one-in-Him. The only conflict between us we can truly and fully "get over" or "get beyond" is the resolved conflict that flows from our reconciliation in Him, our *oneness-in-Christ.* This means any conflict left unresolved between us remains between us. More than that, because we are one together in Him, our unresolved conflict remains in us. Because we are in Him together, and He is in us, our unresolved conflict remains in Him as well. Because we all belong to one another in our oneness in Christ, any unresolved conflict between any of us remains in all of us, for we are all one-in-Him.

This reality is difficult for many of us to understand, due to the degree of our conformity to the world pattern. So let me put it this way: Imagine your body has a cancerous growth in the bowel. And let us allow for each part of your body to have its own individual identity. Can you imagine your arm declaring that it is free from cancer because the cancer is in the bowel? I can hear the arm now: "Cancer? What cancer? I'm not involved in any of that cancer. I'm just tending to my own business, being the arm."

Now do you understand the gravity of this issue?

Because those of us who make up this body of Christ in the world today so often fail to recognize this reality of being one in Christ, we have parts declaring their disconnection from one another in every corner of the world. Maybe even in your corner. But we need to understand the only conflicts we can truly and fully "get over" and "beyond" are those we approach together in Christ. Otherwise, we take them with us wherever we go, or stay, and the fallout infects more and more parts of His body.

Avoid the Conflict and Avoid Him

The Lord does not call us to avoid our conflicts. He calls us to approach them—together—in Him. When we avoid our conflicts, we avoid far more than just the conflict. We avoid opportunities to experience Him more fully. We avoid opportunities to more fully experience who we are in Him.

When we avoid our conflicts rather than approaching them together in Him, we conform our lives to the world pattern, rather than to the life of Jesus Christ.

We also need to recognize the world is watching. Rather than seeing the members of His Body deal with our conflicts in ways different from them, the world often watches His Body dismember itself. No wonder so many have such a difficult time believing God sent His Son to the world, and that He loves the Church as He loves His Son. When we conform to the world pattern of reacting to conflict out of our *self* rather than responding together in Him, we don't do ourselves any favors. We don't do the Church any favors. And we don't do the world any favors either.

5 Fear and Avoidance

As soon as Mike got off the phone with Jack, he began to search for Kevin Ward's number. Locating it, he pressed the call button on his cell phone, and within moments Kevin was on the line.

"Kevin . . . this is Mike Hanson. Listen, I don't know if you heard about the big blow-up at the meeting at church . . . Yeah, it was ugly, man. Jack was trying to promote the needs for the new youth center, and all the old folks blew a gasket . . . Yeah, it was something. Anyhow, Jack walked out, not that I blame him. I just got off the phone with him . . . What? . . . Yeah, he's pretty upset. Anyhow, we're going to try and get together a meeting of like-minded folks to see what we can do to make some leadership changes around here, get some forward-thinking folks who aren't always trying to relive the glory days of thirty years ago, know what I mean? . . . Exactly! So, you interested? . . . Great, man! I've got a bunch more calls to make, so when I know more, I'll call you back . . . What? . . . Yeah, call everybody you think will be interested in getting this church moving forward for a change . . . Yeah, I'll call you back when we get a set time and place. See ya later."

As soon as he ended this call to Kevin, Mike began to scroll through his phone list, looking for the next person he could call and enlist on his side of the battle he could see coming.

As pointed out in the previous chapter, our experience has shown us that most Christians react to conflict by conforming to the world pattern of avoiding it. Admittedly, not too many folks enjoy dealing with conflict, and most try to avoid it like the plague. We can create it easily enough, sometimes without even trying. But we don't usually invest much of ourselves in the work involved to deal with it in a healthy manner that reflects Jesus Christ in us and through us.

After hundreds of interviews with Christian brothers and sisters in conflicted churches, we've found the major reason for avoiding conflict is fear. It comes in many different forms, but the roots can all be traced back to that Garden of Eden scene we shared in Chapter 2. Why did Adam and Eve hide from God? Fear. Why did Adam blame Eve, and Eve blame the serpent? Right again; it was fear. And it all comes from perceiving, understanding, and experiencing life by means of the Tree of the Knowledge of Good and Evil. Now hang on to that thought for a moment.

The Fear of Not Knowing How

The fear that motivates our conflict avoidance takes many forms. One of the most common we have heard is the fear of not knowing how to deal with our conflicts *in Christ.*

Each time we present one of our training seminars, we ask for a show of hands of those who have had any previous training in resolving conflict. I remember one situation where four individuals in a group of 150 raised their hands. We have been with churches where no one in the group had any formal training in conflict resolution. Those with training usually receive it as part of their job training. Few church leaders have ever received any formal training in conflict resolution. In fact, of the dozens of churches with which we have had contact, only three pastors have had any formal training in dealing with conflict, and none received it in a Christian setting of local church, college, or seminary.

The Church is behind the curve in equipping her members with information and skills for dealing with conflict in a way that manifests the Lord by expressing the health and wholeness that is ours in Jesus Christ. This sad reality is amplified when you realize Christians not only have the Prince of Peace dwelling within, but also that the Scriptures reveal many of the fundamental principles practiced by mediators throughout the world. If any group in the world today should have a handle on a healthy approach to dealing with conflict, it is the Church, the living body of the living Christ.

Unfortunately, you have a better chance of receiving this kind of teaching and modeling in the secular world than you do in the Church. While many of the principles and methods are the same, the spirit in which it is accomplished, and the purpose for which it is done is far different in the secular world than what the Lord has given His Church.

Fear of Hurting the Other Person

Many fear hurting the other person if we approach him or her about the conflict or our hurt feelings. On occasion, this has been literal, as we have had folks tell us the reason they did not confront the other person is they were afraid their anger would lead to physical violence. While I'm glad they chose not to express their anger in such a fashion, it saddens me to know the only two solutions they could think of were to smash the other person or avoid him or her altogether. Even when we're afraid of hurting feelings instead of faces, it's still a concern that the only other option many of us can think of is to avoid the person and the situation.

Fear of Getting Hurt

Another expression of the fear that prevents us from approaching conflicts *in Christ* is the fear of getting hurt. You only have to witness someone "blowing up" at a church meeting—or at a family member in the parking lot—to convince you to avoid approaching that person about a conflict. Sometimes those fears flow from past conflicts in our families, with friends, or on the job. Because those situations didn't go well and resulted in pain, we start getting a bit jumpy whenever we feel conflict in the air.

We have a dear sister in our Lake Shore Community gathering who used to volunteer in the baby nursery during every church meeting. That was her method for avoiding personal and church-related conflicts that didn't go well over the years. I was much more willing to face the potential of some angry brothers and sisters than a nursery full of babies and toddlers. But that's just me. I'm happy to report this sister no longer avoids dealing with conflict. The Lord has done a marvelous work in her over the years, and now she often serves as a peacemaker.

Fear of Damaging a Relationship

Another fear is that of damaging the relationship. I've never been quite sure what kind of a relationship we're trying to protect by pretending all is well when it isn't. What kind of relationship do we think it will be if it's built on disobeying the Lord's clear instructions to deal with our conflicts in a direct manner? The fact we hear this reason as often as we do may say a lot about the health of the average relationship believers experience in the body of Christ today.

The Idol of Being Nice

We call this fear reaction the "Idol of Being Nice." Now I'm all for being nice. I think my parents did a pretty good job of teaching me social manners that included how to be nice to others. Using "please" and "thank you" is being nice. Saying "excuse me" when you need to interrupt someone, or get through a space they are blocking, is being nice. I even walk on the street side when walking with my wife. I was taught that is being nice. So is holding the door for others.

That reminds me of an incident that took place on one of our family trips years ago. We were taking a lunch break along the way and stopped at a McDonald's. We have a large family, and at that time they were all fairly young. While I was trying to help a couple of the children clean the table, and assist our son who navigates in a wheelchair, my wife, Launda, was shepherding the others out the door and toward the van. Her hands were full, balancing leftover food and drinks while trying to hold the hand of one of the youngest. As Launda approached the front doors of the restaurant, a man stepped in front of her and pushed through the doors, allowing them to start closing on her as she came closer. At the last moment, he looked back and noticed her and quickly caught the door before it crashed against her and our young daughter. As he caught the door he said to her, "Oh! I'm so sorry. I thought you were my wife." By the time I got out to the van, Launda was still having a good laugh. When she told me the story, we both laughed. I then suggested we better pray for that poor fella. Launda suggested we pray for his poor wife.

I guess it was nice that the man caught the door before it slammed in Launda's face. But it wasn't nice if he was unconcerned about his own wife. Apparently he wasn't sure what was nice and what was not. I think a fair number of us do know, so we should understand that avoiding conflict out of a desire to be nice is not nice. Avoiding conflict so we don't damage our relationship with another person is not nice. Avoiding conflict for fear of hurting or being hurt is not nice. They are all acts of worship at the altar of the "Idol of Being Nice," which in itself is far from being nice.

Avoiding out of fear is about putting our own agenda before the Lord's. It is making the situation about us, not Him. Avoiding out of fear also damages the relationship, the other person, ourselves, and the body of Christ. It damages our relationship with Jesus Christ, for it disobeys His clear instructions in Matthew 5:21–24 and Matthew 18:15–17.

Matthew 5:21–24 says,

> You have heard it said to the people long ago, 'Do not murder, and anyone who murders will be subject to judgment.' But I tell you that anyone who is angry with his brother will be subject to judgment. Again, anyone who says to his brother, 'Raca,' is answerable to the Sanhedrin. But anyone who says, 'You fool!' will be in danger of the fire of hell. Therefore, if you are offering your gift at the altar and there remember that your brother has something against you, leave your gift there in front of the altar. First go and be reconciled to your brother; then come and offer your gift.

Matthew 18:15–17 says,

> If your brother sins against you, go and show him his fault, just between the two of you. If he listens to you, you have won your brother over. But if he will not listen, take one or two others along, so that 'every matter may be established by the testimony of two or three witnesses.' If he refuses to listen to them, tell it to the church; and if he refuses to listen even to the church, treat him as you would a pagan or a tax collector.

Fear of What Follows Matthew 18:15

Another fear used as an excuse to avoid dealing with conflict is concern about the implications of Matthew 18:15. This is the text (shared above) that lays out a process of dealing with issues directly and personally. If the conflict isn't resolved, it allows for others to be brought into the process. Apparently the Lord knew we'd have conflicts, and we'd need guidance in dealing with them. But because this process is often mishandled—resulting in everything from church splits to lawsuits—many folks would just as soon avoid the confrontation in the first place; they just hope it all blows over.

Unfortunately, as we have often experienced, it doesn't blow over as often as it blows up. If we haven't been personally involved in a blow-up related to the application of this text, most of us know folks who have. Even their second-hand accounts convince us we don't want to go there anytime soon. Right?

This is an unfortunate reality for a number of reasons. First, as pointed out above, this fear motivates us to disobey the Lord, and not approach our conflicts in Him, as He commands. I hope we all recognize the folly of that approach. To think that disobeying the Lord will lead to healthier relationships and healthier churches is foolish, if not sinful.

Second, I believe most applications of this text fail to capture the context in which it is found. Because so many Christians view their life through the world pattern of right and wrong, they often apply this text to one another with the gentleness and love of a sledgehammer, or the judgmental swiftness of a lynch mob. These approaches do not fit the spirit in which Jesus presented this message.

Look again at Matthew 18:12–14, where Jesus said,

> What do you think? If a man owns a hundred sheep, and one of them wanders away, will he not leave the ninety-nine on the hills and go to look for the one that wandered off? And if he finds it, I tell you the truth, he is happier about that one sheep than about the ninety-nine that did not wander off. In the same way your Father in heaven is not willing that any of these little ones should be lost.

Having planted in their hearts a word picture of love, compassion, recovery, and restoration, He then goes on to describe how we are to approach those who sin against us. In sinning against one another, we wander from the relational way of the One who made us one in Him. Therefore, when prompted by the Lord, we who have been sinned against are to approach the other person, not to blame, judge, or punish, but to "find" the one who has "wandered off." We are to carry in our hearts the Father's love that seeks to find and redeem the sinner, all the way to the step described in verse 17, if necessary.

Fearing the results of following the Lord's commands in Matthew 18:15–18 is unfortunate because, when we avoid approaching our conflict, we avoid a powerful and unique opportunity to experience Jesus together, on a much deeper level. After commanding His disciples to approach their conflict with one another in a spirit of humility, and in a loving and redeeming way, Jesus then declares this promise: "For where two or three come together in my name, there am I with them."

Do you want to involve yourself in an activity in which the Lord promises to be with you? Then approach your conflicts with one another in Christ, and He will be there right in the middle of things. We'll have more to say about this promise in a later chapter.

We've heard other Christians list other fears about obeying the Lord and approaching their conflicts with one another in Him, but these lead the list. The bottom line is this: we were not called to live our lives motivated by fear. Instead, He gave us His life so that we may live lives motivated by love.

God's Solution to Our Fear—Even Our Fear of Conflict

First John is a powerful little letter. It's filled with principles that reveal Jesus Christ. The letter's major theme ("love one another") flows from our Lord's heart. But 1 John 4:18 deals specifically with the fears we use to excuse conflict avoidance: "There is no fear in love. But perfect love drives out fear, because fear has to do with punishment. The one who fears is not made perfect in love."

That is a powerful statement. This letter is all about love. It's about God loving us, and us loving Him and one another. Then John proclaims there is no fear in love. No fear in love. Does that register in your heart and spirit? If fear is the motive of our avoidance, then there is no love there. Not God's kind of love. That really sets the whole "be nice and avoid" thing on its ear, doesn't it?

Perfect love drives out fear. That is an awesome proclamation, isn't it? The word "perfect" here carries with it not so much the freight of moral perfection as that of being whole or complete. It reflects the wholeness or completeness that comes with being one together in Christ. The love that reflects this kind of wholeness and completeness drives out fear. I love that. When we relate to one another in and through perfect (whole and complete) love, then fear is not on the radar. We will no longer fear approaching our conflicts. Instead, we will see this activity as an act of love that reflects and strengthens the wholeness, the completeness, and the love of our oneness in Christ.

John proclaims this kind of love drives out fear ". . . because fear has to do with punishment." This statement travels to the very heart of a fundamental theme we have been looking at in the previous chapters. Punishment comes out of that flow of good and evil or right and wrong. When seeing life through the filters of good and evil or right and wrong, we turn to punishment to reinforce the "right-ness" of right, and the "wrong-ness" of wrong. At the same time, we also fear this punishment. Sometimes we fear exercising it. Most of the time we fear receiving it.

We also fear being wrong; thus, we react by competing as we try to prove ourselves right. Or we react by withdrawing and avoiding, so as not to be held accountable. We do so, I believe, because we tend to see things by the world pattern of right and wrong, rather than through what is life (Jesus Christ), and what is not life.

We are also fearful of doing wrong, so we react by avoiding, convincing ourselves that at least we aren't doing anything wrong by doing nothing at all. However, to avoid these issues between us is to disobey the Lord.

God's Love Leads Us to Completeness Together in Christ

The love that makes us whole and complete—the love that flows from our oneness in Christ—drives out this fear. I like the picture described here. Love drives out the fear that gets in our way of being whole and complete as the body of Jesus Christ. This ain't no mamby-pamby kind of love. It's a driving force. It's not afraid of conflict. God's love engages conflict. God's love transforms conflict. God's love uses conflict to build the body of Jesus Christ stronger and stronger, more fully reflecting the glory of His Son into this world.

I'm glad this love He shares with us drives out the fear of punishment, because John also tells us ". . . the one who fears is not made perfect in love." As we saw earlier, the word "perfect" here means being made whole, complete, or fulfilled. John is saying here that those who operate out of the fear that comes from the world pattern of right and wrong are not made whole and complete in His love. This may be why so much of the Church is fragmented, with unresolved conflict. It's not really a conflict issue as much as it is a lack of love issue—God's love, rather than the world's.

But it doesn't have to be this way; we do not have to operate out of fear when approaching conflict. We can learn to approach conflict within our oneness in Christ. When we do, His love picks us up from that path of right and wrong and punishment, and sets us on His path of life, truth, and freedom. Rather than unresolved conflicts or broken relationships, we can experience strengthened relationships, because we were able to resolve the conflicts in and through His love. Is there any greater witness of Jesus Christ more needed in our world today?

Jack, Mike, Alice, Bill, and all the others sucked into their growing conflict, have reacted to conflict out of fear more than responding in Christ. Jack has been fearful of being wrong, and often reacts by defending his "right" position. Mike shares a lot of that fear as well. He also wants to be seen as a "nice" guy, so he does most of his reactionary work behind the scenes. Alice has always been afraid of doing wrong, so she avoided approaching Jack until that fateful meeting where her emotions got away from her and she verbally attacked Jack. And Bill has wanted to approach Jack numerous times, but just didn't know how to do it without making matters worse. Meanwhile, the environment they helped create has set the stage for some very un-Christ-like behavior on all their parts, resulting in untold damage to individuals, relationships, ministry, and the Christian witness in their community.

Approach—Don't Avoid

As Christians, we do not have to react to conflict out of fear, or any other self-focused reaction. As Christians, we don't have to follow the world's extremes of smashing someone in the face, or disconnecting from them completely.

When faced with an unresolved conflict, Jesus commands us to "Go" and approach the other person directly and personally. The world pattern allows us to avoid approaching the core of the conflict, by either fighting or fleeing. Jesus does not. His command is to go and approach the other person; and in so doing, experience our reality in Him together. We will look at the elements of this approach in Chapter 10.

6 Truth: A Thing to be Possessed—or a Person to be Experienced?

Time: 6:35 A.M., approximately 14 hours after "the incident" at the Mission Committee meeting
Location: Meeting room of the Corner Café
Purpose: Weekly Men's Group Prayer Gathering

After everyone had shared what he knew about the blowup at the Mission Committee meeting Sunday afternoon, elder Lawrence Johnson spoke up. "I think it is obvious what this situation reveals. A number of us have been concerned for some time about the influences some of these young families have been bringing into our church family. And while I agree it's a blessing to have the church growing—and I realize it takes young families—it has not been lost on me how much we older members have had to give up in order to attract these young folks to our church." All the men who were gathered for prayer murmured in agreement.

Lawrence continued, "I think we must now recognize the fact that, in our attempt to save our church, we may be losing it to these young folks and their modern, worldly ways."

From across the table, Benjamin Hoff replied, "That's the truth, Larry. So what are we going to do about it?"

Time: 7:45 P.M., five days after "the incident" at the Mission Committee meeting
Location: The home of Virgil and Elaine Swanson
Purpose: Meeting called by Mike Hanson, to organize a movement to change leadership and renew the life of the church

"The truth of the matter is," Mike went on to summarize the views he'd been sharing with the others in the room, "Alice, Bill, and the rest of their group, have been running the show for far too long. It is time for new life, new direction, and new leadership. This whole thing is about more than just defending Jack. The future of the church is at stake here."

"That's the truth," added someone from the back of the room. Other voices chimed in, and plans began to be made regarding how to remove much of the church leadership and replace them with new "forward-looking" people.

The Truth, the Whole Truth, and Nothing but the Truth

Perhaps at a time like this, it would be helpful if a person would arise to repeat the question Pilate asked of Jesus so long ago: "What is truth?" I'm not sure just how interested Pilate was in the answer to his question, as it doesn't appear he hung around long enough to engage Jesus in a conversation about it. Perhaps, like the prayer group above, or those gathered with Mike, Pilate thought he already possessed the truth. This is often an element of the world pattern we discover in conflicted situations, and is most reflected when truth is seen as a thing to be possessed.

We tend to throw the word "truth" around like we do the word "love." The word "love" means many things to many people in a host of different situations, and yet the same word is used. *I love ice cream. I love my wife.* But I'm hardly communicating the same love in each of those statements. The word "truth" is like that. It tends to mean different things in different situations, but the same word is used. So what do I mean when I use the word in the context of this book?

It might help if I first define what I do not mean. When speaking of truth as a thing to be possessed, I am not speaking of what many refer to as God's truth, or absolute truth. I'm not referring to the truth of Scripture, or doctrinal truth. I absolutely believe in the absolute truth of God.

What I'm speaking of when referring to "truth as a thing possessed" is the personal, individual views and perceptions we each have regarding the elements involved in our conflicts with one another. Our perceptions of the things said and done, the feelings attached to these memories, our own desires, interpretations, judgments, and assumptions, all create this "truth." We base our future perceptions, attitudes, behaviors, and feelings on our own creation of this "truth."

I have chosen to use the word "truth" rather than "story," as others do when speaking of these personal perceptions and feelings. I do so for three reasons. First, we often feel our perceptions and feelings are totally accurate, factual and, therefore, "true." Second, we also tend to believe what is true for us is true for everyone. Third, the word "story" carries a connotation of being made-up, fictional, and, therefore, not true. So, for these reasons, I refer to this collection of personal perceptions, beliefs, and feelings, as the "truth we possess" when dealing with one another.

Lawrence and Benjamin have their individual "truths," which were shared in one degree or another by the other men gathered for prayer. Their truth includes the modern world's "threat" to the church, introduced by the young families who have joined their church in recent years.

Mike has his "truth." Mike's "truth" is that a number of leaders in the church need to be replaced, so new life and new directions can be introduced. In Mike's "truth" these folks are obstacles to be removed—deadwood to be trimmed away. As he stated in the meeting of like-minded folks he convened, "They are old-fashioned and unable to engage the present, much less the future. The Lord is breathing new life into the church these days, and this group doesn't get it. They've had their day, but a new day has come. The Lord is leading in new directions. A lot of work needs to be done, and these folks are far more interested in keeping things as they were than doing what the Lord wants done today. They need to go." There is a lot more to Mike's "truth," but you get the drift.

By the way, while it will often be lost on Lawrence, Mike, and many of the rest of us, everyone else connected with this situation has his or her "truth" as well. Even those who openly agree with Lawrence's general truth—or Mike's—will have different specifics. In fact, these differences in specific elements of shared "truths" often lead to conflict among the very folks who claim to agree with one another today. Of course, their truths are not the only truths involved in this conflict, as Alice, Bill, and every other member of the church has his or her "truth" as well.

Which means each pictures his or her conflict to be in defense of *THE truth*; their "truth." To change their position in any way would be seen as admitting their truth was more than just wrong, it was actually a lie. No wonder they were able to turn so quickly from loving brothers and sisters to battle-ready warriors; they were defending the truth, after all.

TRUTH: A THING TO BE POSSESSED—OR A PERSON TO BE EXPERIENCED?

In an earlier chapter I mentioned a natural reaction to conflict; we call it "fight or flee." God gave our bodies a safety system to protect us when we are at risk. It works wonderfully when we perceive our life and/or limbs are at risk. Without a conscious thought, the adrenal glands begin to pump adrenalin into our blood system. Other glands and organs begin to pump a mix of different chemicals and hormones as well, creating an interesting brew, which in turn impacts other systems and organs within our body. The heart pumps faster, and the lungs breathe faster and shallower, in order to rush more oxygenated blood into the arms and legs, preparing to fight or flee the threat. As the blood levels and corresponding blood pressure begin to build in the arms and legs, they begin to drop in other parts of the body, including the brain. The upper, reasoning parts of the brain lose blood as it is redirected to the "survivor" area of the brain stem, as well as to the arms and legs. In the process, the brain's ability to reason normally is significantly impaired. After all, when life and limb are at risk, what is there to reason? Survival is the goal, and fight or flight is the means.

Unfortunately, this system does not discriminate the perceived threat of a relational conflict from other forms of danger. Thus, when dealing with the relational conflicts that arise in our relationships with one another, this "fight or flight" system is more of a hindrance than a help in moving to solutions, peace, reconciliation, and living out our oneness-in-Christ.

The impact of this reaction on the reasoning parts of the brain also impacts our ability to take in the full picture of what is taking place around us. As a result, our ability to fully and accurately record what we and those around us say and do is impaired. Have you ever been in a situation where it feels as though everything has gone into slow motion, and your vision is tunneled, excluding everything except the one thing you are focused on? The authors of *Crucial Conversations . . . Tools For Talking When Stakes Are High* describe this as being "doped-up" and "dumbed-down".[1] In other words, this flood of chemicals and hormones powerfully impacts our ability to know the whole and objective "truth of the matter" regarding who said and did what in such circumstances.

A long time ago, in a galaxy far, far away, in a place called college, I took a social psychology course, of which I remember one class in particular. The professor had arranged for a stranger to enter the lecture hall during the lecture, rush to the front table, grab the professor's briefcase, and bolt for the door. Needless to say, there was quite a commotion in the room when this all played out. Most of us sat frozen in our seats, not really comprehending what had just taken place. A couple football "jocks" leaped to their feet and were preparing to pursue the "thief" (I suspect these guys would qualify as "fighters" in a conflict), when the professor called them back and began to settle the class down.

He asked us what we all had just seen. At first, students described the intruder's actions. Then the professor asked for more descriptive details, such as what he was wearing, and exactly what he did and said. What unfolded was a lesson I'll never forget. Some described him as being at least six feet tall; others pegged him as much shorter. Some described him as a blond, while others saw dark hair; and the hair length varied quite a bit as well. He wore everything from a red, to a blue or black baseball cap. Or he didn't wear a cap at all. His clothing varied from a windbreaker, to a jean jacket, to a plaid shirt. Some said he yelled something. Others didn't hear a thing. You get the idea. We got the point. And I've questioned eyewitness testimony ever since.

Under the best of conditions, our brains collect bits and pieces of all the input received at any given moment. We then thread these bits and pieces together with our own internal

[1] Kerry Patterson, et al., *Crucial Conversations . . . Tools For Talking When Stakes Are High* (New York: McGraw-Hill, 200

editing system, another process of normal brain function, and we create our "truth" about what has taken place. Because we each have different filtering systems collecting different input, we can experience the same event and come away with very different memories. Married folks know exactly what I'm talking about. Teenagers and their parents do, too.

But the important point we need to realize is this: even on a good day our "truths" are going to differ from one another, even when experiencing the very same event. So perhaps we shouldn't be so confident in our "truths" that we are willing to go to war over them at a drop of a hat. When we are under the stress caused by conflict, causing brain function to be negatively impacted by the combination of lowered blood pressure and the flood of chemicals and hormones preparing for "fight or flight," we may want to follow mom's instructions: "stop, take a deep breath, and count to ten." That's actually pretty good advice. There are other options to consider, which we will describe in following chapters.

Over the years, we've listened to many brothers and sisters, and their "truths." We've observed a number of similarities among those who treat truth as a possession in their personal and individual perceptions, understandings, and experiences.

The Higher the Stakes, the Greater the Reaction

First, the greater the stakes are in the conflict, the more reactive we become regarding our "truth." Sometimes this emotional ramp-up develops quickly, and leads to sudden outbursts that catch us by surprise. Other times it develops slowly, involving numerous unresolved situations over a period of time, each one adding to the growing emotional reservoir within us. Some react by turning to silence. Others react with violence. Both reflect the world pattern of reacting in our *selves*, rather than responding *in Christ*. Often these emotions control us more than our will, mind, values, or even the Lord.

Many of those we've worked with who left shocking voicemails, or wrote hurtful letters and e-mails, often wondered later how they could have done such things, as that kind of behavior is not who they are, nor how they normally behave.

At one point in our time with some brothers and sisters in Christ, we began to describe what we saw "from the outside looking in." Many were shocked and brought to tears. A sister volunteered this observation: "It appears so ugly when you describe it." But she, along with others, admitted we were simply reporting what they had each been describing to us during our interview sessions with them.

It is interesting how defending or promoting this "thing" we call "truth" can lead to behavior we later question, or even call "ugly." This "ugliness" comes from reacting in ourselves, not responding in Christ.

From Cooperation to Competition

A second similarity we often encounter when brothers and sisters in Christ see truth as a possession is this: it often leads to a competitive environment of "right or wrong" and "win or lose."

If I see my view as the "true view," then that means my view is "right." If I'm right, then that means you are "wrong," and also "not true." If I am right and true, and you are wrong and not true, then my goal is to "win," in defense of everything that is right and true, and the defeat of everything that is wrong and not true. Amen, and pass the ammunition!

A few years ago, as part of a mediation team called to come alongside a body of believers in deep conflict, I was seated in a room with two of the most intensely conflicted groups in this local expression of the body of Christ. They sat on opposing sides of the conference room table, and you could feel the anxiety and tension in the air. The only sounds we heard were quiet murmurings among persons sitting beside one another. Suddenly, everyone's attention was drawn to the doorway, as the leader of one of the groups noisily struggled to enter the room. The racket he caused was due to the heavy load he carried: five three-ring-binder notebooks, containing church meeting minutes going back years, complete with a rainbow of colored sticky-tabs marking no less than a dozen places in each notebook. He made his way to his group's side of the table, plopping his load down when he arrived at his open chair. Without any prompt from either of the mediators, he announced to us: "I assumed you would be interested in the truth, so I brought all the evidence you will need to get to the bottom of things here."

This brother was prepared for battle. Shooting from the hip, or just blowing off some steam wasn't enough for him. He had done his research. He knew his facts. He knew his "truth." He knew his "enemy" and their "untruths." He was prepared for anything they threw at him. He was ready to defend "truth" as he knew it and defeat any and all who challenged it. He was "right," and they were "wrong," and if he had anything to do with it, "right would win" and "truth" would vanquish all its foes. Of course, the truth in this case was the "truth" he possessed. And who were the foes in this battle? They were his brothers and sisters in Christ who did not share his "truth" but had their own. That fact was very evident in their faces and body language as he sat down.

We All See it the Same Way—Right?

This situation also illustrates the third similarity we find when brothers and sisters in Christ see "truth" as our personal possession; we tend to believe everyone on our side shares our "truth"—as should everyone else. That perception is obvious by the effort we put into trying to win over to our side those who disagree with us.

What isn't always so obvious to us is that—often with some very surprising results—we also tend to assume that everyone on our side of an issue sees and believes things the same way we do. Our Peace Connections team was meeting with a group who had all signed a letter they made public to the church, detailing a number of issues they had with the pastor. The content of the letter was presented as representing the views of all those who signed it. But in listening to their "truths," it became obvious to us that few of them were in full agreement with everyone else's "truths" in the letter. In a couple of situations, some open disagreement emerged among them. As the reality of this fact was brought to their attention, they were all a bit surprised, if not shocked. One of the group leaders said it best when they concluded, "I think I need to reconsider my position in all of this."

If Ya Ain't with Us, Then Ya Must be A'gin Us

Some of their attitudes and behaviors toward one another reflected a fourth similarity we find when brothers and sisters in Christ see "truth" as a possession: we tend to dehumanize or demonize those who disagree with us, along with their "wrong" views, positions, interests, behaviors, and motives.

We start the dehumanizing process when we begin relating to others on the basis of our labels according to our "truth" about them. Often this dehumanizing begins rather innocently, with the label of "them" or "those people," reflecting our "truth" that they are different and separated from us in some way. With that simple label, we set out upon the world's path of disconnecting emotionally, relationally—and in some cases physically—from those with whom we are actually "one in Christ." From here, it's an easy slide from describing them as different from us to labeling them according to our "truth" about their behavior, motives, beliefs, and, eventually, their relationship with Jesus Christ. From labeling them as disagreeable, we begin to label them as difficult, manipulative, liars, power hungry, and other labels that actually have more to say about our own hearts than about them. We start by labeling them as "negative," then they become "selfish, judgmental, out to get their own way in everything," and much more. Though they were once seen as a "friend, brother, or sister," they eventually become a "sinner," and often their relationship with Jesus Christ falls into suspicion as well.

Once we travel far enough down this path to see people according to the labels of our "truth" about them, it is but a small step further to demonize them as the enemy. For some of us, this path is a downhill slide taking but an encounter or two. Sometimes we get there simply on the say-so of someone who has already labeled that person as an enemy, based upon their "truth" about him. For others, it's a much more drawn-out affair. But if we stay on this path long enough, we gain a sense of freedom to treat these folks in ways contrary to our beliefs, commitments, inner values, or our normal behavior. In such settings, what the Bible calls wrath is no longer seen as a sinful expression of rage and malice directed toward brothers and sisters in Christ. Instead it becomes "righteous indignation" directed at the enemy, in defense of God and "truth." They are the enemy, sinners attacking "truth," and we feel free to treat them as such. After all, we are right, for we have the "truth" of the matter, and, since we can't both be "right," then they are wrong. It's a "win or lose" battle, and "truth" must win—our "truth," that is.

This oft-repeated process not only illustrates the environment of "right or wrong" and "win or lose" that is created when we see truth as a thing to be possessed, it also reveals a fifth similarity we have encountered in these situations. This view of "truth" as a personal possession often leads us on a path away from Jesus.

At the cross, Jesus made us "one in Him." Back in that room, where two opposing groups were preparing to meet with the mediation team, brothers and sisters in Christ who had once been closest of friends no longer spoke with one another. As we would later learn, many of them were guilty of gossiping, backbiting, slander, rage, and malice toward one another. At the time of this meeting there were few, if any, expressions of forgiveness, patience, kindness, or extending grace toward those with whom they were in conflict. As they competed to see whose "truth" would carry the day, they were behaving less like Christ and more like the world. After months and even years of accumulating unresolved conflicts between them, they were not experiencing more of Christ, but less. In their attitudes and behaviors, they were manifesting more of the world, and less of Jesus. Many of these people were considered the leaders of this particular expression of the local body of Jesus Christ, but we must wonder where exactly they were leading. It certainly wasn't leading any of them to experience more of Jesus. Treating our "truth" as a possession leads us on a path to disconnection rather than to more of our life in Christ.

So when we conform our lives to the world pattern and treat "truth" as something to be possessed, then the higher we perceive the stakes to be in the conflict, the more reactive we become regarding our "truth." This competitive view creates an environment of "right or wrong" and "win or lose." In this environment, we begin to dehumanize or demonize others by labeling them according to our "truth" about them. This allows us to behave toward them in ways contrary to our core values, faith, or normal behavior. In the process, we move increasingly farther down a path not of Jesus, experiencing less and less of Him along the way.

There is truth—and there is TRUTH

Fortunately, there is a better way. His name is Jesus. Not only is He the way, He is the truth as well. Oh, yeah, He's the life, too. So if we were looking at our conflicts from His perspective, the important thing would not be that we possess the "truth" of the matter regarding the issues between us, but that the Truth (Jesus) possesses us. Wouldn't you agree?

Here is another important element in all of this: Jesus, who is the Truth, does have us—together, as one in Him. We've been taught that He has us separately, individually, independent of and separate from one another. But as we have seen, that is not how the Scriptures describe it. There are many parts, but one body. And each of those parts (that's us) belong to all the others.

We can possess our individual "truth," and go to war with one another. Or we can experience Truth (Jesus) together. Two choices, two paths, are before us. One conforms to the world pattern. It begins at the Tree of the Knowledge of Good and Evil and flows toward death. The other path begins at the Tree of Life. Its very flow is life itself. His name is Jesus.

7 Many Parts—One Body—One Life

As was their habit every Wednesday, a handful of student leaders from the church youth group gathered for lunch. Squeezed around a table in the far corner of the high school lunchroom, they often used this time to prepare for that evening's youth group meeting at the church. Occasionally they were able to share personal needs with one another, and even spend some time in prayer. But this day, the conversation had centered on the growing level of conflict in the church.

"Well, like I said, I just don't get all this stuff. Like, Mrs. Morgan is like a grandmother to me. She's got to be one of the sweetest people I've ever known. And I just can't picture her being the kind of person so many people say she is." Becky shook her head in disbelief as she reached for her water bottle.

"I know," Gary replied. "It just blows me away, you know, to watch these folks I've always looked up to as spiritual leaders . . . and . . . like now you wonder just how deep their faith really goes. Ya know what I mean?"

"So let me try this idea on you guys, okay?" Melissa leaned forward so everyone at the table could hear what she was about to say. "I've been wondering what could be done to help things, and I've been praying, and this is what I came up with. You remember the winter retreat a couple years ago when the theme was being one in Christ?" Most of the group nodded their heads. "And do you remember that skit the Seniors did? . . ."

"Oh, yeah," Aaron interrupted excitedly! "I remember! I thought I'd split a gut when they all came out dressed like different parts of the body." Everyone in the group laughed as they remembered the skit.

"So, Melissa," Gary asked, "Are you suggesting we create a skit like that to present to the church?"

"Exactly," Melissa responded. "Don't you remember the impact that had on all of us when we realized that Jesus died to make us one with the Father, and one with one another?" Again a number of heads nodded in agreement.

"So you're thinking the adults need to be reminded of who they are in Jesus?" Gary asked.

Aaron leaned forward, "Either reminded, or possibly learn about it for the first time."

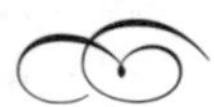

We find Paul's letters filled with descriptions of our oneness in Christ and its impact in our lives as brothers and sisters in Him. I find it very interesting that Paul focuses on this reality of who we are in Christ whenever he is confronting unresolved conflict within the local church. The world pattern leads us to focus first on ourselves, and to perceive, understand, and experience the conflict from a self-focused position. This reactionary pattern flows from the Tree of the Knowledge of Good and Evil, and therefore has nothing to do with those who live in Jesus Christ. That's why, whenever he was confronting an unresolved conflict in a local church, Paul always began by focusing their attention on Jesus, and who those believers were in Him.

One of these references is taken from Paul's thoughts offered in the midst of what appears to have been unresolved conflict between some Jews and Greeks in the church in Rome. You remember that flap, don't you? It's the one where both groups had their own perceptions and positions regarding certain foods and holidays, and what it meant to be a true Christian. Talk about a conflict! It makes arguments over what songs to sing, or the color of the carpet, seem like small stuff in comparison.

So in the midst of his thoughts about it, and on the heels of telling them to no longer conform their lives to the world but be transformed by the renewing of their minds, Paul wrote the following in Romans 12:3–5,

> For by the grace given me I say to every one of you: Do not think of yourself more highly than you ought, but rather think of yourself with sober judgment, in accordance with the measure of faith God has given you. Just as each of us has one body with many members, and these members do not all have the same function, so in Christ we who are many form one body, and each member belongs to all the others.

In just these few words, shared with a church made up of at least two very divergent groups, Jews and Gentiles, Paul connects a specific pattern of relational attitudes and behaviors with the fact we are all members of the one body of Jesus Christ. Over the next sixteen verses in this chapter alone, as well as most of what follows in his letter, Paul goes on to describe different attitudes and behaviors that flow from Christ, and our being one in Him together. A number of these attitudes and behaviors in verses nine through twenty-one have a direct bearing on how Christians are to deal with conflict together in Christ:

- "Love must be sincere. Hate what is evil; cling to what is good. Be devoted to one another in brotherly love. Honor one another above yourselves" (verses 9–10).
- "Be joyful in hope, patient in affliction, faithful in prayer" (verse 12).
- "Bless those who persecute you; bless and do not curse" (verse 14).
- "Live in harmony with one another. Do not be proud, but be willing to associate with people of low position. Do not be conceited. Do not repay anyone evil for evil. Be careful to do what is right in the eyes of everybody. If it is possible, as far as it depends on you, live at peace with everyone. Do not take revenge, my friends, but leave room for God's wrath, for it is written: 'It is mine to avenge; I will repay,' says the Lord" (verses 16–19).
- "Do not be overcome by evil, but overcome evil with good" (verse 21).

These exhortations all reveal the transformation that flows from the life of Jesus Christ. And as Paul points out, it is to take place in the church environment where all the members of His body "belong" to all the others. Paul wrote of a level of Christian connection we have not often found in the Church today.

From Old to New

Many members, one body. We get that, right? Each of us is a member of the one body of Jesus Christ. As such, we belong to Him. We're not our own; we're His. So pretend you are His left foot. I saw those eyes roll, and heard the groans. But humor me. Okay? And by the way, those of you who would rather be his right hand, or left, you'll have to get in line behind James and John (see Mark 10:35–37).

To help facilitate this illustration, I'm going to call you Lefty. So Lefty, as His left foot you have life, but it's not really your life, it's His life. You used to have an existence that you were born with—it was your own, and it flowed from the Tree of the Knowledge of Good and Evil. It was an existence that was headed toward death. And weren't you proud of yourself at the time? You really thought you had it all together back then, didn't you? You were an individual, independent of and separate from all other individuals. Your entire life revolved around being an individual left foot that was independent of and separate from all others.

At some point in your existence you encountered Jesus Christ and the life He desired you to experience. An exchange took place: your old existence for His new life. Actually, He provided for all of that to happen, as He chose you before you chose Him. But the point is, an exchange took place. He took your old existence and gave you His eternal life by including you in His body. What a deal!

At that moment, two important things took place. First, your old existence of death died. I know, your heart never missed a beat, and you never stopped breathing. The way you feel and act some days, you wonder if anything ever happened at all, right? But trust me, at the moment you gave your individual *self* to Jesus Christ, that old existence met its just reward of death, just as God said it would way back in Genesis 2.

Oh, by the way, along with this old existence that died, so did all of its old patterns; everything flat-lined. This means everything that flowed into you and through you from the Tree of the Knowledge of Good and Evil, from the moment you were born as an individual left foot, died. All the world pattern stuff in you died. Your existence as an individual, independent of and separate from other individuals, also died. Focusing on differences, and who's right and who's wrong and trying to figure out where to lay the blame also died. Everything having to do with that old-existence-nature died. While some of the patterns from that old nature continue to influence your new life, the reality is that the old nature is now death to you. Actually, it always was.

Second, and certainly the most exciting part of all this is, in exchange you received His eternal life. Now I realize this may seem like one of those "Duh!" moments. Like, who doesn't get it that when Jesus Christ saves us we go from death to eternal life? But here's the point that many of us miss; you did not get your own, individual, eternal life. You got His, as His is the only eternal life there is. There is really only one Christian life. That is the life of Christ. As He said, He is the life. And all of us who believe in Him are included in this same, *one*, eternal life.

To accomplish this, He placed all who trust Him in His body. By the way, the Bible tells us He has only one of those as well. I guess at some point He decided He needed a left foot, saw you and said, "You're the one for Me." At the moment you said, "Okay," your old self died. You no longer existed independently, separately, and headed toward death. Now you live as a part of Him, by means of His life, eternally. Can you believe it?

But here's the best part: because you live by means of His life, and are now in Him and He is in you, none of that old dead stuff has any control or influence in your life anymore. Truth is, you don't have a life of your own. The life you now live is His life flowing in you and through you. Because He is victorious over all that world pattern stuff, so are you. The world's nature is no longer your nature or reality. Your nature is His nature. Your reality is His reality. His life is your life. Isn't that awesome? Paul wrote about this a lot. I especially like what he had to say about it in the sixth through eighth chapters of Romans. Check it out.

Lefty, I hope you realize your story is not unique. All the other parts of His body share in the same basic story. Though He found all of us in different places along the path flowing from that world-pattern existence, we were all headed toward the same destination: *death*. He has placed all of us who trust Him in His body, together, living by means of His eternal life. It is as Paul writes in Romans 12:4–5a: "Just as each of us has one body with many members, and these members do not all have the same function, so in Christ we who are many form one body. . . ."

The point is, Lefty, your reality in Christ is a corporate reality. By that I mean your *life/reality* is no longer yours, independent of and separate from all the other parts of His body. Nor is my reality in Christ mine alone. Our reality is Him. His reality on earth is us—together—one body with many parts. All the parts share in the one life—His eternal life.

The Next Level in Belonging to Him

But there's more to this relationship than just everyone together being members of His body. If that was all there were, we could still maintain our own independent and separate position in Him, something akin to our seat in the local church sanctuary or auditorium. I suspect you know what I mean. Belonging to His Body would seem no different than belonging to the Rotary Club or PTA. Of course, the purpose and activities would all be different, but the sense of belonging would be the same. We'd all be in Him, together, but everybody would have their own little piece of Him to claim as their very own. While gathered together, we could each enjoy our own personal relationship with Him, separate from and independent of everyone else's relationship with Him. What's more, we could relate to one another in the same way. We could talk and sing about our unity as Christians. But in reality, it would really be more of a level of cooperation among the independent and separate parts. Paul speaks to that in 1 Corinthians 12, which we will attend to later. But you get the picture, don't you?

While that picture may tend to reflect the church life commonly experienced today, it does not reflect the dynamics Paul described in the rest of the Romans text referred to above. Romans 12:4–5 states, "Just as each of us has one body with many members, and these members do not all have the same function, so in Christ we who are many form one body, *and each member belongs to all the others*" (italics added).

In the body of Jesus Christ, every member not only belongs to Him; they also belong to one another. That's what Paul wrote. Each member belongs to Christ. Each member belongs to all the other members. So, Lefty, not only do you belong to Christ, you belong to all the other members that make up the body of Christ today. In fact, because Paul did not put any limitations on this reality, I guess you belong to every person who is in Christ, including those who have already died in Him, those living in Him today, and those yet to be included in Him. This also includes all those with whom you have ever been in conflict, are in conflict, or ever will be in conflict. You belong to them. They belong to you.

I love the moment this reality hits home in a group of Christian brothers and sisters who entered the room in a state of conflict with one another. I've actually seen folks who have not been at all nice to one another actually look at one another and offer a smile. It's a painful smile sometimes, but it's a smile nonetheless. Of course, I've seen heads droop, stern looks shared, and heard a few moans and groans as well, as participants contemplate the full impact of this truth.

I can only imagine what the reaction would be with Jack, Alice, Bill, Mike, and the others in our story. Imagine looking at Jack, and then Bill, and then saying to them, "Yep, that means you guys belong to one another." Makes me smile just thinking about it.

While you're imagining that, you might want to take a moment to picture the folks with whom you are one in Christ.

Make sure you include the ones you don't easily connect with, and especially those with whom you may have some unresolved conflict. As you picture each one, speak this truth in your heart: "Yep, in Christ you belong to me, and I belong to you—and together we belong to Christ." Are you smiling yet? I strongly suspect He is. And honestly, so am I.

When Alice saw what she interpreted as Jack trying to take support away from the missionaries and programs she had worked so hard to maintain, Alice reacted out of her *self*. Because she was a *conflict avoider*, she had developed the pattern of suppressing her fear and anger. This is a part of the *passive avoider* reaction to conflict that flows from the world pattern. If she did share her feelings and opinions with someone, it was always someone other than Jack.

Jack was just as passionate about the mission of the church. His individual focus was on the community's teenagers, partly due to having teenagers in his own home at the time. He, too, was an *avoider*, but rather than being one who flees, he was a "fighter." So he would bulldoze his way through any obstacle that got between him and the goal of reaching the community's teenagers for Christ. Unfortunately, Jack perceived Alice and her missionaries to be in the way.

If they had recognized their "oneness in Christ," and the degree to which they belonged to one another, and if they had focused on the Lord rather than themselves, then they could have seen His passion for reaching the lost and worked from their oneness in Him. They could have had conversations to share their different views regarding the long-term support of the missionaries, as well as the development of new opportunities with the teens. Together, along with the other committee members, they could have then sought to discover the mind of Christ in the matter.

But they did not do so because they did not see who they were, together in Jesus Christ. Instead, they conformed themselves to the world pattern of operating as a group of independent and separate individuals, reacting out of themselves, rather than as members of the body of Jesus Christ—members who belong to Him and to one another.

Their experience is not what Jesus prayed for the Church in John 17. Nor is it the early Church reality reflected in the "one heart and one mind" experience described by Luke. Nor is it reflective of Paul's concept of the church as the living body of the living Jesus Christ, where all the members belong to Him and to one another. Our reality as Christians is that we are one in Christ, even in the midst of our disagreements and conflicts—perhaps especially then.

I know we often throw around the concept of "belonging to Jesus," and we do so with a sense of gratitude, praise, and love. But how often have you realized that, in belonging to Jesus, you also belong to all the others who believe in Jesus, and together with them share in the fellowship of "oneness in Him"? To the degree you are not your own in your relationship with Jesus, you are not your own in your relationship with your brothers and sisters in Christ.

Now I realize that doesn't preach well in our culture, where all of life tends to be focused on and through ourselves. And we certainly don't have much experience in walking out this "belonging to" one another in much of the Church today. But, it is what Paul declares here and elsewhere. This "oneness" is not about the individual "you" and the individual "I" joining the same Christian organization and cooperating out of our individual relationships with Jesus, as well as our individual beliefs, views, and positions. That's just a setup for experiencing the very same patterns of conflict found in the world. Instead, this is a relationship of belonging to Him and to one another, and together living His life. The former is based upon the world's self-focused pattern. The latter flows from the single life of Jesus Christ experienced in His one body, and lived out together by all those made one in Him.

In living His one life together our minds are renewed and our lives transformed. It is as Paul described it in 2 Corinthians 5:14–20:

> For Christ's love compels us, because we are convinced that one died for all, and therefore all died. And he died for all, that those who live should no longer live for themselves but for him who died for them and was raised again. So from now on we regard no one from a worldly point of view. Though we once regarded Christ in this way, we do so no longer. Therefore, if anyone is in Christ, he is a new creation, the old has gone, the new has come! All this is from God, who reconciled us to himself through Christ and gave us the ministry of reconciliation: that God was reconciling the world to himself in Christ, not counting men's sins against them. And he has committed to us the message of reconciliation. We are therefore Christ's ambassadors, as though God were making his appeal through us.

As good as that is, it gets better as we continue reviewing Paul's teachings regarding who we are in Christ.

The World is Not Our Reality—He is

As we've seen, when Paul approached the subject of unresolved conflict in the Church, he often began by focusing their attention on Jesus Christ and who they were in Him. To assist them in understanding the relational impact of their reality, Paul would describe the Church in terms of being the body of Christ. It's important we not allow that truth to be lost to us. When dealing with unresolved conflict, Paul did not get believers to focus first on the conflict, their issues, their self, or one another. He focused first on Jesus Christ, and then on who they were, together, in Christ. That's not the world pattern, but it does flow from the life of Jesus Christ.

Like the church in Rome, the brothers and sisters in Corinth had their conflicts as well. The Corinthian believers—not unlike many churches today—functioned through a world pattern element in their relationships that, when exposed to conflict, resulted in a perceived relational disconnection between them. As we have pointed out earlier, the void created by this disconnection soon became filled with numerous attitudes and behaviors that reflected the world, rather than Jesus Christ.

In 1 Corinthians 12:12, Paul writes, "The body is a unit, though it is made up of many parts; and though all its parts are many, they form one body. *So it is with Christ*" (italics added).

Many parts, but one body. Seems like that's the same point he made in dealing with the unresolved conflict in the Roman church. He didn't start with the conflict, or with them. He started with Jesus Christ, and who they were in Him.

As we noted earlier, when we look at the body of Christ, we recognize He is made up of many different parts. His parts do not have a life apart from each other. There is life and function in the parts as they "belong" to one another in the body. Many parts—one body. "So it is with Christ." This isn't theoretical or philosophical; it's real. It's practical. It's real practical.

It is also now, in the present. "So it *is* with Christ," he proclaims (italics added). He does not write it in the past tense, looking back to some historical moment. Nor does he look forward to some great moment in future glory. The phrase, "So it is with Christ," speaks of the ever-present now. This is our present reality. As Christians, we are one, together in Him, now, today, and forever.

We are His Reality in the World

Our reality together is also all about Him, not us. Paul wrote about Christ's present reality more than he wrote about ours. You will note Paul did not write, "So it is with you." He states Christ's reality: "So it is with Christ." Jesus Christ is the one body made up of many parts. We are the parts that make up His body in the world today. He walks this earth *in and through us, together*. He continues to say what the Father tells Him, and does what the Father shows Him, *in and through us, together*. As much as our reality is in Him, *His reality in the world today is in us, together.*

It's important we really get that last point. Reflect on those brothers and sisters with whom you are connected in His body today. Picture the ones who make you smile, and recognize, "So it is with Christ." Picture the ones who make you frown, cry, or twist your innards in a knot, and recognize, "So it is with Christ." All of you together are an expression of the reality of Jesus Christ in your world today. And please know this as well: the world is watching.

Our Differences are often Him

Paul goes on in verse 13: "For we were all baptized by one Spirit into one body—whether Jews or Greeks, slave or free—and we were all given the one Spirit to drink." I'm not exactly sure who Paul would use to make this point if he were writing this letter today. But in his day, he could not have chosen parts of his culture any further disconnected from one another than the ones he chose. The Jews and the Greeks were disconnected ethnically, culturally, religiously, and in a host of other ways. Their perceptions and values were very different. Their understandings and positions were different. Their customs and values were different. Their languages were even different. And yet, Paul wrote that, when the Holy Spirit baptized them, they were one in Christ. Together, they were one body. Together, they were Christ's reality in Corinth.

They didn't lose their individuality as individual Jews or Greeks when they were baptized into the one body of Jesus Christ. In reality, they each gained the fulfillment of being a Jew, or a Greek, plus a whole lot more. The Jews gained the elements of Jesus that could only be expressed through Greeks. The Greeks gained the elements of Jesus that could only be expressed through Jews. And with all the other parts of His body, they gained the fullness of Him, *together.*

Their God-created individuality continued as creative and necessary expressions of the many parts of the body of Christ. In fact, as Paul pointed out in Romans 12, and again here in 1 Corinthians 12:1–11, they also gained gifts of Jesus' character and ability given them by the Spirit for the mutual benefit of the entire body. What a deal! Can you believe there are people who pass on this offer?

So what changed when they became believers in Christ and were baptized by the Holy Spirit? What changed is this: they were no longer independent, separate individuals existing individualistically. They were no longer self-focused individuals, living separate and independent lives, even when grouped together in a common activity. They became "belonging" parts of the living body of Jesus Christ, belonging to Him and to one another. What they saw as differences from their world pattern views were actually opportunities to experience different elements of Christ.

For the Greeks to experience the fullness of Jesus, they needed those unique elements of Him contained in the Jews. And for the Jews to experience the fullness of Jesus, they needed those unique elements of Him contained in the Greeks. Being made one in Him brought all those elements together for them to experience the fullness of Him together, not as independent, separate individuals.

It appears a couple of other groups (the slaves and freemen) in the Corinthian church may have had difficulties figuring out this many-parts-one-body thing. Like the Jews and Greeks, these groups lived at opposite poles of the society in Paul's day. I suspect there were actually more worldview differences disconnecting them than the differences between the Jews and the Greeks. Slaves were not held to be human beings as much as livestock, owned and used by freemen. But again, in Christ, there was more about Him to be experienced in these differences than there was the condition of being either slave or free. Whether slave or free, they were one in Christ, belonging to one another, and expressing His reality in their world.

Each group brought different elements of Christ to the table for all to enjoy. They should have had a "Jesus Christ smorgasbord," featuring dishes from the Jews, Greeks, slaves, freemen, and every other "different" person and group included in Him. But rather than sitting down with one another and digging in, they had a "relational food fight" with their differences. What a waste.

Obstacles—or Opportunities

Recently I was in a gathering of pastors and church leaders, listening to a wonderful presentation dealing with conflicts that often arise in local church transitions. During the presentation, a couple of people made observations or asked questions regarding specific situations in their local gatherings. Finally—with a bit of frustration in his voice—one of them asked the presenter, "Are you going to share with us what we can do to deal with the difficult people who keep derailing the growth of the church?"

"Yeah," the other added, "What do we do about these obstacles preventing our vision from going forward?"

It's easy for us to see those who disagree with us as "difficult," "obstacles," and a number of other dehumanizing and negative labels we might use to describe them. Once we attach these labels and further our sense of disconnection from them, it's that much easier for us to treat them accordingly. After all, if we can question their status as Christians—which happens with all too much regularity in conflicted situations—then we can also question their views and positions and treat them as "not of us." It's amazing what we're capable of in our treatment of others whom we label as "not of us."

But what would occur if we saw ourselves as one with them in Christ? What if we recognized we belong to each other in this reality of *oneness* in Christ? What if we saw and acted as Paul observes in 1 Corinthians 12:15–27:

> But in fact God has arranged the parts in the body, every one of them just as he wanted them to be. If they were all one part, where would the body be? As it is, there are many parts, but one body. The eye cannot say to the hand, "I don't need you!" And the head cannot say to the feet, 'I don't need you!' On the contrary, those parts of the body that seem to be weaker are indispensable, and the parts that we think are less honorable we treat with special honor. And the parts that are unpresentable are treated with special modesty, while our presentable parts need no special treatment. But God has combined the members of the body and has given greater honor to the parts that lacked it, so that there should be no division in the body, but that its parts should have equal concern for each other. If one part suffers, every part suffers with it; if one part is honored, every part rejoices with it. Now you are the body of Christ, and each one of you is a part of it.

I won't even pretend I understand God's wisdom and purpose in putting some of the combinations together we find in different gatherings of the Lord's body. We come from different cultures, backgrounds, education levels, and life experiences; and all these differences can get in the way of us all agreeing with one another. And yet, none of this is a surprise to God. It's not like He suddenly notices our conflicts and exclaims, "Oh, my, what have I done in putting these folks together?"

Yet it seems that church members are regularly surprised by these differences. In fact, not only are we often surprised, we tend to react in the way Paul describes in 1 Corinthians 12:15–21. Paul describes a scene we've encountered numerous times. Let me describe it using an analogy based on the picture Paul presents.

First Church of the Conflicted Differences is made up of a bunch of different parts of the Lord's body. As in most local churches, some members exercise more power and authority than other members. Sometimes this is due to their individual personalities, community status, or position in the church. At First Church of the Conflicted Differences, Eye is a strong leader, with a strong and clear vision for the church. Because of Eye's personality and position in the church, Eye is able to influence a number of the other body parts to see the same vision. They've all been cooperating, working hard to make this vision become a reality for the entire local body.

But as Paul observes, there are always other body parts that function differently, thus they often have other perceptions, understandings, and experiences. At First Church of the Conflicted Differences, Ear, Nose, Hand, Foot, and Head would fit this description. Given the self-centered world pattern described earlier, you can imagine what is going to occur within this body, can't you? On the surface, it appeared that this group of individuals has been cooperating and getting along fairly well. But as so often happens, reality goes far deeper than what appears on the surface. Looking a bit deeper, we find that Ear has been tuning out Eye. Nose had a twitch over the vision, but has stayed out of Eye's business thus far. Hand was a little slow in responding to the vision, but eventually got involved, but from a hand's perspective. From the very beginning, Foot didn't like the direction of things, especially Hand's involvement. So, initially Foot reacted by kicking back and watching how things developed. Head just tried to stay on top of things.

Things went along, and all looked calm and peaceful at First Church of the Conflicted Differences. But one day, Ear heard some gossip he didn't like, and started a slow burn. Apparently, Foot said something that took quite an editing spin by the time it was passed from Ankle to Knee to Hip to Shoulder, and was finally shared with Ear. When Nose caught wind of all this, he went to Hand, who reacted by sticking himself into Eye's business. Foot got a kick out of that, but continued to soak on the sidelines. Meanwhile, Head got dizzy trying to sort it all out.

Eventually, Ear had heard enough, and proposed a different vision based on what Ear heard Jesus saying. As the conflict between Ear and Eye grew, Ear decided if the body was going to conform to Eye, Ear could no longer remain. Ear was above continuing this fight, and decided he would just move on and put it all behind him.

Because Nose was close to both Ear and Eye, Nose had a dilemma. If the whole body became either an Ear or an Eye, where would the body's sense of smell be? Nose began to smell big trouble in the air, but decided to pull back and let Ear and Eye settle things on their own. It never dawned on Nose that by taking this action she was robbing the body of its sense of smell anyhow.

Before Ear left, Eye and Ear had it out at a church meeting. It wasn't pretty. In a heated exchange, Eye declared he didn't need Ear, and if Ear didn't like it, then too bad. Hand—who already had had some crossings with Eye—reacted with a clench and came to Ear's defense. Thankfully, Head cooled things down.

Foot couldn't believe the way everyone was acting, and told them so. Unlike Hand, Foot was not a fighter; he threatened to walk away.

Unfortunately, by this time other body parts, led by Head, decided Eye was right, and let Foot know they didn't really need Foot either. "It's the Eye way or the highway," they proclaimed. So Foot and Ear walked out and started looking for a new body to join. And the rest of this body hopped along and struggled to hear what the Lord was trying to say to them.

Is any of this familiar?

How different would things be if we realized we're connected with all who comprise our particular expression of His body, because He has placed us here, "just as he wanted (us) to be." If we see others as difficult, then might we begin to wonder what the difficulty is, and what the Lord would have us experience of Him in approaching it together? Or if we see others as obstacles, then might we reflect on the fact the Lord placed those obstacles before us for His purposes, and seek Him together to figure out what that's all about? I may even find out I am the difficulty, and an obstacle to what the Lord wants in my part of His body.

The point is that our differences are about Him, not us. The fact that we are together in the same local expression of His body—with the differences that are present in each one—is also not about us; it's all about Him.

In our story, Jack, Alice, and Bill found themselves at odds with one another. We're not talking about Jews and Gentiles, or slaves and freemen here, but we might as well be. Like all of us, these folks came to their church experience with a whole pile of differences that led them to disconnect. There were differences of generation, personality, perceptions, values, understandings, experiences, politics, Bible interpretations, and the list goes on and on. Foundational to that list was the self-centered focus of the world pattern, where they saw themselves as independent of and separate from each other.

Any one of these differences can divide us, some a whole lot quicker than others. When we don't recognize we're one in Christ, it's just a matter of time before one or more of these differences leads to conflict. When we react out of ourselves, the world pattern is continued and expanded. If we respond to our conflicts in Him, then the experience of His life is continued and expanded for everyone—including the world—to see.

The week before their incident, Alice, Bill, and Jack joined with the rest of their church to sing the old favorite, "Family of God." At this point, they were calling one another names other than "brother and sister." There weren't too many "smiling faces" in their midst anymore either. Recently they had concluded sharing communion by singing these words: "We are one in the bond of love, we are one in the bond of love. We have joined our spirits with the Spirit of God. We are one in the bond of love." Now they felt anything but a bond with, or a love of, one another.

Unfortunately, they conformed to the world pattern of reacting out of themselves, rather than responding in Him. They reflected the pattern of the world, rather than the life of Jesus Christ. If only they had realized that their situation, perceptions, and feelings did not and could not change the reality they had failed to recognize thus far. They were one in Christ. They belonged to Him, and they belonged to one another. They were one in Him and belonged to one another prior to this recent blowup. They were one in Him, and belonged to one another as they reacted to one another. And they would remain one in

Him and belong to one another, no matter where their feelings and actions took them. They, like all who believe in Jesus, are one in Him and belong to one another.

8 Is Christ Divided?

As pastors arrived at their scheduled prayer gathering, there was the usual banter of catching up on personal news since their last gathering, along with discussions regarding everything from the local high school football team to the latest scandal on the news. Eventually, the visiting subsided as they prepared to share any prayer needs and then spend the rest of their time praying together.

As the room quieted, Pastor Edward looked at Pastor Tim and asked, "So how are things going with you and the church, Tim?"

Tim was quiet at first. Then the room grew quiet, as each pastor there knew the difficulties Tim had faced these recent weeks. They'd been praying for him and the church since Tim first shared about the growing conflict there.

Following a few moments of uncomfortable silence, Tim spoke: "I wish I could report that things were getting better. Unfortunately, I can't. If anything, things are getting worse. I learned yesterday of another private meeting that took place among a group of folks. I have no idea who all was there, or what their purpose was, but I have to assume it reveals yet another division in the church."

Tim lowered his head as a wave of grief and despair rolled over him. A hand came to rest on his shoulder. When he looked up to continue, he could tell a number of the pastors were already praying, and the others were staring at him with tears in their eyes.

"I don't know what to do . . . or even what to think anymore. It's as though the entire church has divided into separate camps. Groups are already waging war against one another, or are preparing to enter the battle in some way. And then there are those who seem to be lying low, trying to stay out of it. The whole thing is breaking my heart. And I know it must break the Lord's heart. But I don't know what to do anymore. I'm afraid we're one incident away from a major split."

The church in Corinth was like many of our local expressions of the body of Christ today. They also naturally tended to conform to the world pattern in dealing with their conflicts. Paul seemed to have been addressing that concern as he began his letter to the Corinthians. First Corinthians 1:10–12 says,

> I appeal to you, brothers, in the name of our Lord Jesus Christ, that all of you agree with one another so that there may be no divisions among you and that you may be perfectly united in mind and thought. My brothers, some from Chloe's household have informed me that there are quarrels among you. What I mean is this: One of you says, "I follow Paul"; and another, "I follow Apollos"; another, "I follow Cephas"; still another, "I follow Christ."

I have to admit, I'm not surprised there would be such quarreling going on in a local church, especially this one. What does surprise me is Paul's radical idea that they could all agree with one another so there would be no divisions among them, and they would be perfectly united in mind and thought. Could he possibly have meant what he said? Could he actually have believed it possible? If these Corinthian brothers and sisters were anything like many church groups today, there would be more views and positions than the number of folks belonging to the church at the time. Yet he expected they could experience being "perfectly united in mind and thought."

In the verses that immediately follow this challenging statement, we discover Paul was referring to a division in the church involving individuals with differing perceptions, understandings, and experiences. It appears they were conforming to the world pattern by competing with one another over their differences within this local expression of the Lord's body. Sounds familiar, doesn't it?

It Only Takes a Spark to Get the Fire Going

Do you remember the song called "Pass It On"? We used to sing it around campfires years ago. It speaks of the impact of God's love and the desire to share it with others. The song has a nice message, and it's a wonderful experience when it occurs. Unfortunately, it only takes a spark to get a firestorm of conflict going as well. I suspect that's what Paul hoped the opening of his letter to the brothers and sisters in Corinth would head off.

We don't have enough information to know clearly what the full issues were. We do know, however, that at least four individuals or groups (I suspect the latter) claimed independent and separate connections with Paul, Apollos, Cephas, and Christ.

We also know the conflict was large enough to get the attention of the Corinthian church that met in Chloe's house. The situation caught Paul's attention, earning lead-off position in his letter. If the problem involved just *four individuals*, then why would Paul use a public means such as a letter to the entire church to attend to such a private matter?

We also know Paul described their behavior as quarreling, which speaks of a contentious strife between them. This was not a civil debate. Later, in 1 Corinthians 3:3, he identifies "jealousy" as a primary emotional motive for their behavior. We've found that when personal divisions grow to this level there are always more people involved than the original conflicted parties.

Impact = Involved x Ten

Regardless of the total number involved, the impact of this unresolved conflict was certainly not limited to the original four individuals involved. We know it affected those who gathered at Chloe's house. They were concerned enough to seek outside help in dealing with it, so they contacted Paul. There is something important for us to recognize in this: with rare exceptions, there are almost always far more people directly impacted by the conflict—or who know about it—than are directly involved in it.

I remember working with a congregation in which two different leadership boards were in conflict. Both groups were convinced they had protected the congregation from the conflict, but during the intervention process we discovered there were few, if any, members who didn't know about and feel effects of the conflict. This included the young people in their high school group, who also requested the opportunity to visit with our Peace Connections team. They were very aware of the conflict—in some cases painfully so, when it involved their parents.

We returned to work with this congregation a number of times during the next two years. During that time, we frequented a local café near the church facilities. One day, while taking our order, the waitress asked, "So, tell me, are you guys helping (church name) at all? They sure do need it." She then went on to mention that in the course of waiting on tables, she had heard plenty of conversations involving church members, as well as other residents of the community who were not members of this particular church. She also had learned about us, and what we were attempting to do. Church conflicts can impact the entire community.

Another piece of this world pattern activity needs to be recognized. Most of this "information sharing" is in the form of gossip. It takes place over the dinner table, at the water cooler or break room at work, over the neighborhood fence, in the grocery store line, over the Internet, and, as mentioned above, at the local café or coffee shop. Each time a story is shared, the impact spreads further and further. And the further it travels from those who were directly involved, the less accurate the stories become.

Now, back to the Corinthian church. Assume this conflict is still in its early stages, and limited to four individuals in the church. If so, we can learn another important lesson here. Paul was concerned enough to address the situation directly and forcefully. Today's churches need to be as concerned and attentive when conflicts arise between individuals in our midst. We need to seek assistance from someone qualified to help. Instead, in the spirit of being nice, we tend to avoid these situations like the plague and hope they blow over soon. But rather than blow over, they often blow up.

In the contemporary scenario we're following, the initial conflict began between Jack and Alice, and quickly included

Bill and then Mike. Within hours the conflict spread to include those who agreed with Jack and Mike's view. They believed the old leadership had to go in order for the church to move forward. As Mike promised, he spent the rest of that day calling those he was confident shared his view and position. By the middle of the week, Mike had a list of nearly thirty members who expressed varying degrees of willingness to support his plan. A meeting was scheduled to take place the following Saturday evening.

Of course this activity and the buzz it created didn't take place in a vacuum. Word of the blowup between Jack, Alice, and Bill traveled quickly, as did Mike's calls. And the situation was the main topic of conversation during the men's early morning gathering in the back room of the Corner Cafe. Fact and fiction were spun together to create quite a story. Before the group disbanded that morning, it was determined "their church" was under attack, and it was going to be up to them to save it.

Do You Want to be Right or Relational?

Knowing what we know about the Corinthian church, I'm amused that Paul would appeal to this bunch to ". . . be perfectly united in mind and thought." Knowing what we do about the church in our story, I want to say to Paul, "You are kidding, right? Perfectly united in mind and thought; this group?" You might be thinking about your own church group and wondering the same thing.

But Paul didn't stop there. If what he had just said wasn't difficult enough, he then took it a step further. He asked this question in verse 13: "Is Christ divided?"

I wonder what the impact of that question was when they first read it. It stops me cold every time I read it. His question should stop us all, for who of us has not been in such a conflict with a brother or sister in Christ? Perhaps you find yourself in such a place at this very moment. And when we have found ourselves in such conflicted situations, how many of us have given a great deal of thought to being one in Christ with our "opposition"? How often has the thought crossed our mind that we belong to them and they belong to us, and our life together is in Him? Is Christ divided at such a time as this? Can Christ be divided? How is that possible if He is one, and we are one in Him?

There's another reason I'm stopped cold by Paul's question in 1 Corinthians 1:13. I expect him to begin defending himself and the individual or group aligned with him. Come on, Paul, rally the troops! Send out the e-mails! Make the calls! Hold the special meetings! Defend the truth! Attack those views different from yours! Don't allow the church to get sidetracked by these other individuals with their different views. Slap on the labels, such as *those other people, wrong, sinners, unbelievers*, or *enemy*! In other words, conform yourself to the world pattern and behave as though you are an individual—separate from these other brothers and sisters.

Instead, Paul asked if Christ was divided. Is He?

So, if Paul wasn't going to defend himself, then shouldn't he have attacked the others by pointing out how wrong they were? Shouldn't he have pointed out the sin of their positions, and the danger they were introducing into the church? After all, if it were not for Paul, this church may not have existed at this time. Who were these folks, coming in and trying to take over by promoting their own leaders, views, and positions?

If he wasn't going to defend himself or attack the others, then why didn't he threaten to pack up his tent and find some other church in which to serve God? Oh yeah, I forgot. There was only one church in Corinth, though it appears they may have gathered in different groups and locations. But there were options. He could have broken new ground and started a new church with those in Chloe's house. Or he could have worked hard to get a bunch of the Corinthian church to take his side, and then gone off to start a whole new work in some other part of town. When he did, he could claim he was above the division, and was simply putting the conflict behind Him to continue His service to the Lord.

He could have conformed to the world pattern and reacted in any one of those fashions. Instead, in verse 17 he went on to mention he had not previously come to them preaching words of human wisdom. Later, he said he did not come to them preaching with eloquence or superior wisdom or wise and persuasive words, but with weakness, fear, and much trembling. What does that have to do with this conflict? Perhaps the conflict formed around the content and styles of the mentioned leaders and their preaching. I suspect they were all different in some ways. As it often is today, I suspect there were folks in the Corinthian church who preferred Paul's style and content, while some preferred the other leaders.

No doubt some viewed Cephas and Christ as "old school," with ties to the old ways of the past. Perhaps they were seen as no longer promoting the new, cutting-edge future of the church. Furthermore, some may have seen Paul and Apollos as leading the church astray from its Hebrew roots, with new Gentile concepts and models to adopt. This is all conjecture, but I suspect these folks weren't all that different from us. And this is exactly what takes place in many gatherings of the body of Christ today.

Conflicts are often all about personal preferences, which is just another way of saying "It's all about me." We have seen this played out many times in what we refer to as "The Worship Wars." Oh, how we've bloodied ourselves on that battlefield. One group is battling to preserve the purity and holiness of the classical hymns, while the other is dying of boredom and pushing for the Christian version of MTV.

I remember when we were gingerly picking our way through some of the minefields of that battle within our own church a number of years ago. One dear brother expressed his concern that we were singing more choruses than hymns, and he let everybody know he didn't like it. It wasn't Christian, as far as he was concerned. Church just didn't feel like church to him anymore. During the discussion, one of our worship leaders asked him what his favorite hymn was, so she could make sure we included it in the future. His answer was "Amazing Grace." That's one of my favorites too.

I chuckle about that now; having enjoyed the wonderful experience of traveling with family to Germany in 2004, including a trip to Oktoberfest in Munich. Imagine my surprise when, as we were eating lunch, the crowd jumped to its feet with beer steins raised high, and the band and trumpets began to belt out the tune for Amazing Grace! I have to tell you; they sang with as much gusto as I've ever heard it sung in any church back home. Then our hosts reminded me that the tune for this wonderful hymn was adopted from a traditional beer-drinking song. Talk about a scandal!

At Lake Shore Community Church, we've learned that personal preferences are wonderful; they add to the fullness of our experience in Christ. But when our personal preferences become more important to us than our relationship with Jesus and one another, they're no longer about Him. We can either be right, as we define it individually, or we can be relational. We believe the Lord has called us to a relationship of being one, together in Him.

I also suspect the folks in Corinth were much like the folks in churches today, who quite easily see their differences in terms of "right and wrong," thus the quarrelling and division among them. Remember how broad is the path of seeing things in terms of "right and wrong," and how easily it leads to destruction. It appears these brothers and sisters in Corinth were hoofing it double-time down this path by the time Paul heard of it and wrote his letter to them. They were dividing themselves individually, or possibly into camps of individuals, sharing particular elements of their individual perceptions, understandings, and experiences. Is Christ divided?

There is another intriguing dynamic to ponder in all of this. In his appeal for them all to "be perfectly united in mind and thought," why would Paul include the individual or group claiming to be following Christ? If any group in the church could claim the position of being "right" in all of this, wouldn't it be those who claimed to be following the Lord rather than these other influential leaders? Yet Paul included this individual or group as well. Why? I think it's because these divisions are more about our relationship in Christ together than what we claim about Him individually. Unity is about being the body of Christ, *together*, rather than a group of independent, separate individuals with our own opinions and positions. Is Christ divided?

The unfortunate reality in the church today is that often we'd rather be right than relational. But that kind of *right-ness* reflects the world pattern of independent and separate *selves* more than it reflects Jesus Christ and our relationship of being one in Him.

Jesus Christ was fully, totally, and perfectly "right." Yet He allowed Himself to be scorned, spat upon, beaten, scourged, and eventually murdered. Why? Because God is all about life lived in the relationship of "one." Jesus willingly laid down His "right" so that we could enter the relational fellowship of "being one" with Him and His Father, and with one another. Hallelujah! Isn't that awesome?

Paul captured this thought in Philippians 2:1–8, when he wrote,

> If you have any encouragement from being united with Christ, if any comfort from his love, if any fellowship with the Spirit, if any tenderness and compassion, then make my joy complete by being like-minded, having the same love, being one in spirit and purpose. Do nothing out of selfish ambition or vain conceit, but in humility consider others better than yourselves. Each of you should look not only to your own interests, but also to the interests of others. Your attitude should be the same as that of Christ Jesus: Who, being in very nature God, did not consider equality with God something to be grasped, but made himself nothing, taking the very nature of a servant, being made in human likeness. And being found in appearance as a man, he humbled himself and became obedient to death—even death on a cross!

The Foolishness of the Cross—and its Connection with our Conflicts

I find it interesting that Paul introduces the power of the "cross of Christ" not in the context of spiritual warfare or conflict with the world, but with the issue of this particular conflict and division *among the church body.* Have you ever noticed that before? "The message of the cross is foolishness to those who are perishing, but to us who are being saved it is the power of God. For it is written: 'I will destroy the wisdom of the wise; the intelligence of the intelligent I will frustrate'" (1 Corinthians 1:18–19).

Could it be that the wisdom of the wise and the intelligence of the intelligent is simply another reference to the world pattern of handling things? For the remainder of this portion of this letter, Paul compares the wisdom of this world with the "foolishness" of Christ crucified. He seems to be saying to the Corinthians, "Look at yourselves; you are living proof of what I am saying." Verse 26 says, "Brothers, think of what you were when you were called. Not many of you were wise by human standards; not many were influential; not many were of noble birth."

Weapons or Tools?

Why would the observation listed above be important for Paul to point out to the Corinthian church? I suspect it has a lot to do with the fact that these "human standards" translate into power positions in the world's pattern of dealing with conflicts. As such, they are often used as weapons that injure and divide, rather than tools that heal and connect.

In the world pattern, those who are "wise" use their knowledge to establish a stronger position in the conflict. In the world pattern, knowledge is power. Because the world pattern of dealing with conflict places conflict in terms of good or bad and right or wrong, it becomes a win-or-lose competition. Thus within the conflict, power in any form is an important resource to have on your side.

In the world pattern of dealing with conflicts, some can use their influence to get others to join their position. If they're effective, they can even get others to believe the idea was their own, rather than that of the person who influenced them about the position.

In Paul's day, those of noble birth had the advantage of social position and financial strength. Power, title, and money still provide advantages in most social circles today. Unfortunately, they often make quite an impact in the local church as well.

The point is, these world pattern standards often divide us, rather than unite us, when used against one another in the one body of Jesus Christ. Apparently, most of the Corinthian folks lacked such worldly measures of power and strength, and Paul wanted them to recognize God's wisdom and power revealed in their lack of such things. Rather than seeking after or using such worldly influence—which focuses on our individual differences, rather than on Christ—Paul was driving toward an important observation. He goes on in verses 27–29:

> But God chose the foolish things of the world to shame the wise; God chose the weak things of the world to shame the strong. He chose the lowly things of this world and the despised things—and the things that are not—to nullify the things that are, so that no one may boast before him.

In the world pattern, things like knowledge and wisdom, strength and power, title and status are all valued more highly than the Lord's pattern, which is seen as "foolish, weak, lowly, and despised." By the world's standard, the cross of Christ communicates a message of foolishness and weakness. It was a lowly, despised death, far from reflecting a position of wisdom, strength, and title. These "human standards" are some of the "things that are" in this world. But God chooses the "things that are not"—things usually seen as foolish, weak, lowly, and even despised, to "nullify the things that are."

You may have some of the world's "things-that-are" bumping around in your head regarding Jack, Mike, Alice, and Bill. Perhaps you picture Alice and Bill as dead wood needing to be trimmed. Or perhaps you have them pegged as true defenders of the faith. Jack and Mike could be seen as forward thinking. Or they could be feared as willing to adopt modern, worldly practices that present a danger to the church.

Remember two things. First, remember Jack and the others aren't real. And the fact you may have such thoughts about make-believe people points to the second important thing to remember. You have these thoughts because you have your own individual filtering system that produces such opinions based on the information you receive, sometimes without much conscious thought. Kind of scary, isn't it?

How would your views be affected if you discovered that Alice and her recently deceased husband are well-respected, successful entrepreneurs and philanthropists who also provide nearly 30 percent of the church's annual financial support? What if you knew that Alice's friend Bill is the president of the local community college? What if Jack is a used car salesman? Sorry, nothing personal about that. One of my friends is a car salesman. In fact, he used to be a pastor. Moving right along, what if you learned Mike is unemployed? Does any of this information change your views?

Now, let's turn it around. How about if Alice and Bill are both retired, barely getting by on Social Security and small pensions? Let's make Jack the successful businessman and Mike a highly regarded professor at a local Bible college. How do those changes adjust your feelings and opinions about this group of folks and the positions they've taken?

Remember that most of our observations, opinions, feelings, and judgments of other people say a whole lot more about us than they do the other person.

The point is this: regarding human standards of wisdom, strength, and status, there are "things that are," and there are "things that are not." Our natural human inclination is to be attracted to the "things that are." God chooses the "things that are not" to nullify "the things that are." Why? Because it's not about us; it's about Jesus. Relationships are not about what we value and the positions we take, and who's right and who's wrong, and who's going to win and who's going to lose.

Relationships are about Christ crucified, and the power released in us and through us by means of His crucifixion. Community is about us living in Him, together, for His purposes and glory. Life really is about being relational—about being one in Him.

The Cross Changes Everything

So why did Paul focus on Christ crucified in this Corinthian conflict? Because in willfully submitting to the cross rather than reacting like the world, Jesus provided the means for us to be "one in Him." Rather than reaching for the sword or calling for an army of angels, He opened His arms wide and was nailed to the cross. By our Lord's sacrificial act, our independent, separate, disconnected *selves* were reconciled to God and one another. Our reality was changed from "me" to "us." Life was changed from "mine" to "His." Paul went on, "It is because of him [our Heavenly Father] that you [plural] are in Christ Jesus, who has become for us [collectively us, not individually] wisdom from God—that is, our righteousness, holiness and redemption. Therefore, as it is written: 'Let him who boasts boast in the Lord'" (1 Corinthians 1:30–31).

The Corinthians' boasting of their allegiance simply revealed their individualistic hearts. Because they saw themselves individualistically, and not as "one in Christ," they boasted and quarreled over their differences. Some were followers of Apollos; others were followers of Paul, Cephas, or Christ. Paul called their behavior "quarreling." They were quarreling about their different perceptions, understandings, and positions, and were reacting in divisive manners toward one another. Rather than one body, they were acting like individuals, independent of and separate from one another. They were conforming to the world pattern. And each time we act like them, we are, too.

9 God's Secret Wisdom: The Corporate Experience of the Mind of Christ

Excerpt from a private conversation between two members of the church council, seated beside one another during a council meeting:

"It sounds to me like everybody thinks God is on their side. But how can that be when they're so far apart in how they all see things? Who's right, and who's wrong?"

"I don't know . . . I just don't know. I try hard not to take sides. I figure everybody probably has some things right, and some things wrong. But it's just a big mess trying to figure it all out."

"I just wish the Lord would show us what to do."

"He might, if we stopped arguing long enough to listen."

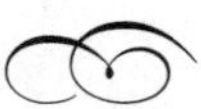

As discussed in the previous chapter, Paul began his letter to the Corinthian church by addressing a conflict—a division—among them. Beyond simply disagreeing with one another, they were reacting out of their jealousy and quarreling about their differences. So Paul pleaded with them: "I appeal to you, brothers, in the name of our Lord Jesus Christ, that all of you agree with one another so that there may be no divisions among you and that you may be perfectly united in mind and thought" (1 Corinthians 1:10).

I'm not sure what the folks at Chloe's house expected Paul to do or say about this conflict when they first contacted him. Nor do we know what the church expected when it was reported that Paul had been contacted about it, and he had responded. If the Corinthians were like many of the churches we have worked with, they probably expected him to declare who was right and who was wrong. A person loyal to Paul was involved in the ruckus, so some may have expected to hear this person declared the winner.

Picture this scene as the scroll is opened and the letter is read. Feel the anxiety begin to rise in the room. As the four conflicted positions are identified, hear the discomforted fidgeting and throat clearing, and notice the sidelong glances shared between folks.

Then the question is read: "Is Christ divided?"

Silence.

The reader continues, as Paul remembers those of the group he personally baptized. He speaks about the cross of Christ, and the degree to which God has made foolish the wisdom of the world. The group listens, as they hear Paul's comments about the world's standards of power and wisdom, and how short they all fall when measured by such things. A few puzzled looks are exchanged around the room. Those who didn't like Paul or his style shake their heads.

The reader continues. Paul goes on to speak about his own lack of eloquence and persuasive preaching, and a murmur and giggles are heard throughout the room. When the reader reaches the point about the demonstrations of the Spirit's power—which accompanied Paul's previous time with them—the murmurs and giggles cease, and someone proclaims a loud "Amen."

Throughout the room people wonder, "What about the conflict, Paul? What are we supposed to do about the conflict? How are we to deal with these differences that threaten to split us in four different directions?"

The reader continues Paul's thoughts about the "message of wisdom," a wisdom far different from the wisdom of the world and its rulers. The murmurs and fidgeting begin anew. People begin to wonder what any of this has to do with the conflict, much less its solution.

The reader continues: "No, we speak of God's secret wisdom. . . ." The reader stops, interrupted by the sudden commotion as the entire room comes to attention as one and focuses on the reader and the scroll in his hands. Many of them wonder what they just heard. Secret wisdom? What secret wisdom? Many look at one another, perplexed.

The reader realizes every eye in the room is suddenly on him. He clears his throat and takes a deep breath. Returning to where he left off, he begins the sentence again: "No, we speak of God's secret wisdom, a wisdom that has been hidden and that God destined for our glory before time began." Again, the room is filled with commotion as people react to what they are hearing. Paul is writing about a secret that God has hidden until now. Perhaps this secret is the solution to the conflict in their midst. Everyone in the room strains to hear the next words from the letter. Even the children are silent.

The reader continues Paul's letter: "None of the rulers of this age understood it, for if they had, they would not have crucified the Lord of glory." Again, there are puzzled expressions on some of the faces. "However," the reader continues, "as it is written: 'No eye has seen, no ear has heard, no mind has conceived what God has prepared for those who love him.'"

The reader pauses for a moment. The sense of mystery and excitement is palpable. Glancing over the top of the scroll, he looks out at his brothers and sisters and sees their expectant faces glowing back at him.

Focusing on Paul's letter once again, he continues to read: ". . . but God has revealed it to us by his Spirit." A stunned silence dominates the room. He stops, and quickly reads the line again: "No eye has seen, no ear has heard, no mind has conceived what God has prepared for those who love him." Again a short pause, ". . . but God has revealed it to us by his Spirit."

For a moment the silence continues, and then the power of this truth crashes in on the room. Suddenly shouts of praise and celebration fill the air. Some people hug those next to them. Excitement surges through the room like pulse waves. "The secret," someone shouts! "Revealed to us," another yells! For a moment it seems the very building is shaking with their excitement.

Then everyone becomes aware of the reader holding Paul's letter above his head. Of course, there is more to be read, more secret to be described. Once the room quiets, the reader begins again: "The Spirit searches all things, even the deep things of God. For who among men knows the thoughts of a man except the man's spirit within him?" This thought is greeted by a sound of agreement and nodding heads. "In the same way no one knows the thoughts of God except the Spirit of God." Again, signs of agreement fill the room. "We have not received the spirit of the world but the Spirit who is from God. . . ." Someone interrupts with a loud "Amen," as many heads nod in agreement.

The reader begins the sentence again: "We have not received the spirit of the world but the Spirit who is from God, that we may understand what God has freely given us. This is what we speak, not in words taught us by human wisdom but in words taught by the Spirit, expressing spiritual truths in spiritual words." Again, the room becomes silent, as brothers and sisters soak these words deep into their spirits, and ponder them in their minds.

The reader continues: "The man without the Spirit does not accept the things that come from the Spirit of God, for they are foolishness to him, and he cannot understand them, because they are spiritually discerned. The spiritual man makes judgments about all things, but he himself is not subject to any man's judgment: 'For who has known the mind of the Lord that he may instruct him?'" Again, the reader hesitates a moment before proceeding. It seems the entire room is holding its breath, awaiting his next words. Taking a breath himself, he reads the next sentence: "But we have the mind of Christ."

The collective breath is released, suddenly, as the room bursts into shouts of praise and celebration. "The secret is revealed!" someone from the front shouts. "We have the mind of Christ!" another cries out. "Together!" many voices shout in unison.

After a time of great joy, a loud voice is heard above the din. "I must ask you, my brothers and sisters, why did our brother Paul not tell of this mystery before this?" The raucous din subsides in a moment. The brother pushes to the front of the gathering. Many recognize him to be one of the four involved in the conflict Paul has written about. "Please, tell me; if this secret revealed is cause for so much joy in our midst, why would Paul not tell us about it when he was first with us?"

The man's challenge is met with a hushed silence in the room. The reader speaks, "Perhaps, brother, you would allow me to continue Paul's letter, as I believe he speaks to your question in his next comments." At this, the brother rejoins the crowd, signaling for the reader to continue.

The reader looks over the crowd, allowing his gaze to remain on the brother for a moment. He then begins to read: "Brothers, I could not address you as spiritual but as worldly—mere infants in Christ. I gave you milk, not solid food, for you were not yet ready for it. Indeed, you are still not ready. You are still worldly. For since there is jealousy and quarreling among you, are you not worldly? Are you not acting like mere men? For when one says, 'I follow Paul,' and another, 'I follow Apollos,' are you not mere men?"

The brother slowly makes his way to the back of the room, as the reader continues sharing Paul's letter.

Paul's letter is real; the rest of the story above is just a product of my imagination. But I do wonder about some things. I wonder how many of the Corinthian folks walked away wondering what Paul meant when he wrote about God's secret wisdom being revealed to the church. I wonder how many of them wondered what having the mind of Christ meant, and what it had to do with the conflict they wrote him about. I wonder how many of you wonder the same things.

Perhaps it might help if we spend some time looking a bit closer at what Paul has written. As we do, let's not forget he's responding to the conflict he described in chapter 1, verses 11 and 12. Paul says he came to share Jesus Christ crucified. He came to share "God's secret wisdom" recognized by those mature in Christ, but missed by those focusing on the world pattern of the "things that are." We looked at those in the previous chapter.

Paul mentioned the rulers of the age being one group who missed God's secret wisdom. Do you wonder why Paul would refer to them in this context? After all, he wrote to the church about a conflict in the church. What is it about world rulers that would provide Paul the right illustration to reveal the attitudes in the Corinthian church conflict?

Rulers tend to rule by exercising power. In other words, their way is THE way; they are right, and they are the winners. Rulers are the folks who get to determine "the things that are" for everyone else. What they say goes for all they rule over. They're the ones who declare, "My way or the highway!" Unfortunately, we encounter these "ruler" types in conflicted churches all the time, usually at the very center of the storm. I've actually heard the above declaration made in group settings, and watched the impact it has had on those in the room. Trust me; I've never seen it resolve a thing. But I've often watched it make things a whole lot worse than they were moments before.

I remember one meeting where the pastor was wearing the "ruler" hat, though that isn't always the case. Just as it appeared the energy in the room was beginning to turn toward Christ, rather than conflict, the pastor made one last stab at declaring his position of leadership. He concluded that as far as he was concerned it was his way or the highway. Unfortunately, a handful of key leaders chose the highway and left.

> When the ten heard about this, they were indignant with the two brothers. Jesus called them together and said, "You know that the rulers of the Gentiles lord it over them, and their high officials exercise authority over them. Not so with you. Instead, whoever wants to become great among you must be your servant, and whoever wants to be first must be your slave—just as the Son of Man did not come to be served, but to serve, and to give his life as a ransom for many."
>
> **Matthew 20:24–28**

If the quarreling folks in Corinth were anything like

many in the situations we've encountered, I suspect each of them was hoping their individual view would become the ruling view that determined "the things that are" for the Corinthian church. Sounds like a church leadership model very familiar to many of us; even though Jesus shared a much different model with the apostles in Matthew 20:24–28. By the way, what Jesus said in this passage came out of a situation involving a similar leadership-power-struggle among the apostles.

Paul refers to the rulers missing God's secret wisdom, and then quotes this thought: "No eye has seen, no ear has heard, no mind has conceived what God has prepared for those who love him" (verse 9). Look at this statement and remember the following: First, Paul wrote this about the conflicted situation in the Corinthian church. Second, he shared it in the context of God's secret wisdom. Third, he shared it in reference to their day's world rulers, who missed God's secret wisdom.

With that in mind, note the singular, individualistic focus of the sentence: *no eye has seen, no ear has heard, and no mind has conceived.* Certainly this singular, individualistic focus would characterize the rulers of their age. But these were the very rulers who, because of this singular, individualistic focus, missed God's secret wisdom.

Remember, God's secret wisdom is not made of "the things that are" of the world pattern. God's secret wisdom is made up of those things that appear to the world to be "the things that are not."

Think again about the world rulers Paul mentioned earlier. They would be represented by the single eye, ear, and mind. The way they saw, heard, and perceived things would become the "things that are" in their rule. His or her individual views and perceptions would be THE way for everyone else. This was the approach Paul saw developing among the conflicted folks in the Corinthian church, as they quarreled over whose views were right and whose views would "rule"—those of Paul, of Apollos, of Cephas, or of Christ?

It actually wouldn't be all that different from what was going on between Jack, Mike, Alice, Bill, and many of their brothers and sisters. Individuals, and/or groups of individuals, were trying to "lord it over" all the others, just like the world rulers Paul mentions in his letter, and just like those the Lord instructed His followers not to be like.

It's very natural for some of us to fall into this "ruler" mentality and relate with others in such a fashion, especially when in conflict. I suspect that's another reason why Paul introduced the cross-of-Christ theme at this moment. There is a whole lot of our independent, individualistic *self*, involved when trying to "rule" or "lord" over others in the body of Christ. And nothing less than the cross of Christ, and all it represents, will set us free from it.

Having the Mind of Christ—Together

So what is the Corinthian church to do? They have four different factions—each operating from the self-focused motive of jealousy—"quarreling" over their views and alliances. I suspect they all argued that their view was God's view; at least, that's how such quarrels we deal with today usually present themselves. Each individual thinks he sees what God has prepared. Each one thinks she hears what God is saying. Each one thinks, "I've seen the vision." Each one believes he has the truth of the matter. Paul declares, *No, you don't, not individually.* For no single, individual, human being has been given that capacity. *"But God has revealed it to us* [plural] *by his Spirit"* (verse10, italics added). He didn't reveal this to individuals, but to "us," the community, the body of Christ, who gathers together in Him; seeing, hearing, and conceiving what God has prepared for us is a corporate, community, "us" experience. That's the core of God's secret wisdom.

The community of being-one-in-Christ—the spiritual man shown in chapter 2, verse 13—has been given the capacity to see, hear, and conceive the things of God. Isn't that awesome? We who experience our being-one-in-Him together (the Church, which is all of us who gather together in Him) have been given the capacity to see, hear, and conceive what God has prepared for us. It's a natural spirit process when the body (us) works in unison, responding to the head (Jesus).

We Have the Mind of Christ

Did you catch that part of Paul's thoughts captured in chapter 2, verse 16? We (the Church) have the mind of Christ. He doesn't say we might get Christ's mind. He doesn't even say we will get Christ's mind. He says *we have Christ's mind.* The Corinthian church already had the mind of Christ. They didn't each have His mind individually, independently, and separately. They had His mind corporately—*together,* in Him. The local expression of His body in Vancouver, Washington, known by the name of Lake Shore Community Church, has the mind of Christ. The local expression of His body of which you are a part has His mind as well. We're all recipients of God's secret wisdom. May I please have a big amen and hallelujah!

Church life is not about the individual or group views "quarreling" with one another. It's not about the individuals and their individualistic views (truths) in any individual group. It's about Jesus, who is the head of His body, the Church, of which we are all parts belonging one to another. It's not about Jack's truth, or Mike's, Alice's, or Bill's, apart from the others. None of them has the capacity to see, hear, and conceive of God's things apart from the others, nor does any one group, independent of all the others. Only when they all come seeking

His mind, together, do they have opportunity to see, hear, and conceive what God has prepared for them, for He sees them as being one in Christ.

This is especially true when we find ourselves in disagreements and conflicts with our brothers and sisters in Christ. Paul must have thought so, as he is the one who introduced these thoughts into the midst of dealing with the conflict in the Corinthian church. We certainly have found it to be true when working with conflicted churches today. When the body parts get their eyes off of themselves, one another, and their differences, and start focusing on Jesus, they all can experience His mind together. We've witnessed some profound relational miracles as a result.

We were invited to work with a congregation that was suffering the impact of unresolved conflict among its staff. The new senior pastor had been the associate pastor for a number of years. Because he and the previous pastor had worked well together for years, everyone assumed the transition would go smoothly. Unfortunately, reality was anything but smooth. The result was a breach in their personal relationship, the resignation of a third staff person, and additional conflict among the elder board and congregation.

The conflict boiled down to which vision the church was going to follow. Were they going to keep following and building on the vision established by the former pastor? Or were they going to begin the new vision introduced by the present pastor? The elders and most of the congregation were divided by their loyalties to these two leaders.

Fortunately, the two pastors were able to set aside their differences and focus on Jesus and His vision, rather than themselves. Once they did, many of the conflicts were resolved quickly, and a plan was designed to approach the remaining issues in a healthy, Christ-honoring way. They ended that time together with tears of relief and joy, and an anticipation of what the

Lord had in store for the church. I was additionally blessed to attend a meeting in which these two brothers stood before the elders and openly confessed their individual contributions to the conflict and asked the elders to forgive them. This led to additional confessions among the elders, as well as expressions of forgiveness and tears of joy. Together, they all began to get their eyes off of themselves and on Jesus. As they did, the things of the world grew "strangely dim in the light of His glory and grace."

It's the same for you and me and the folks we gather with *in Him*. It's the same when you and I have a conflict over something. The conflict is not about you and me competing over whose truth is going to win, or whose view is going to rule. It's about us coming together to seek His mind in such matters. I don't have the capacity to know the whole truth of the matter, and neither do you. But because Christ dwells within us, and we dwell in Him, there are elements of His truth in our truths. Therefore, as we come together to share our truths—listening to one another, working to understand one another—we position ourselves to see together, hear together, and conceive together what He has prepared for us in that moment.

Imagine what different path the Corinthians could have taken had they chosen the way of being one in Christ, rather than the individualistic, "right or wrong" and "win or lose" approach illustrated by their jealousy-fueled quarreling. In their oneness in Christ, they had always had the "mind of Christ." This was their reality. It's our reality as well. Individually, they had their separate, disagreeing, competitive, quarreling views. As you read on in Paul's letter, you can see what their independent, individualistic approach produced in their midst.

Imagine how different things could be for Jack, Mike, Alice, and Bill, as well as the rest of the body of Christ of which they are a part. Rather than giving themselves to the draining activities of warring with brothers and sisters, they could have been building up the body of Christ, by investing themselves in dialogue with one another and the Lord. Rather than experiencing the death and destruction that comes from eating of the tree of right and wrong, and traveling down the broad path of independent individualism, they could have experienced the life of Christ together, by seeking and discovering His mind in the matters before them.

Imagine how different things could be in your gathering of His body.

It's not about the tree of right and wrong; it's about *the Tree of Life*—His name is Jesus.

It's not about your path or mine; it's about *the path of life*—His name is Jesus.

It's not about my truth or your truth; it's about *the truth*—His name is Jesus.

It's not about us individually; it's about us *together* in His body—His name is Jesus.

Jesus is the head of the body, of which we are all parts. All the parts of His body belong to each other. We (plural) are in Christ, and Christ is in us (plural). We (plural) are one in Christ, and Christ is one in us (plural). As the world saw the Father in seeing Jesus, the world sees Jesus in seeing us (plural) together. He prayed in John 17 that when the world encountered us, they would encounter the very oneness shared by the Father and the Son. He prayed this encounter would bring the world to a place of believing in the Father's love expressed in sending His Son into the world.

How do you think the Church is doing so far? How about you and the folks you gather with *in Him*?

10 From *Me Versus You* to *Us in Him*

Mike was encouraged by most of the responses he'd received thus far. He was still frustrated with Jack's unwillingness to help lead the meeting he was setting up with like-minded people, but he was still hopeful Jack would come around eventually. The first meeting he'd scheduled had gone better than expected. It was standing room only, and it appeared the vast majority agreed with Mike and his desire to do whatever was needed to move the church forward. Because of the growing interest, a second meeting was now scheduled. A handful of folks who attended the first meeting volunteered to attend the second one and share their views as well. This excited Mike, as it would communicate a broader involvement than just his voice trying to rally the troops. Mike recognized the similarities of this experience to the time he led a major change in the leadership of the local little league group who, like the older church leaders, were not interested in new ideas and ways of doing things. Perhaps, he thought, he was more of a leader than he had given himself credit for being.

IS CHRIST DIVIDED?

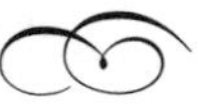

Albert Einstein once said, "The world we have created today as a result of our thinking thus far has created problems that cannot be solved by thinking the way we thought when we created them."

I couldn't agree more, especially when dealing with the way Christians and congregations commonly react to conflict. As we've seen, the unfortunate reality is that many of us conform to the world's pattern of reacting out of ourselves rather than responding in Christ. The result is that within the body of Christ we have as conflicted an environment as we find throughout the world. And the world is watching.

One of the more common reactions we hear when coming alongside Christians who are dealing with unresolved conflict is their surprise at how quickly things moved from relative peace to painful, unresolved conflict. There are a great many reasons for this, some of which we've already looked at. Failing to see ourselves as one in Christ—and as parts of the body of Christ belonging to one another—certainly put us on the path toward potential unresolved conflict. Not recognizing Jesus as an involved party in our relationships, including our disagreements and conflicts, assists us along this path. Not availing ourselves of the wisdom and power of seeking the mind of Christ together in such situations is also a contributor. Another factor is treating our "truth" as a personal possession to use competitively against one another, rather than together seeking Him who is truth. Making relationships about our differences rather than about the Lord also moves us toward conflict rather than peace. Moving into a "win or lose" mode, where we compete over "right and wrong" issues rather than the real issues of life in Him, places us on the downhill slide toward conflict.

So if we are to create an environment in which conflict and the process of resolving it is an opportunity to experience Jesus together—and to reflect Him in the world—we need to make a conscious, Christ-centered decision to respond in Him rather than reacting out of ourselves. This environment will take a different kind of thinking than we may be used to. It will take a thinking transformed by the indwelling power of Jesus Christ.

Conflict: Sin or Friend?

When I was growing up, people often told me things I just knew they didn't believe themselves, so neither did I. I'm sure you've had moments like these as well. I remember hearing on more than one occasion—as my father prepared to spank me—that it was going to hurt him more than it hurt me. Yeah, right.

Or what about the visits to the dentist or doctor, when they brought out those huge needles and told you it would only hurt a little bit? Sure. You didn't really buy that, did you? Neither did I. I bring up these fond memories, because I'm wondering if that's your reaction when you read that conflict is our friend. Yeah, right.

That's often the reaction we get when sharing that bit of truth during the trainings we do with local congregations. But, at the risk of sounding like my father, the dentist, or a doctor, "Trust me."

Conflict is our friend, and here's why: if you knew someone who, each and every time you encountered them, consistently presented you with the opportunity to experience more and more of Jesus, would you not consider that person to be one of the best friends you ever had? And if every time you were with that person, you were given the opportunity to gain a deeper sense of who you and others really are in Jesus, would this really be someone you would fear and avoid as if he carried the plague? Well, let me introduce you to your friend, conflict.

In approaching conflict in Christ we have a grand opportunity to experience Jesus in ways unique to that very situation. In these experiences, we can discover and experience more and more of Him and who we are in Him. Along the way, minds are renewed and lives are transformed from worldly forms to the life that is ours in Jesus Christ.

Can you imagine how your feelings and responses to conflict might change with just this simple transformation of your view of conflict and its value in your life? The Lord spoke powerfully to a single mom, who confessed to me during a break in a training session that she was scared to death of conflict, especially with her oldest teenage son. As she struggled with the idea of conflict being her friend, she began to question the power she was giving it through her fear, and the unhealthy impact it was having on her relationship with her son. Later that week she came to me, smiling and tearful, to share a miracle that had taken place in her relationship with her son. A recurring situation took place between them, but rather than avoid the potential conflict, she approached it with her son. Though it was but a start, she tearfully described a conversation with her son that lasted nearly thirty minutes and ended with him giving her a hug.

A mind was renewed, and the transformation of two lives and a relationship was begun. And it all began when a single mom no longer conformed her thinking about conflict to the world pattern, but allowed Jesus to renew her mind and begin to transform her life.

From Competition to Cooperation

In conforming to the world's reaction to conflict, we can easily slip into a competitive mode of right or wrong and win or lose. This is especially prevalent within the American church because of our highly competitive culture, but it certainly is not limited to us. While the idea of winning and losing plays a big part in much of our lives, from sports to politics and much more, the competitive nature it breeds does not reflect who we are in Jesus Christ. We are each part of His Body, where collaboration reflects health and wholeness, and competition leads to disease.

We easily see the reality of this in our own physical bodies. When all the parts are working together in a healthy state of cooperation, our bodies reflect wholeness, oneness of balance, health, and well-being. In such a state we're strong, able to achieve great things, and withstand all kinds of attacks against our good health. But when parts are not cooperating, and instead are competing within the body, then we become susceptible to all kinds of life-threatening situations. Cancer is but one illustration, as one uncooperative cell competes with the rest of the body and eventually risks the health and well-being of all the other parts. We have witnessed the disease that is spread by the spirit of competition in local bodies time and time again. It's not a pretty sight.

In his letter to the church in Ephesus, Paul reminds us we don't fight against flesh and blood, but against powers and principalities. We especially need to remember this fact when we're tempted to see our brothers and sisters as the enemy, and wage our win or lose battle against them. We're one in Christ, not enemies. When we compete against one another, we're acting like the renegade cancer cell that decides to take on the whole body. While I don't worry about any such disease threatening the life of the body of Christ, I can tell you we do damage to the parts of the body and His witness in the world by our competitive fights with one another.

From Being Certain to Being Curious

When we treat our "truth" as "the truth of the matter" concerning conflicts, we're usually very certain of our facts, positions, motives, and assumptions. Often, from our positions, we're not motivated to learn much about the other person, nor their facts, positions, motives, or assumptions. If we're interested, it's usually only to learn the weak and vulnerable places of their positions, where we can attack them with our truth. Acting from this place of certainty limits the exchange of important information between the parties. This position is dangerous in itself. But it's only through sharing our "truths" that we can begin to comprehend His truth, which makes this "individual certainty" tragic, if not sinful.

We recently had a prime example of the damage such "certainty" can have on individual lives, as well as on an entire congregation. During a number of interviews with conflicted church leaders, we learned of a particular situation that was a battlefield of their struggles. We heard no less than three different versions of this situation, shared by more than a dozen people "certain" of their facts. Though each version shared enough "facts" to be identified as reflecting the same incident, they disagreed in a number of important elements, including the name of the person responsible for the action taken. Then we heard the story from the person who confessed to being responsible for the action. Interestingly, this person's name was not given in the other three versions of the story we heard; those whose names were given all denied being responsible.

Brothers and sisters in Christ were angry and upset with one another. Relationships were being damaged. Ministries were being negatively impacted by leader resignations and loss of financial support. A right-or-wrong and win-or-lose battle was in full bloom, and being waged against one another by brothers and sisters "certain" of their facts, positions, motives, and assumptions. Not once did we discover anyone who was curious enough to check out their "facts" with those they assumed were responsible. They were "certain" they were right. On the basis of that certainty, they were up to their eyeballs in unresolved conflict.

As Christians, we should be very curious to hear and understand one another's "truths"—very likely they have elements of Jesus. He dwells within each of us, revealing Himself and His truth through us. Our curiosity is the gateway to encountering more and more of Him.

From Debate to Exploration

Time and time again, we have listened to conflicted parties limit their communication with one another to a debate. You know how this goes: one party gives a volley of their facts, and the next party volleys back with theirs. Sometimes they even wait for each other to finish their thoughts rather than interrupting or talking over the top of one another. Sometimes they aren't quite so respectful, and just have at it verbally. It's like how we used to argue about whose dad was bigger and stronger, and, eventually, over whose dad could defeat the other's dad. Depending on the safety factors and value of this kind of interchange, I'm often tempted to let the fighting parties tire themselves out with verbal punches.

We were mediating a conflict between two brothers in the Lord when they slipped into the debate mode and began lobbing verbal barrages at one another. I finally called a truce and asked them to consider what would be the most important gift each of them could receive from the other at that moment. They were both silent for quite awhile. Then one replied, "I want to be listened to. That's the most important thing I need right now." I asked why, and he replied: "Because I don't think he's really listening to me . . . he doesn't understand me." He then caught his breath, looked at his brother and said, "And I guess I'm not really listening to you, either."

We then began to discuss what it would be like to listen to one another, and for each to begin to explore the other's concern. They both had to admit they were interested in the *exploring* idea, but they had no idea where to start. I told them they had already begun when they put aside their debate and became interested in listening and understanding one another.

As stated earlier, if we listen when debating our "truths," it's usually only to discover the weaknesses we can attack in the other person's truth. But usually, very little listening takes place in a debate. The goal is to win, not to learn, not to be understood, and not to understand. Because of this, the shared information is kept at a minimum, which also limits the opportunities to discover the Lord's truth in the matter. It is His truth that holds for us the keys to resolution and reconciliation that will renew minds and transform lives.

From Simple to Complex

When we hold to our "truths" as *the truth*, we also tend to see the conflict in very simple terms: *I'm right and you're wrong.* Rarely, if ever, are conflicted issues this simple. Our personal filters, which serve to select the elements of our "truths," are part of a very complex system involving different parts of the brain, nerves, emotions, and other functions of the human body, not to mention the involvement of our spirit. There's nothing simple about how we develop our "truths"; therefore, it's unrealistic to believe the conflicts that arise between those "truths" could be simple either.

During mediation sessions, we've filled pages full of notes while listening to people "unpack" an issue one or both of them had identified as "simple" to resolve. As they begin to consciously and actively listen to one another, they often discover new information they've never heard before. They also discover new elements of their own truths they hadn't considered before. As this exploration of the issues expands their understanding, they're often better able to resolve their conflicts in creative ways.

From *Either/Or* to *And*

When we get into the conflicted position of dueling "truths" we tend to see everything from the positional polarities of either my truth or your truth. Our "truths" and everything about them are often seen to be either right or wrong. As one brother declared in the midst of a group facilitation, "I've heard everything you've had to say, but as far as I'm concerned, it's either my way or the highway." You could feel the hearts and minds of others in the room slamming shut.

Often we're not as blunt as was this brother, though the reactions are often the same. When someone says they have heard what we had to say, and then goes on to share his or her views, such as, "But, this is what I have to say," we often feel they have rejected us and everything we said. Recently, I was working with a church staff when one of them stated they "absolutely agreed with" another staff member. She then took a breath and continued, "But . . ." When she finished her statement, I asked the other staff member if he felt she "absolutely agreed" with him, or not. "Not at all," was his reply. He then went on to describe his anger and frustration at feeling judged and dismissed by her. She was surprised by his reaction. Her surprise turned to shock when everyone else in the room agreed with him.

I then asked her to restate what he originally had said that she so "absolutely agreed with." He agreed she had captured the meaning and intent of his statement. Then I asked her if she meant to judge or dismiss him or what he said. She responded that she did not. She was simply attempting to voice the reasons for her own views in the matter being discussed between them.

I asked her if she would be willing to try it again, and this time replace the word "but" with the word "and." She repeated what she had said earlier, and paused before saying "and," then continued to express her own views. We all had a chuckle at the conscious effort it took her to substitute "and" for "but." I then turned to the other staff member involved in this conversation and asked him if his reaction to this statement was any different. These were his words: "I can't explain why one word should make such a difference, but, yes, this time I did not feel judged or dismissed. I felt we might disagree, but I also felt she really heard me."

So the next time you are in a conflicted situation and you want to express your feelings about what someone else has said, substitute the word "and" where you may be tempted to use the word "but": "I heard you say this, *and* this is what I say." You will be surprised how different it feels to you and the other person. Rather than declaring him wrong and possibly devaluing him personally, when you use the word "and," you are simply adding your views and feelings to his. Everyone's views and feelings are expressed openly and honestly, which then allows them to be dealt with in a healthy manner.

By creating an environment in which everyone is valued personally, and all views and feelings are expressed and dealt with directly, we also greatly increase the opportunity to hear what Jesus is expressing in and through all of us, *together*. In turn, this increases the opportunity for us to hear His mind in the matter, and to discover His solutions.

From Telling to Understanding

If I make our different views of an issue about right and wrong or win and lose, then I'll tend to invest myself in telling you how I'm right and you're wrong, or at least telling you everything I feel is important for you to understand and agree with. My focus is on the telling part. It's all about talking—*my talking*. But isn't it interesting when God created us He gave us *one mouth* and *two ears*. I wonder which activity He values more, our talking or our listening?

There are a number of elements involved in this "telling" approach to our conversations, especially in a conflicted situation. Whether we consciously intend to reflect a judgmental spirit or not, that's often what those on the receiving end of our *telling* hear. Words, tone inflections, and body language all communicate the judgment that our "truth" is right and the others are wrong, or at least not as right as ours.

When we "hear" that our "truth" has been judged wrong, especially when we haven't been given the opportunity to share it yet, we tend to react defensively, thus "proving" to the "teller" his/her initial judgments about us were correct. With this confirmation, the "teller" tends to become even more fixed on his "truth" than he was before, and the conflict level escalates.

If I singularly focus on "telling" my "truth," then I also tend to "dismiss" the other person's "truth." He then feels that I have judged or rejected him. Have you ever had someone walk out on you in the midst of a conversation, or hang up on you during a phone call? Doesn't feel good, does it? This rejection then escalates our stress. Then, as we've already learned, this stress negatively impacts our ability to communicate on a healthy, Christ-honoring level. But that's exactly what often occurs in those on the receiving end of our "telling" conversations.

I'm not sure how it works in other cultures, but in the American culture, acknowledging another's truth is often equated with agreeing with them. We resist admitting we understand another person's perceptions, understandings, or experiences, as they may interpret this as a weakness and try to take advantage of it. As Christians, we need to get over this fear. Acknowledging is not agreeing. Acknowledging what we understand communicates we are listening. It communicates we value the other person, as does Jesus. Acknowledging the elements of others' truth builds bridges to allow them to listen, understand, and acknowledge us, and the elements of our truth. This process moves us closer and closer to discovering the mind of Christ *together*.

Are there times for the "telling" approach? Of course there are. When instructions are being given, or if the basis of the conversation is simply to pass on information from one person to another, a "telling" approach is very important. When you notice your child in the street, or about to put her hand on a hot stove, a "telling" approach is appropriate and necessary. I can't imagine what would occur if a military officer tried to use an understanding approach in the midst of battle to communicate his orders to the troops. But in the relational context of dealing with difficult and conflicted issues between us, the "telling" approach is counterproductive in leading us to seek the mind of Christ together.

From Limiting Information to Expanding it

Most of the self-centered reactions to conflict that reflect the world pattern limit the amount and quality of information shared between those in conflict. When we react competitively, we tend to be certain of our own truth to the exclusion of others. Rather than cooperating with one another to explore the elements of our truths, we reduce our interchange to a competitive debate. Rather than collaborating together with the Lord in discovering His solutions, we compete against one another about whose solution will win. And rather than exploring the elements of His truth found in each of ours, we tend to see the issues in simplistic, right/wrong views, which lead us to become positional, and then we limit ourselves to either one position or the other.

Throughout the process of reacting to conflict in such ways, we tend to expend most of our energy in telling our truths, and very little energy is invested in understanding the other person. When we follow the world pattern we limit the information shared between us. In doing so, we limit our opportunity to seek the mind of Christ together, and instead conform our lives to the world pattern. And the world is watching.

From *Me Versus You* to *Us in Christ*

Brothers and sisters, we are one in Jesus Christ. While we may react to our conflicts in ways more reflective of the world than of Jesus, our reality remains unchanged: *We are one in Jesus Christ.* We can deny our reality, and continue to conform to the world's ways, making our conflicts about "me versus you," or we can approach our conflicts as opportunities to experience Jesus in ways unique to the situation before us. We can make our life in Christ about each of us individually, or we can make it about us *together* in Him. The former leads to death, and the latter leads to life. I hope we will choose *life together*. His name is Jesus.

11 Approaching Our Conflicts in Christ

"So what are you saying . . . that I don't have a clue what's going on here?" Jack was beginning to feel the same anger rising within him he had felt each previous time he and Kathy had tried to talk about the growing conflict in the church. While they had initially committed to not leave the church, Jack was still struggling with the decision, especially as conditions appeared to be getting worse. During the whole experience thus far, it felt to him that Kathy was never very sympathetic to his position; she wanted him to see things from other people's views.

"No, Jack, that's not what I'm saying at all. You know that. We've had this conversation . . . how many times? I'm just saying that if we've made the commitment to remain in the church, then it seems to me we should do whatever we can to be a part of the solution. And it seems to me in order to do that, we need to try to see things from other people's views as well as our own."

"*My own*, you mean." Jack stood at the end of the kitchen counter, arms folded, and a bit of a scowl on his face.

"No . . . *our own*. Yours. Mine. And ours. We each have our own views on things. . . ."

"That's for sure," Jack interrupted.

Kathy continued with a little more emphasis, ". . . and we have a lot in common. But honestly, honey, what do you really know about Alice Morgan? I know you think she's against the youth center because she's an old lady and doesn't remember what it's like to be young, or that she has no idea of the importance of that center in the lives of teens today. But, honestly, how do you know that? Have you ever had a conversation with her to find out her true feelings about these things?"

Jack studied her for a moment as he tried to sort through the storm of thoughts and feelings being unleashed within his head and heart. He was angry, and wanted to tell her she didn't know what she was talking about, and it would be nice if she took his side for a change. Yet he also knew she was right about how little he knew about Alice, or Bill, or any of the others who were not part of the youth ministry team. He had to admit, he had never thought about trying to have a conversation like that with these folks. He wouldn't even know how to start.

"So I suppose you have some grand plan to tell me about?" Jack pulled out a chair at the table and sat down.

Looking rather sheepish, Kathy responded, "Well, actually I do . . . not so much a plan . . . more like an idea, because I don't know what will happen beyond this. But do you remember when Anna and Beth had that falling out a while ago?" Jack gave her the look that signaled he didn't have a clue, but to go on, so she did. "Well, anyhow, Anna told me that Beth's mom really helped them work through their issues together. And you know, both Jennifer and Dick work with conflicted situations all the time in their jobs. So I was wondering what you thought about bouncing some of this stuff off of them, and see if they can help us figure out how to be a part of the solution." She paused as she studied his face. "So, what do you think?" she asked cautiously.

Jack pushed back his chair, and began to stand up. As he slid the chair back under the table, he replied, "I don't suppose it will hurt anything. Maybe Dick will be on my side." Jack gave Kathy a half smile to let her know he was teasing—a little. "And if all else fails, Dick and I can talk about football." With that, he left the room.

"A fool finds no pleasure in understanding but delights in airing his own opinions" (Proverbs 18:2).

It seems counterintuitive to invest ourselves in trying to understand someone with whom we are at odds. Everything inside us calls us toward a more "telling" approach; you could say it seems more "natural." As well it should, for as we've been learning, it flows from the Tree of the Knowledge of Good and Evil, which has set the natural character of mankind since Adam and Eve first ate of its fruit.

But as Paul declares in Romans 6:1–14, just as Jesus was raised from the dead through the glory of the Father, we too have been raised in Him to live a new life. This new life does not come from the same tree Adam and Eve ate of; it comes from the other tree, the Tree of Life, whose name is Jesus. This life replaces the fallen-death nature of Adam with the risen-life nature of Jesus Christ. To live is Christ, as Paul declared in Philippians 1:21. Therefore, while the *telling* approach may seem more natural to us than the *understanding* approach, we must recognize it is an expression of the fallen-death nature of mankind, not the risen-life nature of Jesus Christ in mankind.

Approaching our conflicts with the goal of understanding the other person's "truth" not only moves us toward that goal, but assists us in understanding the Lord's truth in the matter as well. Remember, He dwells in all those who believe in Him and declare Him Savior and Lord. He reveals Himself through the many parts of His body. Therefore, there are usually elements of His truth resident within the truths of each of the parts who comprise His body. If I'm truly interested in Him and His truth, then I'll avail myself of every aspect of Him in every situation I can. If there are elements of His truth in you, as there are in me, we can both discover more of Him by understanding one another. Then, and only then, are we well able to access His mind in the matter together.

By focusing on understanding one another, we can create an environment in which we may express our truths in a way we will be heard and understood. Rather than a competitive win or lose environment, we can create a collaborative environment in seeking Him together. Rather than an environment in which it's often risky to be open, honest, and vulnerable, we can create an environment where everyone is safe, and free to be the person they are in Christ. Rather than an environment in which we are often controlled by our reactions and the reactions of others, we can create an environment in which we are freely able to respond in Him.

We know the pattern the world uses to deal with conflict. It comes all too easily and naturally. But if we're going to avail ourselves of Jesus' transformative power, then we'll need to replace the world pattern with the new pattern reflecting Him. Rather than a conflict pattern that prepares us to react in ourselves by either fighting or fleeing, we need a pattern that prepares us to respond in Christ, and approach our conflict together in Him and with Him. I believe our Heavenly Father has given us such a pattern in His Word, a pattern that prepares us for such a response. So where do we begin? We begin by preparing ourselves in Christ. And where do we begin our preparation in Christ? We follow the preparatory steps below.

- *Begin with Jesus*
- *Then yourself*
- *Then your brother/sister*
- *Then the situation*

Begin with Jesus

We always, at all times, start with Jesus. We also move with Him along the way, and end with Him as well. He is the Alpha and Omega, the beginning and end, and everything in between. He is life.

Whenever we meet with the leadership of a local body considering calling us to assist them in dealing with their unresolved conflict, we share with them two of the most important tasks we see before us. The first task is to remind them of who Jesus is. The second is to remind them of who they are in Him. Basic concepts, yet these two crucial realities are easily forgotten in the midst of unresolved conflict. Time and time again, when these two truths are mentioned, tears appear in the eyes of many as they suddenly realize what they'd forgotten.

It happens to most of us in the midst of conflict. Sometimes it begins as we approach a possible conflict. As we slip into our own reactions rather than responding in Him, we begin the process that causes us to forget who He is. We don't intend to lose our focus on Him, but it easily happens unless we prepare ourselves in advance. So, toward that goal, let me suggest that you memorize some favorite Scriptures concerning who Jesus is to you, or at least spend enough time reflecting on them to have their meaning well-engrained in your heart and mind.

When approaching a possible conflict, or even in the midst of one, it's important that we refocus in Christ. Reminding ourselves of Jesus—*Son of God, Son of Man, the way, the truth, the life, all in all, over all, through all, in all, King of kings, Lord of lords, Word, Spirit, Prince of Peace, master, ruler, Lord, Messiah*—will help us to focus on Him rather than on ourselves.

Beginning with Him opens our hearts, minds, and spirits to be more receptive to the Holy Spirit's leading. It allows us to experience the renewing of our minds, which Paul referred to in Romans 12:1–2:

> Therefore, I urge you, brothers, in view of God's mercy, to offer your bodies as living sacrifices, holy and pleasing to God—this is your spiritual act of worship. Do not conform any longer to the pattern of this world, but be transformed by the renewing of your mind. Then you will be able to test and approve what God's will is—his good, pleasing and perfect will.

While the Corinthian church tends to get a bad rap for its spiritual immaturity, worldliness, and conflict, a few other conflicted situations drew Paul's attention in the early Church as well. For instance, a couple of sisters in Philippi, Euodia and Syntyche, apparently had a squabble. Perhaps you've heard these two sisters referred to as "You did it" and "So touchy."

After pleading with these two sisters to agree with each other in the Lord, Paul then goes on to offer this counsel in Philippians 4:4–9:

> Rejoice in the Lord always. I will say it again: rejoice! Let your gentleness be evident to all. The Lord is near. Do not be anxious about anything, but in everything, by prayer and petition, with thanksgiving, present your requests to God. And the peace of God, which transcends all understanding, will guard your hearts and your minds in Christ Jesus. Finally brothers, whatever is true, whatever is noble, whatever is right, whatever is pure, whatever is lovely, whatever is admirable—if anything is excellent or praiseworthy—think about such things. Whatever you have learned or received or heard

> from me, or seen in me—put it into practice. And the God of peace will be with you.

Do you want peace? Then begin with Jesus, who is our peace. Rejoice in Him, and His gentleness will begin to flow in you. Your anxiety will begin to decrease as you lift to Him yourself, the person with whom you disagree, and the situation. As you do this, God's peace will guard your heart and mind in Christ Jesus, so that you can more clearly reflect on Him, for He is true, noble, right, pure, lovely, admirable, excellent, and praiseworthy. Truly, the God of peace will be with you in a most profound way. Do I hear a "hallelujah"?

In situations in which we have time to prepare before a conversation we suspect may get conflicted, we can spend time reminding ourselves of who He is. We can also do this when we realize our conversation took a turn, and we've entered *the conflict zone*. While our minds focus on all the elements involved in the situation, our spirits can immediately begin to focus in Him. As you become more and more experienced in this, you'll be amazed at the sense of calm that bubbles up from deep within and pours over your entire being.

As Jesus' calming presence envelops you, you are more able to think clearly, listen attentively, feel empathetically, and respond appropriately. This alone will have a major positive impact on you, the other person(s), and the conflicted situation.

I've been personally blessed to experience this calming peace in the midst of conflicted situations. I've heard from others who have applied this in their own lives and have experienced His transforming power in their lives, as well as the life of the other person and their situation.

Then Yourself

As you can tell, when you begin with Jesus, you're already influencing yourself; or more accurately, He is influencing you.

But there's more self-work to be done; and again, this can be done while you prepare for a conversation, or "on the fly" during a conflicted situation.

Jesus spoke to the wisdom of this step in Matthew 7:1–5:

> Do not judge, or you too will be judged. For in the same way you judge others, you will be judged, and with the measure you use, it will be measured to you. Why do you look at the speck of sawdust in your brother's eye and pay no attention to the plank in your own eye? How can you say to your brother, 'Let me take the speck out of your eye,' when all the time there is a plank in your own eye? You hypocrite, first take the plank out of your own eye, and then you will see clearly to remove the speck from your brother's eye.

The Psalmist captured a similar thought when he wrote Psalm 139:23–24, "Search me, O God, and know my heart; test me and know my anxious thoughts. See if there is any offensive way in me, and lead me in the way everlasting."

We don't often like to admit we've contributed to the conflict. That doesn't mesh well with the "truth" we often construct in which "I'm right and they're wrong." Yet in all the mediations we've been a part of, I cannot remember ever encountering a person who hasn't contributed to the conflict in some way.

Again, we can do this self-reflection in preparation for a conversation we suspect may get conflicted, or when we find ourselves in the middle of such a situation. You might try reflecting on the following questions.

• *What has been my attitude and behavior in this situation?* Perhaps the behavior you're encountering in the other person is simply their reaction to something you said or didn't say, or did or didn't do. While your natural instinct may be to react to their reaction, you may want instead to respond in Jesus, and check out your own heart and behavior first. Who knows, the Holy Spirit may reveal to you an important element in the situation that will turn things from conflict to peace in Him. We're often surprised when He reveals a log in our own eye. And we're often more surprised how clearly we can see the situation when our vision is no longer obstructed with our own "stuff."

Or He may show you the ways you've been reflecting Him in this particular relationship or situation. Such awareness can fill you with a sense of awe, as well as comfort and peace as you rest in Him, trusting Him to use you and guide you in the continuing situation.

• *How does my attitude and behavior reflect Jesus, and who I am in Him?* This question simply takes the information we receive above, and goes deeper and wider with it. Are we reflecting Jesus, the world, or our *self*? As Christians, our desire should always be for Jesus Christ to express Himself in all that we do and say. As Paul declares in Ephesians 5:8–10, "For you were once darkness, but now you are light in the Lord. Live as children of light (for the fruit of the light consists in all goodness, righteousness and truth) and find out what pleases the Lord."

As you live out who you are in Christ, characteristics such as goodness, righteousness, and truth will begin to bubble out of you, and as they do, you will discover what pleases the Lord. He is pleased when His Son is manifested in the lives of His children. I suspect He is extremely pleased when we deal with our conflicts in a way that reflects who Jesus is, and who we are in Him.

• *What can I do to approach this situation in Christ and respond in Him?* Based on the information we discover while reflecting on the previous two questions, we can begin to make conscious decisions that will lead us to respond in Christ, rather than reacting in ourselves. It never ceases to amaze me how the Lord is able to place specific thoughts, Scripture passages, questions, and directions in my mind that, when I choose to act on them, lead the situation to Him. When working with conflicted brothers and sisters, we've witnessed transformations within them as they work through these three simple questions, and their anger, frustration, helplessness, and despair are suddenly replaced with His peace, hope, and joy.

Then Your Brother/Sister

After we've begun in Jesus—being reminded by the Holy Spirit of the truth of who Jesus is, who He is in us, and who we are in Him—then we're ready to begin turning our attention to those with whom we are, or possibly are about to be, in conflict. Again, there are a few questions that will help us in this task:

• *How have I seen this person?* In other words, what is "my truth" about him or her? When we begin to list our perceptions of the other person, it often helps us to begin discerning what is based on observable fact, and what we've created through our own feelings and assumptions. We often discover that very little has to do with observable facts, and much of our perception comes from our own editing of our truth about the other person.

We've seen church members' long lists of "truths" about one another dissolve to a short list of two or three items when they begin to evaluate the list in terms of observable facts, feelings, and assumptions.

Some time ago, I was helping a sister who had a workplace conflict with a coworker. As I initially listened to her "truth" about the situation, I listed at least seven negative individual characterizations she had made about her coworker. As we began to unpack this particular question, I listed each item on a sheet of paper, and began to ask questions to help us determine how she'd come to these conclusions about this other person. Four of them were simply her assumptions, based mostly on her feelings about this person. None of them had been checked out in any direct way. Therefore, she had to agree they may not be accurate. Two others were based on "facts" coworkers had told her about this person. We eventually identified these as the gossip they were, and therefore questionable as well. That left us with one negative characterization, and already her "truth" about this person had changed dramatically.

We then began to investigate other things she knew about this individual, perhaps of a neutral or positive nature. Before long, she had listed another five "truths" about her coworker, and she was beginning to question other aspects of her "truth" about her coworker and the conflict between them. Eventually she was able to have a healthy conversation with this person, and they were able to work out their differences in a way that satisfied both of them.

It doesn't always work out this way, but it's always helpful to check out how we've edited our "truths" about others. As we've already learned, we tend to make them out to be the enemy and ourselves the victim, which always colors our views, at least a bit.

• *How are my perceptions affected when seeing us as "one in Christ"?* This question tends to stretch us more than the other questions. Because many of us are not aware of this, spiritual reality uniting all the parts of His body into One, we don't often see one another in such terms. Add to this the normal disconnecting dynamics present in most conflicts, such as win or lose and right or wrong, where we feel anything but connected with one another, and you can begin to understand the difficulty many of us have in getting our minds around the reality that we are one in Christ with this person. But what a glorious moment it is when this realization occurs.

We call these "Jesus moments." They are moments when someone has a deep encounter with the Lord, often at times and in ways least expected. They often lead to at least a 90-degree change in the direction of the conflict, and sometimes even 180 degrees. I'll never forget one of these "moments" that occurred in the midst of a difficult mediation between two extremely conflicted brothers in Christ. In a private session with one of them, we were discussing this particular subject. This brother was having a very difficult time dealing with the implications of the question. He understood the "oneness" concept in his head, but that truth wasn't living in his heart. After returning to the mediation experience with the other party, we noticed this particular brother was quieter than he had been prior to the break we took to meet with each one separately. Later, in the midst of the other person sharing some thoughts, this brother suddenly exclaimed aloud, "I get it! I get it! We're not just brothers, we're one. We're one in Christ. So when we hurt each other, we're hurting ourselves . . . we're hurting Jesus!" There wasn't a dry eye in the room. Needless to say, the mediation experience changed directions dramatically. And while these brothers still had a great many painful issues to deal with, the spirit in which they proceeded was dramatically different following this "Jesus moment" experienced together.

• *How might Jesus see this person?* In spite of our conflicted "truths" about one another, we often can still accept the fact that Jesus has His "truths" of each of us. But the reality is, we don't often invest much time or interest in understanding them. I suspect we're afraid they'll get in the way of our views. But picture Jesus, right there with you. Picture Him whispering into your ear His feelings for this brother or sister with whom you are in conflict. Listen to Him describe the history involved leading to this person's attitude, and actions contributing to your conflict with them. Listen to Him describe that person "in Him." Now, with this new view of who that person is *in Him*, begin anew your discussion of the conflict.

• *What questions about the person and situation do I have that remain unanswered?* Often, after asking ourselves the previous questions, we suddenly realize we have more questions about the person and situation than we have answers. This should create a curiosity in us to better understand that person and the situation. Hopefully, it will also lead us to set aside for a while the certainties of our own truths, while we contemplate some questions to explore things further with that person.

Now please note, I said to *set aside* the certainties of our own truths *for a while.* I set them aside; I don't throw them overboard, not yet anyhow. I may take them up again, once I gain more understanding. Or I may not. But for now, I'm moving into the "understanding" mode, so that we may eventually seek the mind of Christ together.

• *How can I expand my understanding of us (me, them, and Jesus), and the situation?* Working toward understanding in a conflicted situation is a foundational principle to resolving conflict and reconciling relationships in Christ. It involves creating a conversational environment in which we can ask questions and share answers that expand our shared understanding with one another. This will require creating an environment of safety, which may involve my own demeanor, tone of voice, body language, etc.

These and other elements may be involved in expanding the shared understanding that helps lead us together to understanding the mind of Christ in the matter. The Lord will provide everything needed to accomplish His purposes.

"Ask and it will be given to you; seek and you will find; knock and the door will be opened to you. For everyone who asks receives; he who seeks finds; and to him who knocks, the door will be opened" (Matthew 7:7–8).

Then the Situation

Finally, we turn our attention to the conflict itself. I bet you were wondering if we were ever going to get to this, seeing as how this is where most people normally start. This is all the stuff that ties our stomachs in knots, and gives us a headache and high blood pressure. It's the "who, what, why, when, and how" stuff of a conflict that we turn over and over in our heads, and keeps us up at night. But even here, we need to do a bit more reflecting than we may normally do in such situations. We need to review the situation from three different, but very interrelated perspectives:

• *From your perspective.* If you have preparation time prior to dealing with the situation, you may even write down the "facts" as you know them. It helps to lay it all out with timelines that include who said and did what, and when. Given the reflecting with the Lord that has gone on since beginning in all of this, some of your "facts" may not seem so factual anymore. Or it may be you have a much clearer picture of particular issues, or of your interests, or of the other person's views and positions. Organizing all of this information will be helpful in discussing it with the other person.

• *From their perspective.* This is often more difficult, but take some time to reflect with the Lord, entertaining thoughts from the other person's perspective. How might she see this conflict? What could be behind the position she's taking? What issues does she see, and how does she feel about them? What might be her underlying interests reflected in her positions on these issues?

As mediators, one of the more important values we can bring to a conflicted situation is helping both parties see the situation from the other's perspective. Those who are able to set aside their own perspectives to at least try to see things from the other person's point of view are often surprised by how much they have in common with one another. And, while this "other perspective" may not lead to a change of mind or agreement between the parties at the time, it often leads to the creation of an environment that does allow them to resolve their issues and reconcile their relationship eventually.

• *From the Lord's perspective.* While this may seem difficult for those who have not made a practice of it, I can assure you the Lord desires you to see your conflicts from His perspective. Therefore, if you are willing, He will find a way to make this reality for you. I join Paul in his prayer for the church recorded in Ephesians 1:17: "I keep asking that the God of our Lord Jesus Christ, the glorious Father, may give you the Spirit of wisdom and revelation, so that you may know him better." The better you know Him, the more clearly you will be able to see His perspective. When you begin to see your conflicts from His perspective, they'll appear very different indeed.

When working with Christian brothers and sisters in conflict with one another, we often ask them to reflect on how the Lord may see them and the situation. In one particular situation, when working with a committee of sisters in Christ, this particular question turned the entire experience. When they entered the room, no one was speaking to one another, and even eye contact was minimal. They each selected seats that maximized the space between them. Needless to say, there was not a great deal of love in the air.

After each of them had the opportunity to share their "truth" about the conflict, and in the midst of beginning to deal with the agenda they had agreed on, I asked them to consider how Jesus might see them and the present situation. At first there was a silence that grew more uncomfortable as time passed. Eventually, one of the sisters shared her sense of how it must all be breaking the Lord's heart. When she concluded, another sister offered a view that supported the first. She then described her own attitude and action toward another woman at the table, and concluded that this surely must have hurt the Lord. She then turned her attention to this sister and apologized directly. This, in turn, began a process of confessing and apologizing that lasted nearly an hour. There was yet more work to do, but when they left that day the hallway was filled with laughter. I suspect the Lord's heart was filled with joy. I know mine was.

I recognize moving through these preparatory questions can seem insurmountable on a good day, and perhaps impossible if you find yourself in the midst of a conflicted conversation. But I can assure you, brothers and sisters have gone before you in preparing themselves in this way, with beneficial results. Personally, I believe this is more due to Jesus than the abilities of individual Christians. Remember, He is the one who prayed that we would be one, just as He and the Father are one. And He is well able to bring to completion that which He begins.

Introduction to Section II

Therefore, I urge you, brothers, in view of God's mercy, to offer your bodies as living sacrifices, holy and pleasing to God—this is your spiritual act of worship. Do not conform any longer to the pattern of this world, but be transformed by the renewing of your mind. Then you will be able to test and approve what God's will is—his good, pleasing and perfect will (Romans 12:1–2).

It is not my intent for this book to offer a detailed "how-to" list. That would be a cheap substitute for Him. Rather than focusing on "doing" a list, it's wiser to focus on Him, and "be" who we are in Him. In reality, He is the source of every aspect of our life, including how He will lead us to approach our conflicts in Him, which is why I have continually pointed you to Him, rather than to a list of steps.

As the writer of Hebrews declared, "Therefore, since we are surrounded by such a great cloud of witnesses, let us throw off everything that hinders and the sin that so easily entangles, and let us run with perseverance the race marked out for us. Let us fix our eyes on Jesus, the author and perfecter of our faith . . ." (Hebrews 12:1–2a).

When we take our eyes off of Jesus, we tend to look to the world pattern. I hope you've come to recognize that the world pattern of reacting to conflict "hinders" and "easily entangles" us, preventing us from experiencing His life of renewal and transformation in the midst of our conflicts.

Very early in the process of this book, it was suggested it would be helpful if I described what it might look like when we approach our conflicts *in Christ* rather than reacting to them out of ourselves. That was when I decided to add Section II, which describes what could have happened if Jack, Alice, and Bill approached their conflict *in Christ.*

Their story is not meant to offer any kind of list of steps to follow. Remember, we're not called to follow steps; we're called to follow Christ. Their story is simply a description of their experience in approaching their conflict in Christ. It is shared in the hope it will encourage you to no longer be conformed to the world pattern of reacting to conflict out of yourself, but rather to approach your conflicts in Christ, together with your brothers and sisters. After all, it's not about us. It's all about Him.

12

Things were still a bit icy between Jack and Kathy when Anna returned home later in the evening. Her father was watching television in the family room, and her mother was puttering in the kitchen. At least there had been some moderation in the distance between them, though it didn't appear the walls between them had come down just yet. Anna made her way to the kitchen.

"Hey, Mom," Anna said as cheerfully as she could, hoping to break some of the icicles hanging in the air.

"Hi, honey. I hear you were at Beth's," her mom replied.

Aha, Anna thought to her self. *At least they talked enough for mom to know where I've been.* "Uh, yeah. We had some stuff to go over for youth group on Wednesday."

"That's nice, honey. But I thought you were mad at her for gossiping about you to the new boy in your class."

"Old news, Mom. We got that worked out last week. Nothing's gonna keep the 'Blues Sisters' apart too long, not even a cute boy."

"I'm glad to hear that, honey. You two have been like sisters for a very long time."

Anna noticed that her mother hadn't made eye contact with her since she entered the room. Then she noticed her mother had been crying. "Mom, what's up? You've been crying."

"Oh, it's nothing . . . nothing that concerns you."

"Mom, if it concerns you, it concerns me." An awkward moment of silence ticked by. "And if it concerns my mom and my dad . . ." She left the sentence hanging in the air, hoping her mother would pick it up.

"It's not anything you need to be worrying about, dear. And it certainly isn't anything that is going to cause any real damage to your father's and my relationship. So don't worry, okay?" As she said this, Kathy moved to the far end of the counter and began rearranging the canisters.

Anna came around the kitchen island and drew closer to her mother. "Mom? Does it have anything to do with what happened at the meeting at church this afternoon?"

Kathy turned quickly to face her daughter. "What do you mean? What did you hear? Did Jennifer say something? Beth?"

Anna saw a fear in her mother's eyes, and heard a tinge of anger in her voice. It startled her a bit. "Whoa! Hang on! Mrs. Stevens didn't say a thing . . . not to me, anyhow . . . and not to Beth either."

"So who told you? What did they tell you?" Kathy was now turned completely around and facing Anna. Anna could see that her face was flushed. She didn't know if her mother was about to get really mad, or start crying, or both.

"Truth is, Beth overheard her folks talking in the kitchen. I guess her dad was at the meeting or something." She waited for her mother to acknowledge that as fact. "I don't know if they knew she was listening or not. But anyhow, she said she heard Daddy got really mad at some people and walked out of the meeting. And then Mrs. Morgan was crying, and some other folks were arguing." Anna could see the anger giving way to pain in her mother's eyes. Tears were beginning to form at the corners. "Then I guess Pastor Tim had a prayer and then canceled the meeting. So I guess everybody just went home."

"Oh, great. Just great! This will be all over town by tomorrow," her mother lamented.

"Probably sooner than that," Anna sighed.

Her mother scowled.

"Sorry, but it's the truth. You know how people are. You remember all the rumors and gossip when Beth and I were being stupid over that boy." But she could tell her mother's mind was a million miles away from two sixteen-year-old girls having a tiff over a boy. "Mom. Mom? What's going on? Why are you and dad so upset? Are you mad at each other?"

"Oh, you know your father. Mr. Hothead! He just couldn't sit down and let Pastor Tim take over things. No, he had to push a showdown with two dear old sweet people. What was he thinking? And when I tried to get him to calm down, he treated me like I was some worthless rag. I was so embarrassed I felt like crawling in a hole . . . right after I buried him in it first. Oh, I'm sorry honey. I shouldn't be talking like this with you."

"Probably not. It's Dad you need to be talking to about this. That's what helped me and Beth get through our stuff; when her mom talked to each of us, and then helped us talk to each other."

"I'm glad Jennifer was able to help you, honey. But I'm afraid your father and I will have to settle this one on our own. In the meantime, I hope you will ask Beth and her family not to be spreading any rumors about your father. Knowing Mrs. Morgan and some of her friends, there will be enough of that going on to heat up the phone lines for the next few days." Kathy stepped toward the door.

"I'm sure Beth won't say a thing . . . or her mother. But I'll mention it to her. And, Mom?"

"Yes, dear?"

"I'll be praying for you and Dad—and the people at church."

"That's nice, honey. We're going to need it. Good night."

"Good night, Mom."

As Anna approached the family room to say good night to her dad, he was on the phone, and she could hear his side of the conversation.

"Sounds like you've been busy alright . . . Yeah, that's a lot of calls . . . Really? . . . Well, it sounds like you're getting quite a group together . . . I told you, I just don't know if I want to be a part of that or not . . . Because, I'm tired of it all. Listen, I'll pray about it, and if I feel like I'm supposed to be involved, I will. OK? . . . OK! Call me tomorrow night . . . OK. See ya."

Jack turned in his chair, and noticed Anna standing in the doorway. "Hi, honey. Heading for bed?"

"Yes, Daddy. I just wanted to say goodnight."

"Goodnight, honey. See you in the morning."

As Anna closed the door to her room, her heart was heavy. She was burdened for her parents. She couldn't remember them being this upset with each other for a long time. And she couldn't remember them ever being this upset with anybody in the church before, though her dad was often critical of some of the older leaders from time to time.

Before going to bed, Anna opened her Bible and read a chapter or two. Her ribbon marker opened to John 17, and she began to read. As she did, she felt that warm glow that filled her chest whenever she knew God was revealing Himself to her. As she read John 17:20–26, it was as though the words were burning straight into her spirit.

As she concluded these verses, Anna felt her own spirit cry, "Oh Lord, You desired us to be one just like you and the Father are one. One, just like you. Just . . . like . . . you? And you desired it so the world would believe the Father sent you to us? Oh, Jesus, how it must break your heart when we tear one another apart. And especially when the world watches us treating each other the way we do, and they reject you in the process. Forgive us, Lord. Forgive me. Forgive me when I've made it about me, rather than being one with other Christians and making it about you. Forgive me for my selfishness with my friends . . . my parents . . . my brother and sister. Lord, forgive my parents for being selfish right now. And the folks at church too, Lord.

"We're a mess, but I guess you already know that. Yet you chose us to be yours. Wow! And I know there are others out there who you love. They're going to hear about what happened at our church today, and what my Dad did, and the others . . . and they're going to reject you because of us. So Lord, could you do for my parents, and for our church, what you did for Beth and me? Could you get them to remember who you are, and who they are as the church, and especially who they are as one together in you?

"And Lord, thanks so much for showing me your heart in your prayer for us. I'm so blessed to know you've included me in your fellowship with the Father. Thank you, Lord. Amen."

Anna turned off her light, slipped under her covers, and drifted off to a peaceful sleep.

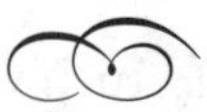

It was getting late, and Mike had just finished his final call for the night. Since arriving home from the meeting this afternoon, and breaking only for dinner and then helping the little one into bed, he had been on the phone constantly. He had a hands-free earpiece for his phone, which allowed him to get comfortable while he left messages or conversed with church members. Many weren't home, so he'd left a message of the meeting plans. At least folks would know what's up and the numbers they had on their side. It was time to move, and Mike could feel the energy building.

While a number of the folks he spoke with had their own gripes to promote, he had learned during the afternoon how to acknowledge their issues and then point out the need to create a voting block of like-minded people in order to get such changes made in the future. By the time each conversation was concluded, the folks on the other end were agreeing with Mike's assessment that a change of leadership was needed, and they were ready to join the cause.

Long after he hoped to be sound to sleep, Mike found it a struggle to turn off his hyper-activated brain. He kept adding more people to his call list. He'd thought through the planned meeting a hundred times. Each time he did, he got a rush of energy, seeing himself leading what could be the single most powerful group in the church. It wasn't about him, he kept convincing himself. It was about Jesus . . . about being the kind of church that attracts people to Jesus, and making more disciples than anyone had ever imagined before. It was about impacting their community, their world, like they had never done before, at least not in the last thirty years. He was tired of hearing about the glory days of long ago. It was time for the church to move forward and create new glories to draw folks to Jesus.

Mike continued to toss and turn for some time, before finally falling asleep.

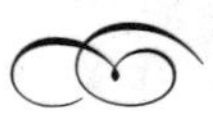

CHAPTER TWELVE

Alice checked the door and turned off the front-room light as she made her way to bed. Her heart was heavy with the experiences of the day weighing on her. The blowup with Jack had upset her a great deal, as had the arguments among some of the others that followed, until Pastor Tim stepped in. She hadn't had to wait too long to find out what the meeting in the parking lot was all about. During the course of the evening, she had received a call from June, sharing in dramatic detail the comments shared by everyone there. None of it sounded good to Alice.

Her fears were confirmed when two friends who had not been at the missions-committee meeting or the parking-lot gathering called to find out how she was doing, having heard all about the episode from others. In one case, the person they had heard the story from was not present at either meeting, but had received their information from someone who had been there. This made Alice the fourth in line for the passing on of that story, all within a few hours. And while the basic elements were fairly accurate, Alice had had to set the story straight that Jack had not actually threatened her, and none of the incident had to do with Pastor Tim or the youth pastor.

Where these people came up with this, Alice had no idea. But the whole thing was getting out of hand. Her sense of guilt and remorse were growing heavier and heavier. Lying in bed with the lights off, Alice began to cry once again. She began to pray: "Father, forgive me for what I've done. I know I should never have said what I did to Jack in public like that. Now look what's happened. I'm so ashamed. I'm sorry, Lord. Please forgive me. I don't know what to do, Lord. Help me. Show me what you would have me to do to fix this, if it's even possible. Help me, Lord." Eventually, she fell asleep.

13

As Tim Matthews joined the weekly pastors' gathering in the café meeting room, one of the members asked, "So what's the report from the front lines, brother?"

"Very funny. I wish there was a front line I could focus on. Right now it's feeling more like an all-out civil war. I just can't believe it." Tim sat heavily in the chair, and placed his head in his hands. A couple of the brothers got up and placed their hands on his head and shoulder. The brother seated next to him grabbed Tim's arm. For the next fifteen minutes, this small band of brothers in Christ lifted one of their own before the Lord in prayer.

"Thanks, you guys. You don't know how much I needed that." Tim wiped his eyes and began to straighten himself.

"Yes, we do. At least a couple of us do. Been there, done that, remember?"

"Yes. Yes, I do. I just never thought I'd be in a place like this. Sometimes I don't even know who these people are anymore. Or whether I should be their pastor or not."

"So why don't you catch us up on all that's taken place thus far. And maybe we can discern what the Lord would have us to do to help you and the church. Remember, we're all in this together. Right?"

"Right," the rest of the group chimed in.

Tim took a sip of his coffee, stared at the cup a moment, and then began: "It's hard to believe it's been less than a month since the first blowup I told you about involving our missions committee. And like I told you then, while it caught us all off guard, I felt confident it was going to all blow over in time. I knew I had some work to do to patch things up between the young guy who blew up and a couple of the older folks, but I didn't anticipate that to be a huge problem."

"Those are the ones that get you every time," added Pastor Lee Thompson, seated across the table.

"Well, I just never would have imagined. Actually, I had no idea there was such an undercurrent of dissatisfaction and outright anger among the congregation like there has been these past few weeks. You wouldn't believe some of the stories I've heard, as members have described how they have been treated by one another."

"Unfortunately, I would." Pastor Edwards was the senior member of this group, having served in the pastoral ministry for thirty-one years, and beginning to think seriously of retirement. "I've been through a number of these storms over the years, and who knows how many smaller squalls. Each time it absolutely broke my heart to see the way Christian brothers and sisters could turn on one another, all in the spirit of somehow defending God or what's right, mind you. I'm very sorry, Tim, that you've been caught up in one of these. I just wish I could tell you it will be your last; or that you've even seen the worst of this one."

"Thanks for the encouragement," Tim responded. The whole group smiled empathetically. "The thing is, I thought I could meet with Jack, get him cooled down. And then meet with the other two, and hopefully get them all to meet in my office to see if we could smooth things out."

"So what happened?"

"At first, Jack didn't want anything to do with any meeting, not even with me. He threatened to leave the church. But I eventually got him to at least pray about that first, before jumping ship. I don't know what we'd have done. He's the backbone of our youth center ministry. And that's eventually what got him to stay connected, though his attendance at church has definitely decreased; and not just his. I'd say attendance is down 20 percent overall. And giving is worse than that. I just can't believe the way people are reacting."

"Any of those secret meetings yet? You know, the ones that are only secret to the pastor, but everybody else seems to know about them?" Pastor Thompson asked. They all chuckled.

"Oh, yeah. The first one took place in the parking lot, immediately after the initial blowup—and after I'd asked everyone to go home and pray for the Lord's leading in this."

"Maybe it was a prayer meeting," Pastor Thompson joked. They all laughed again.

"I wish. That meeting led to a number of meetings organized by the older members of the church, along with some of the younger folks who are related to them. That's now led to a big ruckus in the worship committee, as some of these folks are now demanding equal time for singing hymns. Now the worship leader is threatening to quit if we're going back to the 1950s after the worship committee put so much effort into the slides, choruses, and the worship team format. Do you know that we now have some folks who mill about in the foyer, drinking coffee and visiting, while the worship team sets the mood for worship? Then these people come into the sanctuary after the worship team sits down"

"Ah, the worship wars. Must really bless the Lord's heart, huh," Pastor Thompson said, with a cynical tone in his voice. "Excuse me fellas, but this whole thing brings up a bunch of bad memories for me. I guess I'm still carrying the scars a bit more than I realized."

"We probably all are, Lee," Pastor Edwards responded. "Maybe in helping Tim to work through this present situation, we can help each other find some healing, or at least figure out a way to try and prevent these situations from happening so often."

"I'm with that. So again, forgive me, guys. Tim, carry on." And with that, Pastor Thompson leaned back in his chair to listen to the rest of Tim's story.

"Well, let's see. Where was I? Oh, yeah, along with the emergence of the 'worship war,' as Lee so accurately describes it, there have also been some meetings made up primarily of some of the younger families, and some middle-age folks in the congregation. I'm not sure how many, or who all is involved. Most of the information I've gotten about this group has come through my secretary, whose daughter and son-in-law have attended a couple times. The scary part about these meetings is they don't sound like much more than gripe sessions. I guess people have been airing their complaints about everything from the way the church functions, to the way it doesn't. And what makes me angry—and, I guess I'd have to admit—what really hurts is none of these people has ever come to talk to me about any of this before. Somebody was even complaining about the fact we don't have a clock on the back wall, so I can make sure I don't go past noon . . . ."

"What!" Pastor Thompson jumped in. "You don't have a clock staring you in the face every Sunday? How'd you do that? I made the mistake of mentioning the idea we lose the clock in our sanctuary—during a deacon's meeting one night—and you'd have thought I suggested we desecrate the altar." The rest of the group stared at him. "Sorry. Sorry! I swear I'll remain quiet for the rest of this gathering. I promise. Carry on, Tim. Sorry."

"That's okay. I'm not even sure that many folks noticed it was gone until one of the members mentioned it while complaining about my sermons cutting into his family time at the lake. And before you say it, Lee, I won't be surprised to find a new clock on the wall one of these Sundays." Again they all chuckled. Pastor Thompson grinned while making a gesture of zipping his mouth closed.

Tim continued: "But like I said, it's the way people are treating one another that I just can't believe. Some act like nothing's wrong—*to your face*. And then you hear about all the things they're saying to others behind your back. And the phone messages I've heard about, and the letters and e-mails I've either heard about or read myself, you just wouldn't believe it. Or maybe you would." They all nodded their heads with pained expressions on their faces.

"Wow, that's a lot. So how are you doing personally in all of this?" As he asked this, Pastor Edwards leaned over and placed his hand on Tim's arm.

Tim's head dropped, and his eyes filled with tears. "I'm about ready to throw in the towel, actually."

"You can't do that," Pastor Thompson interjected. "I know, I promised to shut up. But I can't. You can't! You can't give up and let the enemy win! Don't you see? It's not flesh and blood we fight against! It's powers and principalities! There's a spiritual war going on here, and the whole church is being victimized. You can't cut and run; if they ever needed a shepherd to fight the good fight, it's now! You've got to stand up to the ring leaders and tell them to either knock it off or get packing."

"That's just it," Tim replied. "I know the church needs a strong shepherd now more than ever. But when I see the level of anger and dissatisfaction throughout the whole church, and

I realize this has all occurred on my watch . . ." His voice drifted off, as his head dropped, and he began to cry.

Pastor Benson, who had remained fairly quiet during the gathering thus far, spoke into the silence that now filled the room. "I'm not convinced it would be wise for Tim, or the church, if Tim were to go toe to toe with whoever is causing all the trouble in the church. Bottom line is, there doesn't appear to be a clear majority. So if he stands up to all the rabble rousers, it's just going to increase the fallout. More people are going to get hurt, and they're going to get hurt worse than they are now. More will leave. Giving will decrease even more. There could even be a split! Then what? Even if he and the church survive, will it really be a victory when most of the people are injured . . . or gone . . . or both?"

"So what are you saying? He should just run up the white flag and resign; cut his losses and move on to the next place, where it may all happen all over again?" Lee Thompson was back on the front edge of his seat once again, face flushed, and ready for battle.

Pastor Edwards patted Tim on the arm. Slowly, Tim raised his head. Pastor Edwards handed him a napkin, which Tim used to wipe his face. "I wouldn't suggest I know what Tim should do; or what any of us should do in these kinds of situations. I look back over these times in my own life, and there's a lot I wish I'd done differently. There is a lot I think I did right. And there were times I don't think it would have made much difference what I did. But the one thing I do wish I had done more of is this; I wish I'd leaned more on a group like this. I wish I'd had a band of brothers, and sisters too for that matter, where I could do what Tim has done with us today. I wish I'd have prayed more, and sought more counsel until I was sure that what I was doing was what the Lord would have me do, rather than just reacting out of myself and the situation at hand."

"Amen," responded the others about the table—all but Lee Thompson.

"So I'd suggest we go to prayer and seek the Lord's mind in this. Not only for what Tim should do, but to seek the Lord for a clear picture of Himself, and a clearer picture of ourselves." Pastor Edwards then bowed his head, as did the other brothers around the table, and they began to pray.

On his way to the office following the morning gathering with his fellow pastors, Pastor Tim kept repeating a phrase lifted during the time of prayer. "Raise the peacemakers in our midst, Lord. Raise the peacemakers."

14

Within a few days, things between Kathy and Jack had returned to normal, which was part of the problem. "Normal" was simply adding one more unresolved issue to the untold others which had been accumulating during their twenty-two years of marriage. They both avoided dealing with the situation between them by focusing on other things. This time, it was the conflict in the church.

Unknown to Jack, Kathy had been struggling with a situation involving their daughter Anna, and an incident that had occurred at the youth group gathering two weeks before. Anna had come home in tears that night because a couple of the other teens had accused her father of starting the conflict that was spreading throughout the church. Kathy wanted to tell Jack, but was afraid of what his reaction might be. She doubted he'd take any responsibility, and probably would just make matters worse for Anna by verbally attacking the teens or their parents. Kathy painfully remembered a similar situation that had occurred three years earlier involving Anna's older sister Kate. That time, Kate was in tears because of the way

Jack reacted when two boys teased Kate at camp. Still, she felt guilty for withholding this important information about their daughter, and struggled with what to do about the youth group situation. Thus far, it had just been easier to say nothing and hope everything would work out on its own.

It wasn't like Jack's plate wasn't already overflowing with issues. Since the initial incident, Jack spent at least an hour on the phone most evenings. He had no idea his outburst could ignite such a firestorm in the church. It seemed like every segment of the church was in an uproar about something. Jack couldn't believe he could be responsible for all that was taking place now.

The position he'd taken with the missions committee had nothing to do with worship, and yet now there were all kinds of issues regarding the worship service on Sunday mornings. People were complaining about the type of music, and even about the volume. Apparently there was some kind of skirmish involving a group of older members, who had presented the pastor and the worship committee with an eight-page letter of complaints and demands. Part of the worship team had resigned, and others were threatening to do likewise, which led to an uprising among the teens, and some of the young families as well.

Kathy had told him about a recent call from a friend, one of the younger women in the church, who tried to interest Kathy in joining a new Bible study group, scheduled to take place at the same time the women's circle met. When Kathy tried to point out the scheduling conflict, her friend had become defensive and told Kathy she was going to have to decide if she wanted to be a part of the future of the church or stay in the past.

When Jack asked Kathy what her response to the call had been, Kathy looked at him with tears in her eyes, shrugged her shoulders, and walked away. He hadn't known what all that meant, or what Kathy wanted him to do about it, so he did nothing.

He had his own "friend" issues to contend with anyway. Jack's friend Mike had been pressuring him to join the group Mike was organizing, in hope of establishing new leaders and a new direction in the church. And while Jack certainly sympathized with Mike's desire to see the church join the 21st century, he didn't feel good about the way Mike and those who were joining with him were going about it. They had numerous conversations over lunch, golf, and by means of e-mails at home and work, but thus far Jack had refused to attend the meetings Mike's group was having.

Jack's biggest concern was the meetings themselves; they weren't officially sanctioned, nor were they made public for everyone to attend. Instead, Mike and others were personally selecting and inviting those they thought agreed with them. It was very obvious to Jack that serious lines were being drawn between different groups in the church, and these groups were beginning to see and treat each other as the enemy.

Last Sunday had been the first worship service Jack had attended since the initial incident three weeks earlier, and he was surprised by a number of his observations. He could feel the tension in the air as he walked across the parking lot and approached the front doors. Maybe it was paranoia or guilt, but it had seemed a number of folks were staring at him rather oddly. He was convinced June Fredricks and two other ladies with her had intentionally turned their backs to him as he walked through the foyer. This was made stranger by the fact that one of them was serving as a greeter, and was passing out bulletins to people entering the sanctuary—to everyone but Jack.

When he made his way to his normal seat next to the aisle on the left side, saving a place for Kathy, who would join him after making sure things were taken care of in the nursery, Jack noticed a number of people who normally sat around them were missing. It surprised him when he noticed the Murphys and Nelsons were sitting together on the opposite side of the sanctuary. He caught Ed's eye as he settled in. But when Ed looked away without even appearing to recognize Jack, then leaned over and said something to his wife who sneaked a quick look Jack's way, Jack began to get a gnawing feeling in the pit of his stomach. He also started to feel the same tightness in his throat and light-headedness he felt shortly before he lost his temper with Alice and Bill. Not wishing to repeat that nightmare again, Jack tried to focus his attention on the music video being played on the large screen at the front of the sanctuary. Unfortunately, worship was about the furthest thing from his mind at the moment.

When June Fredricks entered the sanctuary, Jack noticed her husband, Bill, stood to allow her to sit next to him. Jack then realized they were sitting right in front of the Nelsons and Murphys, as June greeted them like long lost friends. Maybe they were.

Jack felt a jolt of mixed emotions at the sight of Bill. This was the first time he'd seen him since the blowup at the meeting. Jack was still angry. But he felt guilty as well. He knew he never should have spoken to Bill or Alice as he had. There had been a number of times he'd picked up the phone to call Bill. But he just didn't know what to say, or how to say it. So he said nothing.

He also didn't know what to make of this new seating arrangement, and the apparent grouping of folks on the opposite side of the sanctuary. He also observed they weren't the only ones sitting in new places, or with new seatmates. It all seemed surreal. For the first time, he wondered how Pastor Tim was dealing with all of this.

Kathy never did join him in the sanctuary that morning. It was her month to oversee the nursery volunteers, and part of her job was to arrange for each Sunday's staffing. She hadn't anticipated any problems that day, as those who were scheduled were normally very committed and rarely missed. But this Sunday was different. Two of the three volunteers failed to show up. Kathy was fortunate enough to find a willing mother to remain and help. So Kathy filled in with the volunteer and the willing mother, and together they covered the nursery responsibilities. During their time together, the volunteer shared that she doubted the other two would be helping out with the nursery any longer. When Kathy asked her why, she said she had heard one of the families had left the church because of the conflict over the worship service; her husband was part of the worship team. She thought the other family was planning to leave as well, because they were all friends.

Initially Kathy was shocked, then saddened. Then she began to feel angry. She was angry at the irresponsibility of these two grown women, to leave the church nursery in the lurch as they had. She was angry and frustrated that she would now have to spend most of her week trying to find and train two more volunteers for the nursery. She worried how much more of this kind of thing was going to take place before the entire church fell apart.

She and Jack shared their stories and vented their feelings to each other on the way home. They spoke about it more in the afternoon, while doing some yard work together, and again later that evening after dinner. By then, they had come to some firm conclusions, and had developed a plan. First, they decided they were not going to leave the church, though that was not an easy decision. They both admitted that leaving the church would be the easiest choice. It was tempting to just put this whole mess behind them and move on. But they had come to the conclusion they would not be honoring their commitments by running away, nor would they be honoring the Lord. It was not the message they wanted to send their children, or the kids Jack worked with at the teen center. Second, Jack was going to meet with Pastor Tim and share their feelings with him, and seek his guidance. And third, they were going to invite their friends, the Stevens, to dinner.

Dick and Jennifer Stevens had befriended Jack and Kathy when they first moved to town and joined the church. Their children grew up together, and Anna and Beth had become more like sisters than just friends. Dick was a successful attorney, and Jennifer was the director of human resources for a major software firm in town. They were intelligent and wise people, and strong in their faith in Christ. Jack and Kathy recognized that if they were going to be a part of the solution in the church, they couldn't do it on their own. They were just too invested in the issues in a couple of important situations. They were going to need some help. And they couldn't think of any better candidates for the job than Dick and Jennifer Stevens.

Following the wonderful dinner and relaxed conversation, and after Anna and Beth had exited the dining room for the privacy of Anna's bedroom, Dick, Jennifer, Kathy, and Jack took their coffees into the living room.

As they were getting situated, Jack grew sober and spoke with a serious tone, "So I suppose you're wondering what Kathy and I wanted to talk to you two about tonight."

"I suspected you would get to it in due time," Dick replied.

"Oh, you mean it wasn't our advice about your new deck plans?" Jennifer teased.

They all chuckled a bit nervously. After an uncomfortable pause in the conversation, Kathy spoke up. "It's about the situation at church . . . and what we should be doing, or not doing, about it." Kathy hesitated, looking to Jack to say something.

Instead, Jack gave her a look back that said, "You started it; go for it."

"Well, I know you're aware of the situation that took place at the missions meeting a few weeks ago," Kathy continued.

"Yeah, where I blew it big time," Jack interjected. He saw Kathy's look, and waved her on to continue.

"As I was saying . . . Jack and I have been discussing what we should do; especially in light of all the other issues that have seemed to boil out of this. We felt it would be good to seek your counsel; not only because of our friendship and your skills, but mostly because we've come to recognize you both as very mature Christians, and . . ."

Jack jumped in once again, "And you both definitely know the Word a whole lot more than we do. Oh . . . I'm sorry, honey. Did it again, didn't I?"

Kathy didn't even look his way this time. Instead she looked directly at Jennifer, who responded, "So it sounds like you have some feelings about this entire situation, and perhaps feel you have some important decisions, and you're hoping we can help you sort through all of that. Is that what I'm hearing?"

"Exactly," Kathy expressed with a sense of release and gratitude. Perhaps, with the Stevens' help, she and Jack could regain a sense of balance and well-being within themselves, and their marriage and home—if they could just sort out this whole church mess, and how they should respond to it.

Jennifer looked at Jack. "Does that sound accurate to you, Jack?"

"Uh . . . yeah. We're . . . uh . . . we're just hoping you can help us figure out what we should be doing in this whole mess," Jack responded.

Dick spoke: "Well, Jen and I suspected that might be what this was going to be about. So we've already been praying for the Lord's guidance, and have felt Him leading us to involve ourselves in this with you . . . if . . ." Dick's eyes stared intently into Jack's, and then Kathy's, ". . . if it is in your heart to seek the Lord's guidance, rather than trying to get us to take sides."

"We would never do that," Kathy reacted defensively, and with a bit of hurt in her voice.

"We suspected as much," Jennifer responded. "What Dick is saying is, if it is your heart to seek the Lord's counsel, and if you're willing to submit yourselves to His direction, then we're prepared to do everything we can to help you in this. But if you simply want to get us to be on your side by telling us your stories about fellow church members, then from our understanding, that would be entertaining gossip. We don't want to be a part of that, nor do we want to encourage you, or anyone else to do that, either."

"That's not what's in our hearts," Jack responded.

"We can see that. So what we would propose is this: Why don't each of you share the information you believe would be necessary for us to understand the situation from your perspective. We may interrupt once in awhile to seek more information or clarification. Then we'll summarize what we've heard you say, to make sure we're getting things as you intend them. Then we'll go from there. Sound workable to you?"

"Does to me," Jack said.

"Me too. And I'd like Jack to go first." Kathy smiled at Jack.

Jack fidgeted in his chair, looked to Kathy as though he was going to suggest she go first, and then cleared his throat and began to tell his story.

A little over two hours later, following a great deal of sharing from Jack and Kathy, along with a number of questions and comments from Dick and Jennifer, Dick attempted to summarize what they had heard thus far. "So it appears we've identified a number of different issues and resulting emotions that both of you have experienced in all of this. The strongest feelings I've heard described thus far are frustration, anger, loss, feeling devalued, shame, sadness, embarrassment, and fear. Do those sound accurate to you?"

Jack and Kathy agreed. And as she had often done during the past two hours, Kathy wiped tears from her eyes.

Dick continued: "It sounds like one of the major pieces you're struggling with, Jack, is how you feel Alice and Bill treated you at the meeting. And it sounds as though, closely tied to that, is an internal struggle with your behavior at the meeting, when you apparently lost your temper, said some things you now regret, and walked out."

Looking at the floor, Jack responded somberly, "Yeah. I don't know what got into me."

Dick continued, "And you have struggled with the sense you should do something about all this, but you don't know exactly what to do."

"That's right," Jack responded, looking straight at Dick: "I know I was wrong. . . . Like I said, I know Kathy's right when she says I should go to Alice and Bill and apologize. But I just can't get over the fact that what they did to me was wrong, too. I don't think I'd ever have done or said what I did if they hadn't attacked me first. You know what I mean? I mean, if anybody owes somebody an apology, don't they owe me one?"

Dick responded, "It sounds like you feel Alice and Bill treated you unfairly. And you feel they should apologize to you."

"Yeah . . . that's right. I mean . . . I know I owe them and everybody else at that meeting an apology. But I think they owe me one, too."

"We've heard some other issues that appear to be important to both of you in this. So let's see if we got those as well. Then we can spend time seeking the Lord's mind in each situation and see where things go from there. Is that okay?"

"Fine by me," Jack replied.

Kathy nodded her head in the affirmative as she dabbed at the tears that continued to pool in the corners of her eyes.

About thirty minutes later, Jennifer observed, "It's getting late. You both have accomplished a lot of good work tonight. Plus, we have a couple of sixteen-year-olds upstairs who need to be getting to bed pretty soon. So I'd like to suggest we schedule another get together. How about dinner at our house this time?"

"Are you sure? It seems like you are the ones helping us, so we should be hosting you," Kathy replied.

"No, it's fine. Dick's wanted to try out that new barbeque recipe he found the other day. But there is something you can do."

"Anything. You want us to bring something, a salad, dessert?"

"No. We have some homework we want you to work on before we get together again."

Jack looked a bit shocked. "Homework? Are you serious?"

Dick chimed in, "Very serious. You see, Jen and I have not only come to see conflict as a pretty normal element of life, but we've also come to see it as an awesome opportunity for brothers and sisters to experience Christ together."

Jack's look went from shock to bewilderment. Looking from Dick to Jennifer to Kathy, and back to Dick, he squinted his eyes in puzzlement. "Okay, you're going to have to explain that one, my friend. I always thought God frowned on us fighting with one another. I mean, isn't it a sin or something?"

Dick smiled. "Certainly we can sin in our conflicted situations. As Paul says in Ephesians, we're not supposed to let the sun go down on our anger with one another. In other words, we're supposed to deal with our relational conflicts in a timely manner. But the point that often gets lost here is this: we're going to get angry. We're going to have disagreements and conflicts with one another. That part is normal. It's how we handle them that lead us into sin or not."

The point Dick was making made sense to Jack and Kathy, so Jennifer jumped in. "It's also apparent Jesus recognized conflict was normal; twice in the Gospel of Matthew He instructs us to go to those with whom we have unresolved conflict and get it dealt with directly. In fact, in Matthew 5 He appears to place resolving the conflict between Christians above worship. Here, I've got the reference right here."

Positioning her Bible in front of her, Jennifer began to read Matthew 5:21–24. When she concluded, there was a sense of heaviness in the room, and everyone was silent. Finally, Dick spoke gently to Jack, "You appear to have been moved by that passage."

"Uh . . . yeah . . . I guess I've never really read that passage before. I mean . . . I've read it . . . I've read Matthew before . . . but I've just never seen that passage like this before. You know what I mean?"

"Yes. Yes, we do."

Kathy, who had been fairly quiet for the last half hour or so, spoke up: "You said there were a couple of references where Jesus says something about how or when we're to deal with our conflicts with one another?" She and Jack exchanged nervous glances.

"Yes. The other reference in Matthew is chapter 18, beginning with verse 15. Would you like me to read it to you?"

"Yes, please," Kathy replied.

Jennifer flipped the pages in her Bible, coming to the text she was looking for. "If your brother sins, go and show him his fault in private; if he listens to you, you have won your brother."

Looking up from the Bible in her lap, Jennifer continued, "There's more to what Jesus is saying in this text, and perhaps we can look at all of that later. But the thing that's important to recognize is the reason Jesus gave us these instructions: He knew we'd need them. He knew we'd have disagreements and conflicts, and He wanted us to know there were ways to deal with them that reflected His heart and His Father's heart."

"Exactly," Dick interjected. "You see, Jack, the fact you had some disagreements with Alice and Bill is not, on its own, a sin."

"But letting the sun go down on my anger was?" Jack was beginning to feel the weight of his anger issues in a whole new way. For most of his life, he had gone off at the slightest provocation. But in spite of the work he'd done to control his anger in recent years, he was well aware of the painful impact it had had on his wife and children, and work, and now at church as well. Now he felt the impact it was having in his relationship with God.

"What do you think?" Dick asked.

"Uh . . . I'm starting to think I've got some real thinking to do. I guess I've been so mad and hurt at the way I was treated, I haven't given much thought to my own actions."

Kathy stared at Jack. Now she was shocked. Could this be her husband? Could Jack actually be confessing that he has an anger problem? As she continued to look at Jack, seeing the internal pain he was feeling, her heart toward him began to soften, and her tears began to flow once again.

"That's good to hear. That's part of the homework we have for you both," Dick continued. "We've found it's very important to do some self-reflection in situations like this. So we're going to give you some Scriptures to read and study and some questions to reflect on."

Jennifer spoke again: "In fact, we get this from something else Jesus said in Matthew."

"Oh, oh. I don't think I can take anymore shots from Matthew tonight." Jack smiled sheepishly. The others laughed.

"No, it's nothing like that," Jennifer continued. "But it's interesting that, like you just said, you've been so focused on the actions and attitudes of others that you haven't thought much about your own thoughts and actions—which is pretty normal. We all tend to do that, especially in conflicted situations. But the fact is, Jesus instructed us to start with ourselves, before we start focusing on others. In Matthew 7:1–5, He said,

> Do not judge so that you will not be judged. For in the way you judge, you will be judged; and by your standard of measure, it will be measured to you. Why do you look at the speck that is in your brother's eye, but do not notice the log that is in your own eye? Or how can you say to your brother, 'Let me take the speck out of your eye,' and behold, the log is in your own eye? You hypocrite, first take the log out of your own eye, and then you will see clearly to take the speck out of your brother's eye.

"Geez, I thought you said there wouldn't be any more shots like that tonight." Jack held up his hands, pretending to fend off some blows to his head.

Laughing, Jennifer replied, "I'm sorry. I'm sorry. I forgot about the reference to being a hypocrite. I promise; no more shots tonight. In fact, I believe I'm the one who suggested we call it a night over half an hour ago."

"So, between blows, do you understand what Jesus was getting at here?" Dick asked

"Yeah. I need to quit focusing on what Alice and Bill did to me—and all these other folks in the church who keep trying to suck us into their fights—and I need to do some serious soul searching in my own heart, before I start worrying about them. Right?"

"Right. We've got some questions for you to work on before the next time we get together, and some Scriptures to read and meditate on."

Jack pretended to be offended. "Wow, what a deal. We invite our good friends over for a nice relaxing evening with good food, and good company, and instead I get beat on, and then assigned homework. What a deal!"

"Yep, it's a rough life all right. And may I remind you we are here at your invitation, and we asked if you wanted us to be involved, because it wouldn't necessarily be easy. Right?"

"I know. I know," Jack pleaded. "Seriously, I'm blessed . . . we're blessed by you taking the time to help us with this. I know I'm feeling better already, in spite of the cheap shots from Matthew." This time, Jennifer held up her hands as though fending off an attack. "So what are the questions and the Scriptures? Are we going to need to write these down?"

"That would probably be helpful," Dick responded. Kathy got up and grabbed a tablet from the nearby desk.

"First of all, we've found it helpful to review the stories we tell ourselves about the conflicted incident. So it would be good for the two of you to reflect on the conflicted situations you described earlier this evening. Like with the meeting; you may reflect on what led up to the disagreements and things getting out of hand, and what occurred from there. That you can do together, as you were both there. But, Jack, you can do the same with the situation involving Mike and the group he's trying to get you involved with. Kathy, you can work on the situation with the two ladies' groups, and the conflict you're experiencing with that. Try to recall who said what, and who did what, as accurately as you can. Be sure to write it all down."

"Then ask the Holy Spirit to help you with the next questions. Review your stories, and then ask yourselves what you've edited into your stories, or omitted from them. Be sure to write those down as well. Sometimes we can learn a great deal about ourselves when we begin to recognize how much we edit our own stories to fit ourselves, and then act as though our edited story is the truth."

Jack fidgeted in his chair. "I'm not sure I get that part."

Dick leaned forward a bit and said, “Well, it’s like this. I listened to both of your accounts of the missions committee meeting. Not only did I notice some distinct discrepancies between your stories but, I have to say, having been at the meeting myself, I believe there are some pieces you’ve omitted, and others you have re-edited a bit. And I think it’s having a direct impact on your feelings and your reactions.”

“Like what?” Jack was intrigued now.

“Well, I’d rather get into this next time, as it’s getting late, but here’s an example. Earlier this evening, when relating your stories, you described Alice as getting defensive and verbally attacking you from the moment you began speaking.”

“That’s because she did,” Jack said, with a bit of defensiveness in his voice.

“Yet, Kathy didn’t describe the scene that way at all. She described you as the one who began to aggressively disagree with Alice and escalate the discussion into an argument. While I observed Alice eventually reacting out of her emotions and, as you describe it, verbally attacking you, it appeared to me that she was reacting more to you than she was initiating something against you.”

Jack felt stunned, embarrassed, and angry, but he remained silent, staring at his feet.

Dick continued, “The point I’m trying to make here, which is not to condemn you or make you feel guilty. . . . I’m using this observation to help you see how we all perceive things through our own filtering system, re-edit what we’ve perceived, and create a story that’s factual to us, but in reality may not be accurate in every detail. Physiologically, this takes place in a blink of an eye—and it continues each time we review our story in our mind. During that entire process, our emotional response to our story greatly influences our reaction. In your case, you perceived yourself to be verbally attacked. The feelings you described earlier were your reactions to your story that you were attacked. You felt anger, embarrassment, fear, and frustration. You reacted according to your emotions, which were based on the story you told yourself. And you're still reacting to those emotions, though this event took place weeks ago. When you tell the story, it is as though it just happened. Right?"

"That's true." Jack didn't look up, but kept staring at his feet.

Dick continued, "So tell me, if the story you told yourself about this incident with Alice included her initial attempts to share her views—which were not verbal attacks directed at you personally—do you think it might have resulted in different feelings and a different reaction?"

Dick let his question hang in the air. It hung there for some time, as Jack sat back in the chair, staring at the palm of his hand, which he was rubbing with the thumb of his other hand.

After what seemed like an hour, but was only about fifteen seconds of silence, Jack looked straight at Dick and said very solemnly, "I don't really know. I've had it my mind since the incident that Alice just took off on me, and I was reacting to her. I don't know what I'd think if things were actually reversed, and she was reacting to me."

"That's fair," Dick responded. "But for the sake of our discussion and the point I'm trying to make, what do you think your feelings would be now, if you saw the incident differently, and recognized what you said, how you said it, and how Alice reacted to you?"

"I guess I couldn't blame her for acting like she did. I still don't like it. I don't agree with what she said. . . . I think I've been very supportive of her and her missionary friends over the years." There was another delay and moment of silent reflection before Jack continued. "But I guess I'd like to believe I would have recognized that Alice was reacting to me more than attacking me. Maybe I'd have apologized for ticking her off, if not right then at the meeting, then certainly after things cooled down."

Jack looked at Dick and Jennifer, who were both beaming, and Kathy, who was reaching for more tissues, and sniffling and crying.

"What?" Jack raised his hands in a questioning pose.

"I think we are all being blessed as we watch the Holy Spirit work in your heart, Jack. Think about it. Until this moment, have you felt any sense of compassion or understanding for Alice and where she was coming from in this situation, or how she may have been affected by it?"

"No, I can't say that I have."

"And yet, by entertaining the idea that there may be more to the story than what you created thus far, something inside you led you to consider apologizing to Alice for your behavior. Where do you think that came from?"

"Uh . . . I'm not really sure. It sure didn't come from me, just ask Kathy." Jack reached for Kathy's hand. She leaned toward him and gave his hand a loving squeeze. "I guess it must be the Lord." Jack squeezed Kathy's hand in return. They both gave a smile that said "I love you," without voicing the words.

"If it is the Lord?" Again, Dick allowed his question to hang in the air until Jack responded.

"Then, like I said, I guess I have a whole lot of thinking to do about this situation. Bottom line, I probably owe Alice an apology: Bill, too, for that matter." Jack paused: "But I gotta tell ya, I still think they owe me one, too. They both said some pretty hurtful things."

"I understand that, Jack. And that may yet come. But we can't be responsible for others; we can only be responsible for ourselves. So at this point, I think it would be important to focus on how you believe the Lord would like to respond through you. What do you think?"

"I guess you're right. God knows I've got plenty of my own stuff to deal with. I don't really need to be worrying about other people's stuff at the moment." Jack looked at Kathy once again. Again she responded with that knowing smile. "So, is that it?"

Dick chuckled. "Almost. But there is a bit more we would like you to spend some time thinking about and discussing between you. You've already begun to identify the issues in the situation. So spend some time with the Lord, asking Him to show you why these are issues to you. Why do these particular issues push the buttons in you that they do?

"What's underneath all this, that creates the feelings and reactions related to these particular issues? What you will discover is what we call the interests of the conflict."

Kathy interrupted hesitantly, "I'm not sure I understand what you're asking."

Jennifer interjected, "The issues are the 'what' we're conflicted about. So what was the conflict at the missions meeting? Or what is your conflict regarding the two women's groups, and the conversations you've had related to that? Now the interests are a bit more difficult to identify at first. They are the 'why' of the conflict. Why is the issue you've identified an issue *to you*? And why have you taken the position you've taken, and reacted the way you have? Your answers to those questions will help you identify your interests in the matter."

Jack leaned forward in his chair, "So why is it important to know what our interests are?"

Dick smiled broadly and, getting the go-ahead nod from Jennifer, jumped back into the conversation. "Ahhh, because then we're able to move the conversation from our head to our heart—and our spirit. That's where our conflicts present us with some awesome opportunities to experience Jesus Christ in some very profound ways. We're convinced that's why Jesus told us to deal with the log in our own eye before we deal with the speck in someone else's."

Jack frowned a bit. "I won't even pretend I understand all of what you just said. But what I do understand is this: I see a lot of wisdom in stepping back to take a more objective view of this whole situation. I'll admit . . ." Jack stole a quick look in Kathy's direction, "that's not something I normally do when I'm ticked and the adrenalin is pumping." Jack risked another glance toward Kathy, and found her staring at him with very soft-looking eyes: *very wet*, soft-looking eyes.

"Well, we'll get more into the spiritual side of this next time. But I'm glad to hear you're seeing the importance of stepping back and reviewing these situations, rather than just reacting out of your natural, fleshly reactions. You'll discover that's one of the major things these biblical principles do for us. They help us to move from reacting out of ourselves to responding in Jesus Christ."

Jack's eyebrows rose. "Oh, man, I like that. Instead of reacting out of ourselves, we want to respond in Christ. That's cool."

"Glad you like it. There's more . . . homework, that is."

Jack groaned.

"Next, ask yourselves how you've contributed to each of these situations. This may include attitudes, judgments, and emotions you've brought into these conflicts. Or it may focus on things you've said or done. Some of these will be seen as helpful. Some will not. Again, write them all down. And be as accurate and objective as you can."

Kathy spoke up again. "What if you can't think of anything you've done to contribute to the situation? Like Jack's situation with Alice and Bill: I didn't really do or say anything there. As far as the women's thing, I feel caught between the two groups. So I don't see what I've done to contribute to either of those situations."

Jennifer responded, "It might be accurate that you didn't contribute to the meeting situation at the time. But upon reflection, you may discover there was something you could have done that you didn't. You may ask yourself why. Or you may have omitted something from your story about either of those situations. Honestly, don't try to invent something. But don't dismiss any involvement, either. Go through the process of dealing with the log in your own eye; let the Holy Spirit reveal to you what He knows needs to be revealed into your heart and mind. We'll see where that takes us. Okay?"

Kathy nodded her head in the affirmative, but remained silent.

Jennifer continued, "As you reflect on your stories, as well as your attitudes, emotions, and actions, be mindful of how these reflect your sense of your self. In other words, did your attitudes, emotions, and actions accurately reflect who you believe yourself to be, who you desire to be and, most importantly, who you believe the Lord desires you to be?"

Dick cleared his throat. "Which brings us to the final area of reflection."

"Thank God," Jack responded with relief. "I was starting to feel a bit overwhelmed here."

"We're sorry about that. It truly is not our intent to overwhelm you. In fact, I think when you get started, you'll be surprised how things begin to flow, and thoughts and insights will come to mind; you won't even know where they come from sometimes. That's the Lord at work. In fact, due to a promise He made, I can assure you the Lord will be with you every step of your way as you do all this."

"I think I hear another Scripture coming our way. It's not out of Matthew, is it?" Jack looked at Dick, who had a bit of a grin on his face. "You've got to be kidding me," Jack groaned.

Chuckling, Jennifer opened her Bible to Matthew 18:20. "Do you remember that passage where Jesus instructs us to go to our brother who sins against us? The rest of the text describes what we're to do if they refuse to resolve the issue and reconcile the relationship. Well, at the end of that teaching, in the context of resolving conflicts between Christian brothers and sisters, Jesus makes this promise: 'For where two or three have gathered together in My name, I am there in their midst.'"

"That means," Dick continued, "whenever we're involved in resolving issues and reconciling relationships, we know for a fact that Jesus is right there with us. He's right here, right now. And He'll be with you every step of the way. You can count on that."

Kathy spoke softly, "That's beautiful."

"So the last thing we'd like you to reflect on is how this whole situation may look to Jesus. Prayerfully ask Him what the issues are from His perspective, and what His position is. And listen for His answer."

"He'd say the issue is that I was treated unfairly, and He'd expect Alice and Bill to apologize." Jack saw the pained expressions on everyone's faces. "No? Are you sure? Well, I bet He'd have more sympathy for me than you guys do. Yikes, this is a tough room! I'm only kidding. Really!"

"So let me say it this way," Dick said. "Seriously seek His perspective in each of your situations. And then ask Him how He would like to express Himself in and through you in these situations. Take the time to listen. Listen with your heart and your spirit. Then next time, we'll discuss what you have heard. Okay?"

"Yeah, it sounds like a lot. But I'll trust you guys it'll go more smoothly than I can picture right now." Jack was beginning to wonder what he'd gotten himself into. But he also was aware of this gnawing feeling in his gut that Jesus was in all of this, and Jack needed to be obedient.

"I think it's wonderful," Kathy added. "I can't wait until we can get back together again."

"We look forward to it, too," Jennifer responded. "So Dick, will you close us in prayer, and we'll call it a night?"

15

That barbecue smells wonderful; I can't wait to dig into those ribs." Jack, Kathy, and Anna had just arrived at the Stevens' house. They were going to enjoy Dick's new recipe, and then continue the discussion they'd started ten days earlier.

"Well, I hope you like it. You're my guinea pigs, you know." Dick enjoyed cooking, especially barbecuing. And he was always hunting for new dishes to try, or experimenting with changes to recipes he'd used before. But as enjoyable as that was, Dick was really looking forward to continuing the conversation he and Jennifer had begun with Jack and Kathy. He and Jennifer had both been aware of the presence of the Lord their last time together, and were looking forward to watching Him continue His work of peace in Jack and Kathy's hearts.

As they were all helping to set the table out on the deck, Kathy asked, "So what did you think about Pastor Tim's message today?"

Jennifer and Dick looked at one another, deciding who would answer Kathy's question first. Jennifer responded, "Actually, I'd like to hear what the two of you thought first. And then we can discuss our thoughts about it."

"Sounds like a trap to me," Jack said, chuckling.

As Kathy set down the iced teas, she responded energetically, "I thought it was awesome. Especially since Anna and I were talking about the very same subject during the week. She's been reading the gospel of John recently, and she came downstairs all excited the other day because she'd come across the very same text Pastor Tim used this morning, in John 17."

"That's interesting," Jennifer added.

"I know. It's like the Holy Spirit is revealing the Lord's message to a lot of different people at the same time. Anyhow, when I heard Pastor Tim start talking about the pain with all the conflict in the church, and especially the pain of the disconnected relationships, and then he started to read the Lord's prayer for us in John 17, I felt electric jolts going up and down my spine. I started to shake. . . ."

"And cry. But what else is new?" Jack reached over and put his arm around Kathy and gave her a big hug and smile.

"I know. I know. I cry about everything. But that was really special. It was like I felt God put His arm around me like you just did, and assure me that everything was going to be okay. He's in charge, and if we just look to Him, we're going to get through this. In fact, I think we're going to be the better for it. Is that weird?"

Dick and Jennifer were laughing. "No, Kathy. The Lord spoke to you this morning. Think of that! Just like we said last time, when we involve ourselves in resolving conflicts and reconciling relationships, He promises to be in our midst. He's in control. He's the King of kings, and Lord of lords. I think it's just awesome!" Jennifer gave Kathy a warm hug, and then returned to the kitchen to bring out the salad.

CHAPTER FIFTEEN

"So Jack, what did you think about the sermon this morning?" Dick took a sip of his iced tea and waited for Jack to respond.

"I thought it was pretty awesome myself. I mean, he didn't have to convince me about the level of conflict in the church. I'm well aware of that. But when he read that text, and then started talking about the Lord's final prayer being for us; and beyond that, that we would share the very same relationship that Jesus and His Father experience . . . man, I'll tell you, that just about blew me away!" Jack took a drink of his tea. "I know I've read that passage before, but I just never really saw it like he laid it out today. Can you believe it? The Lord wants us to be one, just like He and the Father are one?"

Dick was nodding his head. "That is quite a thought, that's for sure. Jennifer and I have some further thoughts on the subject we'd like to share with you this evening. But what I'd like to hear is, do either of you see Pastor's message applying to the conflicted situations we've been discussing together?"

"What do you mean?" Kathy asked.

"Actually, I do," Jack interjected. Everyone looked at him, surprised expressions on their faces. "Don't be so surprised. I'm not just another pretty face, you know."

After the laughter subsided, Jack went on. "Seriously, I've been giving this all a lot of thought. Right, honey?"

"He really has," Kathy responded. "I think we discussed the homework you gave us just about every night. And he actually filled one of those wire-ring note pads, writing down all his thoughts. He's been amazing."

Dick gave Jack an ovation of appreciation. "Good job, my brother. I'm impressed."

"Thank you, thank you very much." Everyone groaned at Jack's feeble Elvis impersonation. "But yeah, I've worked on this a lot. For some reason, I feel like this is about more than just my blowup with Alice and Bill. I have to tell you, I've never felt more connected with the Lord than I have the last week or so. I started reading those Scriptures you gave us to reflect on, and I just can't believe how much of the New Testament is all about how we Christians are to treat one another. And I gotta tell ya, I came up short on a lot of 'em. I found myself asking the Lord to forgive me—a lot. And you know something? I think He did. I feel like He did. I mean, I feel better than I've felt in years: lighter, happier. You know what I mean?"

"Yes, we know what you mean," Jennifer responded. "We can see it in you."

Dick cleared his throat to speak, "So Jack, how do you see the message this morning applying to your life today?"

"Oh, yeah. Well, on top of everything I was already feeling because of the homework I was doing, and my Bible reading, it hit me this morning that Jesus wants all of us to live in His fellowship with His Father, and to experience the same oneness with one another that they do. I realized I need to do whatever is necessary to make things right with Alice and Bill. I blew that big time, and I need to apologize and seek their forgiveness."

"What led you to that place?" As Dick asked the question, he moved toward the grill to check on the ribs.

"Oh, man, you know . . . all of this stuff. I know, the first time we met, I was pretty defensive and hurt. And I was blaming Alice and Bill for all my problems. But the bottom line is that I was also feeling pretty guilty and embarrassed. I just didn't know what to do with all of that. I'm still not sure how to even approach them. I just know I need to."

"So it sounds like things have begun to change for you," Dick said as he returned to the table.

"Yeah, I guess they really have. I really don't know why . . . or even what all has changed. I just know I feel a change in me."

Dick settled in at the table once again. "You mentioned you felt you needed to apologize to Alice and Bill. Is that accurate?"

Jack nodded. "Can you explain that a bit more? What do you believe is leading you to that place?"

"I'm not sure what you're asking. Do you mean, is it out of some kind of obligation, or a legalistic kind of thing?"

"It appears you've moved quite a ways from where you were when we first visited. So I'm just wondering if you are aware of what's caused you to come to the place you are at today."

"Well, I don't really feel obligated to do it. I mean, I'm convinced it's something God *wants* me to do, maybe even expects of me. But that's not really the reason I want to do it, not really. It's deeper than that. It's like reading my Bible. I've tried to discipline myself to read the Bible every day, because I've always been told that's something I'm supposed to do if I'm a Christian. But I've never been able to discipline myself to do it every day like that. I watch Kathy, and now even Anna. They read their Bibles every day. But I've never been able to do that. But the last week or so, I've been reading it every day. I even started sitting at the lunch table at work with a guy who reads his Bible a lot during breaks and stuff. Can you believe that? Me! And I want to do it. There's something in me that's different. Before, it was like reading some foreign language. But now there's new stuff popping up everyday; awesome stuff; stuff that speaks to what's going on in my life *right now*. It's like the Lord is talking *to me* through His Word. And not just that either, it's like my prayer life is real now, too. It's just amazing."

Kathy was grinning from ear to ear, as were Dick and Jennifer. "I guess I'm running off at the mouth, aren't I? I don't think I answered your questions yet, either. So I want to make things right with Alice and Bill. I'm convinced the Lord put that desire in me. In fact, I suspect He is that desire, if you know what I mean. I guess that's what led me to where I am right now. That, and all the homework, and the Scriptures, and the discussions Kathy and I have had this week. But the big issue remains for me, what do I do now? *How* do I apologize to

Alice and Bill? What do I say? When? Where? This is all new territory for me."

"Me, too," Kathy responded.

Dick got up to take the ribs off the grill. Jennifer spoke up: "It's new territory for each of us, each time life leads us down this path, Jack. And while Dick and I have an understanding of the process, and the biblical principles that lay it out for us, each situation is new and different. So we're always dependent on the Lord to show us each step of the way."

"Yeah," Dick said, returning to the table with a platter heaped high with his special-recipe ribs, "and the exciting thing is, He's always faithful. When we focus on Him, He leads us exactly where we are to go . . . in His time and in His way."

Eyeing the ribs, Jack said, "So do you think He would mind if we took our eyes off of Him long enough to dig into those ribs? I'm starved!"

Laughing, Jennifer said, "I don't think He'd mind if we enjoy this meal He has provided for us, though I think He might appreciate it if we prayed a blessing first. Would you mind doing the honors, Jack? But before you start, let me call the girls to join us."

After the girls had joined them at the table, they all quieted and bowed their heads. Jack began to pray. "Heavenly Father, how do we begin to thank You for Your love for us . . . for providing us with such wonderful friends . . . and all this great food? Kathy and I don't have a clue where all this stuff in the church, and in our own lives, is going, but we are learning to trust You in it. And that seems like a pretty good way to go. So thank You for blessing us with folks like the Stevens, to help us. And thanks for being with us at all times, especially now. In Jesus' name I pray. Amen. Now, pass those ribs down this way!"

Following the meal, the girls gladly retreated back to Beth's bedroom, leaving their parents to continue their discussion together.

As Jennifer refilled everyone's iced tea, Dick picked up the conversation where they'd left off prior to the meal. "I think we were talking about how you both saw this concept of being one in Christ being applied to the conflicted situations you're experiencing in the church right now."

"Right. Well, for me it ties together the concepts I've been recognizing in the Scriptures you gave us to study. The passages that spoke of Jesus being the head of the Church, and each of us is a living part of his living body; that makes perfect sense when seen in this concept of us all being one in Him. I think it was Romans 12. Or maybe it was 1 Corinthians 12: I don't remember which right now. I know they both spoke about us all making up the body of Christ, but one of them talked about each of us being placed in the body where God wants us to be."

Jennifer interjected, "I believe that's 1 Corinthians 12."

"If you say so. You know the Word better than I do. But when I was reflecting on that this past week, I started thinking about the fact that it's no coincidence that all of us are in the same local church at this particular point in time. I don't understand that. But if God arranges all the parts of the body where He wants them to be, then it just makes sense to me that rather than thinking I need to leave—or wishing others would leave . . ." Everyone chuckled, "Instead, I need to recognize church isn't about me, or what I want, or think is best; it's about Jesus and what God wants."

"Whoa! That's profound." Dick was amazed at what he was hearing coming from Jack's heart. Only a week ago, Jack was hurt, mad, and entrenched in his victim story, stuck in the midst of his unresolved conflict with Alice and Bill. But now he was speaking deep spiritual truth. Dick marveled at the growth of spiritual understanding in Jack in such a short time. Silently he prayed, "May Your work bear forth Your fruit, Lord; not only in Jack and Kathy's lives, but in the life of our church."

"I'm not sure how profound it is. It's sure a new thought to me. But, like I said, as I read all these Scriptures about Jesus as the head of His body, and how we are to treat one another in His body, and relate to Him together as one, it all started making perfect sense. Then, when I started doing the homework questions you gave us, I soon realized the conflicts were more about personal stuff than they were about Jesus."

Dick leaned forward. "What do you mean?"

"Well, like the original squabble over the funding for the youth center ministry. I was the one pushing that on the missions committee because I see it as one of the most effective ministries we have going right now in the church. We're reaching tons of kids of all ages. And not just the kids; we're reaching their families too. Pastor Tim told me not too long ago that 30 percent of those who were baptized or joined the church last year came through the youth center ministry. So I admit, I was pushing pretty hard for more support. I recognize now how Alice and Bill could feel other ministries were being threatened, as there's only so much money to go around. But I was pretty ticked-off too, 'cause every time I brought up anything having to do with the youth center, I'd have to buck their negativity. I guess I just got tired of it, and blew up at 'em at the meeting."

Jennifer leaned forward. "Go on."

"Well, like I said, I now realize that Alice and Bill aren't the enemies I thought they were."

"Hallelujah!" Dick shouted

"Amen," Kathy added.

"You guys are real funny. But I suspect it's not all that different for you when it's you in the conflict, right?" Jack looked around the table. Kathy was looking at the glass of tea cupped in her hands. Dick and Jennifer both had that 'you got me' look on their faces. "That's what I thought. Anyhow, I figured if Jesus died to make us one in Him, then I wanted to give my life to that, rather than giving any more of my life to things that divide us."

"Hallelujah," Dick said, more softly this time.

"Which presents the next problem: I don't really know what to do to take the next step. I mean, I know I need to apologize to Alice and Bill, but I don't know exactly how to go about it, especially when I still have some mixed feelings toward them for some of the things they said about me. Can you guys help me with that?"

"Absolutely. But first, I want to offer the Lord a prayer of thanks for what He's accomplished in your heart in the last week or so, brother. Then I think it would be important for us to seek His heart in this matter, together, seeking His purpose and direction. Is that okay with you?" As Jack and Kathy agreed, Dick reached his hands out to Jack and Jennifer, who then both reached out and took Kathy's hands. Together they bowed their heads as Dick led them in prayer. "Loving Father, we are both humbled and filled with indescribable joy at this moment. We're so thankful for the work You've accomplished in Jack and Kathy, especially that which we have witnessed during these past few days. Thank you, Lord, that You allow these blessed opportunities to discover more of who You are, and who we are in You. We recognize that none of the issues present in our personal lives, as well as the life of our church, are a surprise to You. So we entrust ourselves into Your hands. Our desire is to experience the reality of who we are in Christ, and that He be expressed through us as He desires. We also join our brother Jack in his desire to know how Jesus desires to express Himself through Jack in this particular situation with Alice and Bill. We ask you to reveal to us how You would have Jack proceed. And we give You all the praise and glory." Eventually, Jennifer, Jack, and Kathy all added their hearts' expressions to Dick's prayer.

After they concluded their prayer time, Dick spoke first. "I just can't tell you how blessed Jen and I are by what you've been sharing tonight, Jack. And Kathy, I know we haven't heard much from you yet. . . ."

"That's okay. The Lord's been working a good work in Jack, and I think it is important to go with that right now." Kathy reached over and patted Jack on the forearm.

"I think you're right," Dick continued. "But I didn't want you to think we'd forgotten you in all of this. I know the Lord will lead our time together to focus on your situation as well."

Jennifer reached over and squeezed Kathy's hand.

Dick continued: "So Jack, if I hear you correctly, you'd like our help regarding two things. You want help figuring out how to go about apologizing to Alice and Bill, and you want help figuring out what to do with your feelings toward them for the things they said in the heat of the moment during the meeting. Is that correct?"

"Yeah, that's it. On the one hand I want to make things right. I know I did some things that were wrong, or hurtful. So I want to apologize for those things. But I still don't know what to do with the feelings I have for the things they called me, and accused me of."

"Okay. I'd suggest we start with the feelings first, and then work back to the apology. Jen, what do you think?"

"I agree. How does that sound to you, Jack?"

"Sounds fine to me. Where do we start?"

Dick leaned back in his chair. "You said you've been working on your homework quite a bit. So why don't you first tell us where you are regarding your feelings about Bill and Alice."

"Well, much of it has changed, actually. I'm really not as angry at them as I was. I feel like they've made some unfair judgments about me, and they did it in front of a bunch of other people I have to work with."

"So you feel unfairly judged, and perhaps embarrassed?" Jennifer asked.

"Yes, I do. I guess the fact this was all done in public was really embarrassing to me. I realize that's about me, about my own ego. And I also realize I'm the one who got the whole thing going by ramping up the disagreement into a full-blown conflict. But it doesn't change the way I feel about the way I was treated. Should it?"

"Our feelings are our feelings, Jack. In and of themselves, they're not sin. It's like Paul said in Ephesians 4:26, we can be angry, but we're not to allow our anger to lead us to sin. So it's not so much the feeling of anger that's the issue, it's how we decide to deal with it. Do you understand that?" Jennifer looked at Jack with a great deal of empathy. With his history of anger issues, Jennifer knew this could be a tough process for Jack to work through. Yet she knew it could also make for a profound change in his life, and especially his relationship with Kathy and the kids. She silently prayed for the Lord's guidance at this critical moment.

"Yeah, I think I get that. I've sinned in my anger, a lot."

Dick joined the conversation again. "What do you mean?"

"I just realize that I've had an anger issue as long as I can remember. Like I said last week, I know Kathy and the kids have been on the receiving end of that a lot. I've begun to recognize those parts of myself that don't reflect Christ, especially my anger. And I need His help. I want my life to be His life. You know what I mean?" Jack looked around the room and was met by approving looks. "And you might be happy to know I sat everyone down the other night and apologized, and asked them to forgive me, and told them, with the Lord's help, I'm going to change."

"Really? What was their reaction?" They all looked at Kathy.

"At first, they sat there with their mouths open." Everyone laughed. "Actually, they were all surprised to hear their Dad talk like that. I don't think he's ever done anything like that with them before. We had talked earlier, and he apologized personally to me. And then he explained what he wanted to do with the kids. So I was prepared, but they sure weren't." Kathy smiled at Jack. "Anna and her sister, Kate, were both in tears. And I think Aaron was trying hard to not shed any tears in front of his sisters. But, all in all, the kids were very moved, and they all said they forgave him."

"Yeah," Jack interrupted, "Aaron asked if this meant he wouldn't have to sit through a thirty-minute lecture the next time he got into trouble. I told him I'd work on the anger part first. Then maybe I'd get to the lecture stuff." Again, everyone laughed.

"Well, it sounds like you guys sure have had an eventful week. So Jack, you've come to recognize that your past pattern of dealing with your anger has been sinful. How do you believe the Lord would have you respond in Him as you deal with your anger feelings toward Alice and Bill?"

"I know He wants me to go to them directly, like He says in Matthew 5 and 18. Kathy pointed this out: I recognize that I let my anger build up to the point where I just blow. I think the word you used was avoidance. I avoid, avoid, avoid, and then I can't avoid any longer, so I just blowup. I realize the Lord doesn't want me to do that anymore."

"And do you have any sense of how He would handle things through you?"

Kathy interrupted, "I told him that if he'd just tell me at the time when I've said or done something he doesn't like, or doesn't agree with, then we could talk about it right then, rather than letting it build to a blowup."

Jennifer responded, "Does that seem like a workable plan to you, Jack?" Jack nodded his agreement. "So I'm wondering, Jack, as you look back on your relationships with Alice and Bill, were there times when you experienced frustration or anger but said nothing to them about it?"

Kathy made a low "hummm" sound in her throat.

Jack responded, "I guess you could say that. Yeah, there were plenty of times I came home madder than a wet hen. And I'd share all my frustrations with Kathy, which would usually get her upset, and then we'd get into it sometimes. But yeah, there were lots of times I'd be frustrated, but wouldn't say anything to them about it. That's a common thing with me."

Finally Dick spoke. "So how do you think Jesus would like you to handle this *in Him*?"

"With Bill and Alice?" Jack asked.

Dick nodded.

"Well, I'm convinced He's more interested in our relationships than in who wins." Dick smiled, and Jack continued: "While I was reflecting on what my bottom-line interests were, I suddenly realized that they both probably have their own issues and interests in all of this as well."

Jennifer leaned forward. "And do you have any idea what those might be?"

"Well, from what they said, I know they both feel like I'm a bully or something. So I suspect they have issues with the way I come across when I'm excited about something I feel the Lord wants us to do."

"So what interest do you suspect they might have connected with that possible issue?"

"Uh . . . I'm not sure. I guess from my perspective, I kind of feel they were bullying me. I know some of my interests I identified had to do with wanting to be respected and heard. I'd like them not to react so quickly, but to listen to what I've got to say, and discuss the matters with me. So I suspect they must feel pretty much the same way. I suspect they'd want me to not be so overpowering, probably listen to them more, be willing to discuss things with them and really try to understand one another."

Dick spoke again. "I think that is very insightful, Jack. So tell me, how are you feeling toward Bill and Alice right now?"

"Uh . . . actually, I'm not really angry at all. If anything, I feel bad that I've reacted to them like I have. I realize I've contributed to this situation by not dealing with things as they came up. That same old pattern, you know. I realize I really don't know why they take the stands they do when it comes to budgeting our mission support. So there's probably more I don't know than what I do know. Bottom line is that I'd like to start over with them. Get to know them, and let them get to know me. Then, together—along with the other committee members—work with the Lord to do what He wants."

Jennifer spoke up. "It seems like your story has changed quite a bit since our first discussion—and your feelings, too."

Jack laughed. "Yeah, ain't that somethin'!"

Dick cleared his throat. "So let's talk about next steps. You said you want to go and apologize to Bill and Alice. What might that apology look like?"

"Uh, I'm sorry?"

"Would that work for you, if you received that apology from either of them?"

"Ummmm, probably not."

"Why?"

"Uh, because I'd wonder just exactly what they were sorry about. Were they sorry for the mess that has come out of this? Or were they really sorry for saying what they said, and hurting me?

"So it sounds as though it is important to you that an apology be pretty clear in describing what the person is apologizing for."

Now Jack was smiling. "Yeah, I get it. When I apologize to them, I need to describe exactly what I'm apologizing about."

"Well, it sounds that way. At least, it sounds like that is the way you'd like to be treated in this. So if we are going to follow the Lord's instructions to treat others as we wish to be treated, then it sounds like your apology would be pretty descriptive."

Jennifer entered the conversation once again. "Here's another suggestion to consider. Stay away from using words like 'if,' 'but,' 'maybe,' or any others that tend to take the responsibility off of you."

"Huh?" Jack furrowed his brows in puzzlement.

"Let's say you go to Alice or Bill to apologize, and you begin by saying, 'If I hurt your feelings, I'm sorry.' Or, 'If you wouldn't have said what you did, I wouldn't have blown up at you.' See what I mean? How do you feel when someone apologizes to you for something, then they say, 'But,' and begin to excuse the behavior they just apologized for?"

"That really ticks me off. It's like everything they said before was just a bunch of hot air. It doesn't mean anything."

"Right," Dick added. "So what are the specifics you feel you want to apologize for when you go speak with Alice and Bill?"

"Well, I certainly want to apologize for losing my temper. I really do feel bad about that. I want to take responsibility for contributing to the incident by avoiding situations as they came up in the past, and then letting it all loose at the meeting."

"Anything else?"

"Well, it's not really so much an apology, but I also want to tell them I hope they'll accept my apology. I hope we can start over with a clean slate and work together in the future. I want them to know I really would like to get to know them better, because the Lord has made us one. And I want to learn how to do that; you know what I mean?"

"That sounds wonderful. So it seems the next step is to figure out how, when, and where this is all going to take place. Do you have any thoughts?"

"Actually, Kathy and I were discussing this. I'm worried they won't even want to meet with me, given what they said; certainly not alone, one on one, anyhow. So she was thinking that if I meet with each of them individually, she should go along when I meet with Alice. But then we don't know if Alice would feel ganged up on, being by herself like she is. So we don't know exactly how to proceed. Any suggestions?"

Dick looked at Jennifer, and then at Kathy and Jack. "Well, Jen and I were discussing the matter ourselves. Because of the history you all have had—together with the communication difficulties you've experienced, and especially because of the continued relationship you hope to have in the church—we believe it would be good if a third party was involved to help either facilitate the meeting, or help set it up. And we'd volunteer for that, or you could ask Pastor Tim to help, or someone else that would be acceptable to all of you."

Kathy spoke up first. "I was hoping you guys would help us walk this thing through to the end." She then looked to Jack.

"Yeah, me too, actually. I have to admit I didn't know how we were going to set something like this up with them. I mean, neither one of them has said a word to either one of us since the incident. And I've gotten the cold shoulder from Bill's wife and a few of their friends."

"Yes," Kathy added, "Did you notice that the Murphys and Nelsons are now sitting with the Fredricks on Sunday mornings? I've got to tell you, that really hurts; we've been friends for years."

"Yes, we did notice. And it breaks our hearts when we see such things. But hopefully, with the action you are about to take, we'll start to see a different approach to conflict being modeled."

Jack sat up straight in his chair, smiling, and said, "Yeah, responding in Christ, rather than reacting in ourselves. Right?"

"Exactly." Dick reached over, and the two men gave each other a high-five.

Shaking her head at the men and smiling, Jennifer added, "So I guess the next step is that we need to contact Bill and Alice and find out their thoughts about us setting up a meeting between you and them. We hope they'll be open to that, and we can proceed from there."

"So what happens if they refuse?"

"Let's cross that bridge *if* we come to it. Okay?"

"Okay. So I guess we'll just wait to hear from you then?"

"Yes, we'll make those initial contacts tomorrow, and let you know as soon as we can. In the meantime, we'd suggest you write out your apology and everything you want to say. You might even read it when you meet with them, if you don't feel you're able to just say it all. Sound okay?"

"Yeah, that sounds like a good idea."

Dick spoke once again: "So let's pray. We have a lot to be thankful for, and to praise the Lord for. We definitely are going to need His wisdom and guidance as we move on from here."

Reaching for Jack and Jennifer's hands, Kathy said quietly, "Yes, and I think we need to lift up Alice and Bill, that the Holy Spirit will prepare their hearts for this, like He's prepared ours."

"Amen," the others responded. They began to pray.

16

Jack walked in the door after a hard day at work, and Kathy held out the phone to him as he entered the kitchen. "It's for you," she said. "It's Mike again."

Jack took the phone and walked into the family room to get into his comfortable chair. If this call was going to be like any of the others Jack had experienced with Mike lately, it could be a long one. Thankfully, he could cite his need to join the family for dinner to escape. The last conversation he'd had with Mike hadn't gone very well. Jack had tried to explain what he felt the Lord was doing in his heart regarding the situation with Bill and Alice, but Mike just couldn't understand, or chose not to. Instead, he had continued to try to get Jack to join the group, which was now calling for a congregational meeting to air its grievances. There was talk of asking the Board of Elders, and possibly even the pastor, to resign. It broke Jack's heart, because he could feel the separation beginning to take place as Jack continued to try to talk to Mike about Jesus, rather than the conflicts.

Jack settled into his easy chair. "Hey Mike, how's it going?"

"Not bad. Not bad. So I told you I was going to call and see if I couldn't change your mind about attending our meeting tonight. Most of the rest of your youth center team is going to be there, you know."

"Yeah, I know. But like I've been telling you, Mike, I just don't think what you're doing reflects who we are in Christ, or how He would want us to handle all of this."

"Listen, I don't know about all that Bible mumbo-jumbo stuff you're spouting all of a sudden. I'm happy for you that you've found Jesus again and all that; I really am. But I'm not sure what all that has to do with saving the church. Do you honestly think all these people are suddenly going to just sit down and start loving each other when they're at such opposite ends of things? Geez, man, you admitted yourself you felt the church was dying a slow death the way things were going. So you're just going to sit back and pray and hope everybody gets along, while the whole church goes belly-up? I don't get it."

"I know. I wish I could find the words that would describe how I see everything now."

"Yeah, I know. It's not about us; it's all about Jesus. I've heard it. And the point you don't seem to be getting is that *this is all about Jesus*. What we're trying to do is save the church. You don't think that's about Jesus?"

"No, Mike, I don't. I don't think Jesus needs parts of His body to save His body. I trust He is able to take care of His body quite well, and with a whole lot more wisdom and love than any of us could. That's why it's important for everyone to stop the fighting and bickering, and get together in Him and. . . ."

Interrupting, and with a great deal of exasperation in his voice, Mike responded, "Oh, please! Come on, man! You know dang well these people aren't going to sit down and pray together. They can hardly stand to be in church with each other on Sunday mornings. The line's been drawn in the sand, man.

And it's time everybody decides which side of that line they're going to be on. So what's it going to be with you? Are you with us . . . or against us in this?"

Jack felt a pain grip his stomach. An emotional whirlwind began to twist and turn within him, mixing together anger, guilt, fear, compassion, loyalty, and other emotions he couldn't even identify. He opened his mouth to speak, but no sound came out.

"So what's it going to be, Jack?"

Finally, Jack was able to collect his thoughts and feelings enough to respond to Mike. "Please don't do this, Mike."

"Do what?"

"You know what. We've talked about this enough. You know where I stand on all of this now."

"Listen, man, the days of sitting on the sidelines doing nothing are over." Mike's anger escalated. "And I've got to say, you wimping out like this really surprises me."

Jack was struggling to control his own anger, as he didn't take well to Mike's description of him. "I'm not wimping out, Mike. I'm . . ."

"You're what?" Mike asked, "I don't see you doing a dang thing except trying to walk some spiritual middle ground, which isn't going to help anybody."

"For your information, Mike, I have decided to do something."

"Yeah? What?"

"I feel I need to take responsibility for my own contributions to this mess, and I've got some apologizing to do."

"Apologizing? To whom? Oh, you've got to be kidding me. You're not going to apologize to Alice and Bill, are you?" Mike's question was met with silence. "Oh, man, you are nuts. You're taking this religious thing of yours way too far. They owe you an apology! They're the ones who went off on you. You were just defending yourself. There's not another person in the room who wouldn't have done the same thing you did . . . including them." Jack was silent. Mike continued, "I can't believe this!"

The conversation grew silent for a moment, as both men contemplated what to say next. Finally, Mike broke the silence. "OK. I understand. I know what side of the line you've chosen. Thanks, buddy, I really appreciate it."

The phone went dead. For a moment, Jack sat there with the receiver pressed to his ear, not fully comprehending Mike had just hung up on him. When he did, his heart was filled with sorrow; his head and shoulders slumped forward.

Kathy had been standing nearby, busying herself with preparations for dinner. From Jack's side of the conversation, she could tell things weren't going well. Her concern swelled when the conversation ended so abruptly and Jack reacted as he did.

She wiped her hands and began to approach him. "Jack, what's the matter?"

Jack slowly raised his head at the sound of Kathy's voice. "Huh? Oh, uh . . . he hung up on me."

"You've got to be kidding!" Kathy was shocked. Then she saw the hurt in Jack's face, and the tears in his eyes. "I'm really sorry, Jack. You've been friends for a long time. I just can't believe he could be such a jerk!" She walked over to where he was seated. "I'm really sorry, honey."

"Yeah . . . me too. I guess this is the part where we pick up our cross and follow Him, right?"

"I suspect so. Are you ready for this?"

"Probably not." Jack stood and took Kathy into his arms. "But more than ever before, I know He is." After they hugged one another for a few moments, Jack stepped back. "So maybe we should pray. And then I need to talk about some things Mike said, and get your thoughts on what I should do."

They held one another's hands and bowed their heads. After a moment of silence, Jack prayed, "Lord, I'm trying to sort out just how I feel right now, and what I should do, and I have to admit, I don't have a clue. I'm convinced You desire me to live in peace with everyone. But I'm not sure how I'm supposed to do that when others don't want to live in peace with me." Kathy squeezed his hands to communicate her love and encouragement. Jack continued, "So Lord, I just need You to help me understand how You desire to express Yourself through me in all of this."

Kathy waited a moment for Jack to continue. When it appeared he was done, she began to pray, "Lord, most of all we just want to thank You for who You are; our Lord, our Savior, our strength, our peace, our life, Lord. Thank you, Lord, for being all that and so much more . . . for us and for Mike, and Bill, and Alice, and everyone else who has been made one with you and one another. We trust You and commit ourselves to You. It's our desire to be expressions of You in this situation, rather than ourselves." Kathy then waited a moment to allow Jack to add anything further. He remained silent, so Kathy ended their time with "Amen."

After dinner, Jack and Kathy sat on their deck, enjoying the solitude and beauty of their backyard. Kathy turned to Jack. "So are you going to go ahead and meet with Alice and Bill tomorrow?"

Jack turned to her in surprise, "Of course! Why would you ask?"

"Well, I know Mike's call was very upsetting to you. I doubt you expected you might lose a good friend because you were following the Lord's leading. So I was just wondering if there were any second thoughts or anything. That's all."

"No second thoughts for me. How about you?"

"No, none at all." They both grew silent, lost in their own thoughts. Finally, Kathy spoke again. "Jack, I just want you to know how proud I am of you, the stand you're taking, and the changes you've made. It makes me love you even more."

Jack reached over and took her hand, squeezed, and gave her a warm smile. "I love you, too, honey. I couldn't do it if you weren't with me in this." Within his spirit, Jack spoke to the Lord, "And I know none of this would be possible without You, Lord."

Bill and June Fredricks were just finishing dinner, and continuing a conversation they'd been having since Bill received the call from Jack two days earlier. Bill wasn't completely sure he understood Jack's motives for wanting to visit, but if it was going to help clear the air, as Jack had promised, Bill was willing to hear what he had to say. The next Mission Committee meeting was next Wednesday night, and while Bill was still angry at Jack and upset over what had taken place before, he was not looking forward to the next meeting with things as they were, so he had agreed to meet with Jack and Alice on Saturday morning. June did not share Bill's willingness to meet with Jack, and had been trying to talk him out of it.

June began to clear the dishes and place them in the dishwasher. "I still don't think you can trust him, honey. A leopard can't change his spots, you know. At least not this fast, or this much, for that matter."

Bill pushed his chair in and stood there a moment, using the back of the chair as support. "I know, June. I know. I don't relish putting myself in line for any more of his outbursts, either. But there was something in his voice, not just the words he used. He wasn't angry or bossy. He was almost apologetic."

"That'll be the day! Jack Wilson apologize? Please. You really aren't that naive . . . are you?"

"I don't know what to expect, dear. But I couldn't refuse the man when he said he wanted to talk, and hoped we could settle the issues between us. Could I?"

"No. I suppose not. But even if Jack behaves himself, what makes you think things are going to be any different after you have this meeting. Even if he apologizes and promises to behave differently, what are you going to do the next time he blows up over some little disagreement with you or Alice or somebody else? Then what?"

"I don't know, honey. He's a jerk. Okay? But I've been doing a lot of thinking about what Pastor's been preaching lately. As I told you the other day, since reading some of those verses he told us to study, I've come to realize that, as angry as I've been at Jack, I've done my share of things that added to this whole thing, too."

"Like what?"

"Like the verses that tell us to go to one another when there's an issue between us and try to get it dealt with directly. I haven't done that. Looking back over the last couple years, I realize there were a number of times that I got upset, but I never spoke to Jack about it."

"No, you came home and acted like a bear around here for a couple days."

"You're right. And I apologize for that. That wasn't fair to you." Bill hesitated a moment before sharing his next thought. "I suspect that accounts more for your feelings about Jack than anything Jack has ever said or done directly to you. Don't you suppose?" June stopped what she was doing for a moment, but said nothing. "You know," Bill continued, "there's a whole lot more in the Bible about how Christians are supposed to treat one another than I ever saw before. Some of it seems pretty impossible, actually . . . like the one I was reading this afternoon in Ephesians 4. I don't remember the exact verses, toward the end of the chapter, if I remember correctly. But anyhow, Paul was saying we shouldn't speak badly to one another, but only use words that will help build up the other person . . . according to their needs. According to their needs! Can you believe that?" June stood there and said nothing. Bill continued, "I have to admit, I don't have any idea how you do that. Doesn't seem like anybody thinks that way at all. But there it was, right there in black and white. And I got to thinking what a change that would be if even you and I were more mindful of that when we're talking to one another. Wouldn't you like that?"

"I should be so lucky." June shut the dishwasher, twisted the knob to start, grabbed the dishcloth, and began to wipe off the table.

"So, anyhow, I'm starting to think maybe I've got some apologizing to do myself."

June jerked up from leaning over the table, and blurted, "What! You apologize? To Jack? You've got to be kidding me! Why, that's just about the most asinine thing I've heard yet! For the love of money, Bill, what in the world are you thinking?" June quickly finished wiping off the table and turned her attention to the kitchen counter.

"Now settle down, June. I said I was thinking about it. In that same Scripture in Ephesians, Paul said we're supposed to forgive one another, just as Jesus forgave us. Now think about that a moment. You know that one verse you like to refer to every once in awhile; you know, the one about Him forgiving us while we were still sinners?" June turned a bit, so at least he could see the side of her face, but she didn't turn all the way around to face him. "Well, it just seems to me if that's the way He forgave us, then doesn't that mean that's the way we're supposed to forgive one another? And if so, then if I'm going to follow Jesus in this, doesn't that mean I need to forgive Jack?"

June turned her back to Bill and began to scrub the sink. Her voice was jerky as she scrubbed the sink with a mighty effort. "After all the upheaval he's caused you and this home—and now with everything that's happening in the church—and you're considering just forgiving him." She grew silent as she scrubbed even harder.

After forty-three years of marriage, Bill knew this conversation was concluded. So he thanked June for dinner, and moved into the living room to catch the last of the national news. Along the way, he mulled over their conversation, June's reaction, as well as the growing conflict within his own heart. On the one hand, he was still plenty fed up with Jack's attitude and behavior and—with June's words fueling his own attitude—he wasn't willing to cut Jack much slack. On the other hand, Bill had been deeply impacted by Pastor Tim's recent messages on being one in Christ, as well as his own study of some of the Scriptural references Tim had encouraged the congregation to review. Bill felt his heart and mind being pulled back and forth between these differing influences.

Sinking into his easy chair, Bill reached for the remote control and turned on the television. His attention was immediately drawn to the all-too-familiar scene of yet another war some place in the world.

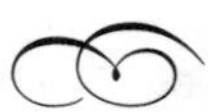

Alice was deeply affected by last week's sermon, based on the content of Jesus' prayer in John 17. It had inspired her to look up all the verses she could find regarding the Church as the body of Christ, and Jesus as its head. It had reminded Alice why she'd given so much of her life to the church. It really was about Him. But somewhere along the way, she'd lost track of that truth. She'd even convinced herself that her undying commitment to missions was singularly due to her faith and commitment to Jesus Christ. But she was beginning to question whether all of her motives were quite that pure after all.

She was starting to realize a lot of her mistrust of Jack—and her defensiveness toward him—had more to do with her longtime commitment to mission committee work than with any clear understanding of the Lord's present leading. For all she knew, God may very well want the church to direct more financial support toward the youth center ministry. But until this week, such thoughts would have seemed heretical to her, an act of unfaithfulness to the Lord. And while she remained committed to the missionaries they'd been supporting for so long, she had to admit she had not asked the Lord about this commitment in years.

Ever since she'd driven out of the church parking lot following the mission committee meeting, she'd felt a sense of guilt over her role in the blowup. At least a dozen times she'd felt she should call Jack and apologize for saying what she had, but she didn't know how. So when he called and requested a meeting, she was eager . . . and afraid. She agreed to meet with Jack and Bill at the church.

Mike left his "new leadership" meeting and walked to his car. The cool air felt good after all the hot air that had filled the room that night. He didn't know whether to feel good or frustrated; at the moment he was just *good and frustrated*. Dealing with these people was more aggravating than he could have ever imagined. About the time he thought they were all on the same page and developing a cohesive plan, someone would raise another personal gripe, and the whole meeting would flare up in another flurry of views, disagreements, and diverging rabbit trails of thoughts and ideas.

He had expressed his own frustration with Melvin Jones who—with a small group of others sharing his complaints and concerns about the worship—had written a letter and submitted it to the Board of Elders. When Mike asked Melvin why he had gone off and done such a thing, Melvin responded he couldn't take another Sunday "singing those stupid choruses, over and over again." The man had no idea what was at stake, Mike thought to himself, nor how to go about saving the ministry of the church. Instead, Melvin was like so many others who had their own little pet peeves and agendas, and Mike didn't know how much more of this he could take. Maybe those who had left the church, rather than stay and fight, had been the smart ones after all.

Then there was Jack Wilson. Just thinking about Jack twisted tighter the knot in Mike's gut. *What the heck was Jack's problem?* Mike thought. They'd been friends for years, hadn't they? They'd played golf together, went camping, and took the high school kids on mission trips to Mexico. What was Jack thinking, turning on Mike like this?

And what was with all this Jesus stuff all of a sudden? Did Jack think everybody was going to believe he suddenly became Mr. Super Christian or something? He'd better rethink that one, if he did think so. Mike knew the old guard wasn't going to trust Jack any further than they could throw him. He'd heard enough of the gossip to know that Bill was probably going to ream Jack pretty good when they met. Mike figured Alice was good for a couple more shots, and a bunch of crying, which would get her friends mad at Jack all over again.

Nope, Mike figured Jack was in for a big surprise with his newfound faith thing. When he got tired of being mistreated by these folks, he'd be joining the renewal movement Mike was heading. Or maybe Jack would just leave the church, like so many others had already done. The way things were going, Mike might join them.

17

When Jack had contacted Pastor Tim to tell him about meeting with Bill and Alice—and to seek Tim's help in securing a private place for them to gather at the church—at first Tim was overjoyed. But then he found himself worrying about all that could take place if the meeting did not go well. Eventually, he came to trust this meeting as the Lord's work, and rested in that. Knowing that Dick and Jennifer had helped Jack prepare for this important step helped Tim to relax as well. Over the years he'd come to respect them both for their spiritual maturity, and how they lived their faith from day to day.

It had been decided that the meeting would take place in Tim's office, as Tim felt that would offer the greatest amount of privacy. Dick had agreed to sit in the outer office reception area to make sure no one else would interrupt the meeting, and to provide ready assistance if called upon. There was a circular table with six chairs in a corner of the office. When they arrived, Alice and Bill took places beside one another, and across the table from Jack. There was a definite sense of anxiety in the room as they settled in.

Jack nervously cleared his throat. His eyes darted from Bill, to the table, to Alice, and to the table again. He fidgeted in his chair, and cleared his throat a second time. Alice and Bill sat quietly, waiting for him to speak first.

"Wow, this is harder than I thought it was going to be," he said. Alice smiled empathetically. Bill watched with little expression.

"Uh. . . . I suspect you're wondering why I've asked you to meet like this. And . . . uh . . . let me first thank you for agreeing to meet with me. I wouldn't have blamed you if you'd refused." Again, Alice smiled. Bill continued to watch, silently.

Jack cleared his throat a third time, and swallowed. "Anyhow, the reason I wanted to meet with you is because I've come to recognize I need to apologize to you both for a number of things; not the least being how I blew up at our meeting, and storming out like I did. I really am sorry for that."

Alice's eyes immediately began to tear up, and she reached into her purse for some tissue. Bill's face registered surprise, but he remained quiet.

Unfolding the paper before him, Jack continued, "Like I said, there are a number of things I feel I need to apologize for. And there are a couple other things I'd like to discuss with you, if you're willing." Jack ran his hand over the piece of paper to lay it flat. "I wrote 'em all down, so I wouldn't forget."

Alice dabbed at her eyes. The hint of a smile showed briefly on Bill's face.

"As I guess you know, Kathy and I have been meeting with Dick and Jennifer Stevens. They've been helping me to deal with my thoughts and feelings about all this . . . and to see the things I've done that have contributed to the conflict between us. It hasn't been easy. And I haven't always liked what they said. But I've come to realize that most of my actions have simply been my own reactions to things. Like Jesus said, I wasn't much concerned with the log in my own eye. Yuh know? In fact, I didn't even know I had any issues myself." Jack noticed the look in Bill's face that seemed to communicate, *If only you knew.* "But I'm starting to know what some of them are now. With what I've discovered so far, I've already apologized to the Lord . . . and to my family . . . and I know I've got plenty of apologizing to do to the both of you." Jack hesitated a moment, as he struggled to find the words he wished to say next. "I . . . I just want my life to not be about me. I want my life to be about Jesus. Yuh know? In fact, I want every part of my life to be about Jesus, including our relationship with one another. Okay?"

Alice nodded; this certainly wasn't what she had expected to hear from Jack. He was different, softer. Based on past experience, she wasn't going to be surprised if Jack tried to defend himself by making excuses, and then try and smooth things over. But he wasn't doing that. Instead, it appeared he'd really taken a serious look at himself in all this. Maybe this conversation wasn't going to be as scary as Alice had feared.

Bill continued to sit quietly, nodding in agreement, but wondering where all this was going. Jack wasn't his normal, pushy self. Was he trying a new strategy? Did Jack hope—by presenting a kinder, gentler version of himself—that he could manipulate Alice and Bill into putting this whole situation behind them, and just move on? If that was Jack's motive, Bill thought to himself, he better think again. Bill was beginning to recognize the fact that he, too, had contributed to this situation and had some apologizing to do. But after listening to June voice her feelings, Bill felt nothing short of a full apology from Jack—and a promise to change his ways—was going to be satisfactory. He wasn't sure even that would satisfy his wife, but he'd have to deal with her later.

"So with the help of Dick and Jennifer, I believe the Lord has used this whole situation to show me a whole lotta stuff about myself . . . about us . . . about the church . . . and, most important, about Him. And like I said, I've come to realize I have some apologizing to do to both of you, and others; and I hope we can talk about some things that concern me as well. I want to promise you, I have not come to make excuses for myself, or to accuse you. So if you think I'm doing that at any point here, please let me know. That's not my goal today. Instead, I hope we can have an open and frank discussion, not only about the incident at the last meeting, but our whole relationship, how we relate and, hopefully, how we want to go forward in all of this. I hope neither of you will hold back. I want to get everything out on the table so we can deal with it as the Lord tells us."

Jack noticed Bill's raised eyebrows. "I know, Bill. I wouldn't blame you for not believing my intent today. All I can say is, I believe the Lord is using this situation to do a profound work in me, and I think He wants to do that same work in all of us . . . to draw us closer to Himself . . . and to one another. And the only way I understand that can happen is to approach this situation directly . . . together. That's what I'm hoping we can start today. So if either of you feels I'm trying to weasel out of something . . . or blame you, then please feel free to draw my attention to that. If you feel that I'm getting angry, or threatening you in any way, I want you to say so. I know I've been aggressive and intimidating in the past. The Lord has shown me that's not Him; that's not Him in me. That's my flesh, which is dead, right? I don't want to live in that anymore. Okay?"

Jack looked at Bill, then Alice. They both looked as though they were seeing something for the first time, and trying to figure out what it was. Jack stifled the smile he felt within his heart. He sensed his spirit speak to the Holy Spirit within him, *"I guess they're seeing You in me for the first time, Lord. Praise your name."*

"Anyhow, like I said, I know my behavior at the meeting was not honoring to God," Jack continued. "And it wasn't honoring to you, or anybody else, for that matter." Jack looked down at the list of things he'd written on the paper. "What I said and what I did were really disrespectful to both of you. I apologize, and I hope you can forgive me." Jack looked up from the paper at Alice and Bill, and then continued.

"I've also come to recognize that I haven't really related to you as brother and sister in the Lord."

Speaking for the first time, Bill asked, "What do you mean?"

"Well, Dick had me study some verses in the Bible that showed me the Lord has made us one in Him. . . . We're each parts of His body, together. But I gotta admit, I've never seen you that way." Jack paused and lowered his head. "I guess I haven't really seen anybody that way, exactly. Instead . . ." Jack had to swallow again, keeping his stare directed at the paper on the table before him. "Instead, I've actually seen you more as obstacles to the church's future than anything else."

Bill leaned forward. "Obstacles?" he asked with an edge to his voice.

Jack glanced up, more due to the tone in Bill's voice than his question. He drew in a deep breath and exhaled slowly. He drew another breath and proceeded. "Sounds harsh, doesn't it? Bottom line, it is harsh . . . was harsh," he corrected himself. "*Was* harsh, because I don't feel that way anymore. I'm not trying to make excuses for myself. I'm trying to explain what I was thinking and feeling, leading up to our clash at the last missions meeting. Instead of seeing you as my brother and sister in the Lord, whom God called me to be one with, I saw you trying to hang onto a time in the church that has passed, and in the process keep us from moving into the future."

Bill began to fidget in his chair and appeared ready to say something.

Jack responded, "I know, I know, Bill. That's not who you are. And it's certainly not who you are in Christ. I know that now. But I'm just saying, I didn't really realize that until the last couple weeks. Like I said, I came to see you guys as obstacles . . . and when I run into an obstacle, I try to figure some way to get around it or move it. I saw you as obstacles to the future . . . at least my version of the future. And I just want you to know I am very sorry for that. That attitude does not reflect the Lord, and it led to a disrespectful attitude toward you on my part. I apologize for that."

Bill leaned forward, placing his arms on the table and interlocked his fingers. "I'm glad to hear you finally recognize the important role we older folks play in this church, Jack. One day you'll understand how painful it is to pour your entire life into the Lord's work, and then have others come along and tell you you're no longer needed . . . or wanted, for that matter." Bill reached over and patted Alice's arm. "And you know, Jack, it's not that we don't value our young people, or see their role in the future of the church. Fact is, if it weren't for Alice, there wouldn't be much of a youth ministry today."

Alice turned, "Bill, please."

"Huh?" Jack was caught off guard by this new information. Moving his gaze from Bill to Alice, and then back to Bill, Jack asked, "What do you mean?"

Bill responded in an agitated manner, "Most of the money in the fund that was used to hire the youth pastor came from a memorial gift from Alice, when her husband, John, passed away twelve years ago. Alice expressed her desire that it be used for the youth ministry in some way."

Jack looked at Alice, amazed. "I never knew. . . ."

Bill continued, "There's a lot you don't know . . . about Alice . . . me, and a lot of the other retired folks that give of themselves behind the scenes around here. You don't know, because you don't ask. You don't ask, because you don't care. And I'm here to tell you, that doesn't feel good. It doesn't feel good at all."

Jack felt his anger rising. He was about to verbally react to Bill's accusations when Alice spoke up. "Bill, please! Your anger is showing, and I don't think it's going to help any of us if we keep reacting out of ourselves all the time." Turning to Jack, she continued, "What I think Bill is trying to say, Jack, is that it's hurtful when we feel we're not valued anymore, simply because we're considered old. It wasn't just John and me who gave into that fund. I happen to know a number of our senior citizens gave; many of them give support to the youth ministry every month. And to be told that you are considered an obstacle . . ." Her voice trailed off as she looked away.

Jack exclaimed, "That's what I'm trying to apologize for! I realize that's how I used to see you . . . but I don't see you that way anymore!" Jack looked at Alice; then to Bill, and back to Alice.

"I believe you, Jack," Alice responded. "I do appreciate your apology . . . as I'm sure Bill does, as well. Right, Bill?"

"If he means it, I do," Bill responded gruffly. He leaned back, crossed his arms over his chest, and stared at Jack.

Jack took a deep breath, trying to follow everything Dick and Jennifer suggested he do if he felt himself growing angry during the conversation. He wondered if Dick heard their voices as he sat outside the door. Jack hoped he had, and he hoped Dick was praying.

Taking another deep breath, Jack spoke directly to Bill first, trying to keep his tone controlled and respectful. "I do mean it, Bill. That's why I asked you both to meet me here today. I realize you've got good reason to be mad as heck at me. That's what I've come to apologize for. I'm hoping we can talk about some of the things that have been upsetting to me as well. But the bottom line is, I've come to recognize I contributed a lot to the conflict between us, and I want to do something constructive about correcting that, and then, hopefully, we can move forward in the Lord, together."

"That sounds wonderful, Jack," responded Alice, who then looked at Bill.

Bill looked back at Alice, and then turned his gaze to Jack. "You said something about us offending you?"

"There's a couple things I'm hoping we can discuss that would help me move forward in this. But, first, I'd like to finish what's on my list, if I may." Jack lifted the paper slightly.

"Go ahead, Jack," Alice said gently.

"There might be some specific situations that you're mad at me about . . . something I've said or done that has hurt you. And I'm more than willing to discuss each one. Okay? But the final thing on my list that I want to apologize for is my past habit of not talking to either one of you when I felt hurt or upset by things you've done or said. . . ."

"Like what?" Bill asked.

"I can share those in just a moment. But I've come to realize that when I react to what others say or do by getting frustrated, angry, or hurt, I tend to avoid dealing with those emotions at the time. The problem is, even after I get past it, I never do go back and deal with it with the folks I'm mad at. Eventually, those feelings build and I either take it out on my wife and kids, or I blow up at the person over some stupid little deal that makes no sense."

Jack took a deep breath, and continued, "I now realize this is not who I really am in Jesus. It certainly isn't who Jesus is and how He would express Himself through me. In Matthew 5, and again Matthew 18, He tells us that when there is something between us and another, we're to go to that person and deal with things directly. That's hard for me, so I haven't done it very often, if it all. There have been times when I'd get frustrated, or even feel hurt by things you would do or say . . ."

Again, Bill interrupted, "When have I ever said or done anything to hurt you?"

Alice intervened once again, "Bill, let Jack finish what he's saying. Then we can get to that. Okay?"

Bill didn't say a thing, but motioned with his hands for Jack to continue.

"Well, the point is," Jack proceeded, "I let things build between us that I shouldn't have, and it all blew at the meeting. I got angry, reacted to what you were saying, and eventually stormed out of the room. I'm sorry for that. Again, I apologize . . . and I hope we can come to some kind of agreement about how we're going to deal with those kinds of situations in the future."

"So you're planning on staying at the church . . . and the committee?" Bill asked, surprised.

"Yes . . . yes, we're staying. Kathy and I have prayed a lot about that, and we feel the Lord would have us stay and try to work things out . . . for His glory . . . you know what I mean?"

"I think I'm beginning to, Jack," Alice replied.

"Interesting," Bill murmured.

"I don't expect either of you to forgive me right away today." Turning to Bill, Jack continued, "I realize an apology is just words until it's backed up with action, right Bill?"

"Right," Bill answered.

"I really do hope you will both come to the place where you can forgive me for what I've done and said in the past. And I hope we can start over . . . start new . . . you know, like when Jesus forgives us." Jack looked at both of them, awaiting their next response.

Alice responded first. "I'd like that, Jack. And I do forgive you. And I hope you will forgive me."

"For what?" Jack and Bill asked in unison.

"I realize Jack's not the only one who contributed to this situation, Bill. I'm guilty, too."

"How do you figure?" Bill asked.

Alice went on to describe her thoughts and feelings since the day of "the incident." Jack winced a few times as she described feeling threatened by his behavior and frustrated with the dismissive attitude she felt from him. Jack felt a stab of guilt and remorse when she described feeling vulnerable due to being a widow and not having a husband who could intervene, or at least someone she could debrief with after being upset by something Jack said or did. She also described her love of children, and how she and John had "adopted" young families in the church family to substitute for their own children's families, who were scattered throughout the United States, the closest living over 1,000 miles away. It was important to her that Jack understood she was not opposed to children, or the youth ministry, as he seemed to think.

She then went on to describe her thoughts and feelings when Jack appeared to be so opposed to continuing the support of the missionaries. She described how, over the years, she'd become close personal friends with many of the missionaries, and the important work she felt they were doing for the Lord—and how dependent they were on the continued support of the church.

During this entire time, Jack remained quiet, and worked very hard to listen, as Jennifer had coached him to do. Jack knew it was very important for him to try to understand Alice's and Bill's thoughts and feelings, so he could more clearly understand the Lord's voice speaking through them. No longer seeing them as the enemy, or even as obstacles, Jack realized that, as parts of Christ's body, Jesus was expressing Himself through them, as He was through Jack.

Jack also remembered what Dick had told him about the importance of listening: that we're most open to listening when we feel we've been listened to. So if Bill and Alice were going to be open to listening to Jack's heart, he was going to need to put all the energy he could muster into listening to them. It was difficult at times, not only because Jack didn't have much experience with it yet, but also because he so wanted to react to some of what he was hearing. Sometimes Alice was inaccurate in her judgments of Jack's motives and beliefs, and his natural reaction was to defend himself by attacking her wrong ideas. But today Jack was aware of the fourth person in the room, the Lord Jesus Christ. Jack turned to Him every time he was tempted to react in himself, rather than respond in Jesus.

"Well, that's a lot more than I planned to say. But I hope you understand my position on the youth ministry, and why I am so passionate about continuing our long support of our missionaries. Jack, I recognize you're not the only one who avoids conflict, and then experiences the negative results of doing so. I do that as well. I've done it with you . . . and I suppose with you, too, Bill." Bill had a surprised look on his face.

Turning back to Jack, Alice continued, "I realized before I left the church that day that reacting angrily by verbally attacking you in front of everyone was the worst thing I could have done. I think I realized it while I was doing it. But I just couldn't stop the words and put them back in my mouth."

Jack smiled, nodding in agreement. In the past he hadn't even thought about the impact of his words. But there had been a few times recently that he, too, wished he could reach out and grab them before they made it to the other person's ears.

"Yeah, too bad He didn't make us with a rewind button," Bill chuckled.

"That would be nice. But, Jack, it was wrong for me to act that way. I want you to know I'm deeply sorry. I confessed it to the Lord that very night, and asked Him to forgive me. I should have called you right away, but I just couldn't. I apologize for that as well. I hope you can forgive me." Alice grabbed a fresh tissue, blew her nose, and then grabbed a second to dry her eyes.

Silence became the cloak covering each person's feelings. No one looked at another, as they sorted through their thoughts and emotions. Jack eventually broke the silence. "I really appreciate what you said, Alice. It sounds like this whole thing has been pretty upsetting to you."

"Yes, it has," she said quietly.

"And it sounds like you have felt threatened in the past by the way I come across. . . . Kathy says I'm like a bull in a china shop sometimes."

Alice nodded. "But I want to correct one thing. It's not like I have felt physically threatened by you. I've never felt you were going to do anything physical; it's been more emotional. Does that make sense?"

"Painfully so," Jack responded. He was crushed at the thought of the impact he'd had on this dear woman. "I'm so, so sorry Alice."

"I believe you, Jack. I can't begin to tell you how healing it is to me to hear you say that, and to see how serious you appear to be."

For the third time in their conversation, they grew silent. But this time, Jack and Alice exchanged smiles. Both felt the pent-up emotion within them draining away in moments. Jack felt the sudden freedom within his heart he'd experienced when he first began to talk things out with Kathy, or the conversation with his children; it wasn't unlike the feeling he had experienced when first saved.

Alice was overwhelmed with relief, and a sense of joy. This experience wasn't anything like what she feared it might be. *"So Lord,"* she thought, *"why did I fear this so much when it is so obvious You are in the midst of it all. Thank you, Lord. Thank you."*

Jack looked at Bill, waiting for him to say what was on his mind.

18

Though he felt relieved and elated about his reconciliation with Alice, Jack was still nervous as he looked at Bill. Jack wasn't sure how to interpret the look on Bill's face, or his body language. He assumed Bill was angry, and perhaps unimpressed by what had just occurred. He also remembered another of the lessons Dick and Jennifer had taught him about checking out his assumptions before acting on them as though they were accurate.

He turned to Bill. "So, Bill, where are you in all of this? Can you share . . ."

Bill interrupted, "I'd like to hear what you think I've done to upset you or hurt your feelings. You've made reference to that a couple times already. And I think what I have to share will depend upon what that's all about." Bill's arms remained crossed. His eyes never left Jack's.

Jack felt anxiety growing, from the restriction in his throat to the tightness in the back of his neck and the knot developing in his stomach. As coached by Jennifer and Dick, he took a couple of long, deep breaths to begin relaxing his body. He also asked silently, *"Lord, please express Yourself through me, and don't let me react from my flesh."*

"If that's what you want, then I guess I can do that now. But I would like to hear what you have to share. I really do want to see if we can work things out between us." Bill remained as he was, continuing his stare at Jack. Jack took another deep breath. "Well, here's the thing; for a long time I've felt that you and Alice saw me as the enemy. Therefore, any idea I came up with, it seemed like you were automatically against it, without hearing me out."

"That's not true," Bill interjected. He uncrossed his arms, straightened himself in his chair, and leaned forward. "I wasn't automatically against your ideas, Jack. I'm not sure Alice was either." He glanced Alice's way. Her head was moving from side to side. "I didn't think so. So you see, Jack, there's something else you didn't know about us."

Bill's comment struck Jack like a knife to the chest. He started to react, as the impulse to defend himself threatened to take control. Instead he gripped the arms of his chair, and clamped down his jaws, until the emotional surge passed. *"You are peace, Lord. You are my peace,"* he prayed.

Bill continued, "I'm not sure why you felt we were against your ideas all the time. Yeah, there were some, from time to time, that seemed a bit out there for our small church. It's like I told you then, it seems like you always wanted to do the same things the big mega-churches do, with all their money. But we're not a mega-church. Probably never will be. But just because some of your ideas were unrealistic for our church, doesn't mean we were against them all. After all, didn't we support the youth mission trips to Mexico? That was originally your idea, wasn't it?" Jack nodded.

"And what about the church softball team? Aren't you planning a softball team for some church league? Haven't we been fully supportive of those opportunities to reach out to our community? And they've all come from you, right?"

"Yes . . . yes, they have," Jack responded. "I've appreciated the support. But how many times have I brought up something, and the first thing you ask is how much it is going to cost?"

"Because I've learned that most of your ideas cost a lot of money . . . money we don't have, I might add." Bill was becoming more agitated, moving forward in his chair, his voice growing louder.

"Bill . . . I haven't come to argue with you. I was hoping we could all share the things that have been hurtful and upsetting to each of us . . . seek some resolution of the issues we have, and hopefully reconcile our relationships to the glory of Jesus Christ, and the health of the church." Jack looked straight at Bill. Bill looked away.

"I hear you saying that you have felt a lot of my ideas were too costly to consider . . ."

"Because they were," Bill interrupted.

Jack took a deep breath, and looked at Alice. She raised her eyebrows, and offered a bit of a smile. *Go ahead, Jack*, she thought, *but be careful.*

"Maybe . . . maybe not. But that's the point I'm trying to make. It seems to me that anytime you feel the idea seems to cost too much, you shut down the discussion. We don't ever discuss any ideas of how to pay for 'em . . ."

Bill interrupted once again: "Because your solution is to stop supporting the missionaries, and use those funds for your youth projects. And we're not about to do that."

"That's not true!" Jack blurted. "I only questioned the continued support of those particular projects because, when I asked around, it seemed like most people didn't even know who they were, or what they were doing with the money we sent them." Jack's pulse was suddenly pounding. His breath was growing shallow and frequent. His throat was constricting, and his mouth was getting dry. At first, he didn't recognize the symptoms Dick had described of someone reacting to stress or a perceived threat.

Bill's agitation was increasing as well. Responding curtly, he said, "Well, I don't know who you were talking to, but all they'd have to do is read their monthly newsletters or attend the annual missions banquet to know all there is to know about the wonderful work the Highlands are doing in South America."

Part of Jack wanted to take a broad swipe at the quality and usefulness of the church newsletter, which so few members read. Jack was aware that Bill's wife, June, helped organize it each month, and he wanted to react by questioning the newsletter's value for informing the church family in a day of e-mails and text messages. Another part of him remembered to say nothing—to relax and focus on Jesus.

A single thought suddenly popped into his mind: *How would Jesus desire to express Himself through you at this moment?* Jack thought to himself, *Yes Lord, how would You like me to respond in You right now?*

Another thought entered his mind: *Bill isn't hearing your heart.* To himself he responded, *Of course he isn't. He's a bullheaded, opinionated . . .*

Another thought: *And you think this is the way I want to express myself to Bill right now?*

Jack was caught short when that thought entered his mind. He looked across the table at Bill, who was visibly agitated. *Please, Lord,* Jack prayed, *help me to see Bill as You see him—and to respond in You rather than react in myself.*

In as calm a voice as he could muster at the moment, Jack looked at Bill and asked, "It sounds to me, Bill, that you think I am opposed to continuing the support of the missionaries, and instead want to use that money for local youth ministries. Is that accurate?"

"That's what you said at the last meeting." Bill shifted in his seat, leaning closer to Alice.

"No, not exactly. I . . ."

"Well, that's what I heard. Isn't that what you heard, Alice?" Bill rose up in his seat and turned to look at Alice.

Alice looked painfully uncomfortable with the development of this conversation, and didn't appear ready to answer Bill's question. So Jack responded, "It may have been what you heard. I'm not arguing that. I can only say that's not what I was *trying* to say. And I'd like you both to know I am not against the Highlands at all."

"So why did you say you were?" Bill asked, confused.

Jack had to deal with the frustration rising within him once again. *Help me, Lord*, he prayed. "I don't believe I did, Bill. I do remember Pastor Tim expressing the need for us to examine our mission budget and review our priorities. And in the context of that conversation, I did ask if that also included the foreign mission support, as well as the local stuff we were doing. It seems to me that's when things started to turn south."

"That's when Alice stood up in support of the Highlands, you mean." Bill looked toward Alice.

Alice was looking at Jack, and when Bill spoke, she slowly turned to face him. "Actually, Bill, that's when I began to defend my own interests." Bill was surprised by her response, and slowly settled back into his chair with a puzzled look on his face.

"What do you mean, Alice?" Jack asked. Jack was as surprised by her response as Bill was.

"As I said earlier, Jack, I now realize neither my actions nor my motives were as pure as I first believed they were. You are right; Pastor Tim did suggest we review our mission priorities, in light of the Lord's direction, as well as the financial issues we've been facing. I'll admit my anxieties began to go up when he first mentioned this at the beginning of the meeting, because

I realize the Highlands receive the major share of our mission budget each year. I was afraid that if there needed to be any cutbacks, we may have to seriously look at this."

Turning to Bill, she continued, "I didn't want to do that, Bill. But that's the real problem. *I* didn't want to do it. Not we, the committee. Not the Lord. Me. My focus that day was really more about me, and what I wanted, or what I thought the Lord wanted, more than about discovering what the Lord wanted . . . or what the committee decided together. Do you see that, Bill? If I would have had my focus on Jesus, instead of on what I thought was best, we may never have had that big squabble in the first place." Alice grabbed a handful of tissue and began to wipe her eyes.

Jack and Bill sat there slack-jawed. An uncomfortably long period of silence followed. Finally Bill said simply, "Well, I'll be."

Continuing to look at Alice, Bill asked, "So you're ready to forgive and forget, and just move on? Just like that?"

"I hope not," Jack interjected.

Bill and Alice both looked at him, surprised.

"I mean that," Jack continued. "I hope we come to recognize what we've done, confess what was our own doing and not Jesus, and repent. And I certainly hope we can come to the place where we can forgive one another . . . completely . . . no matter how long that takes. But I hope we don't just forget all this. I hope we can talk about what got us to the place where we saw each other as the enemy, rather than brother and sister in Christ. Most importantly, I hope we can talk about what we can do differently, so we don't repeat the same stuff and end up having another blowup some day."

Alice was nodding in agreement. Bill was quiet. This entire experience hadn't been anything like what he'd expected. First, Jack was confessing and apologizing, rather than defending and attacking. Then Alice confessed her own contributions to the conflict, rather than blaming Jack. And now she seemed to be taking responsibility for the whole fiasco. Bill was emotionally drained and quite confused. He came into this meeting prepared to hold Jack accountable for every offense he held against him. But much of that fight lost its energy when Jack acknowledged most of those issues, took responsibility, and apologized for his behavior.

Now Bill felt a different struggle going on within his spirit. While Jack earlier acknowledged his contributions to the conflict, Bill was remembering some of the Scriptures he'd been studying, having to do with how Christians were to treat one another. As angry as he had been at Jack prior to this meeting, he had to admit Jack's present behavior was far more reflective of the spirit of those Scriptures than was his own. This was confusing and troubling to Bill—and all the more so when Alice recognized her self-centered motives in defending the Highlanders, resulting in her attitude toward Jack at the meeting.

But what about his own attitude, his own spirit, in all of this? On the one hand, Bill felt right in being angry at Jack for his past actions. But now that Jack had apologized, how could Bill continue to hold that past behavior against him? On the other hand, he still felt offended, hurt, and angry, and he didn't know what to do with those feelings. What would June say if Bill just forgave Jack and decided to try to move forward in their dealings with one another? Bill could hear her now. She'd consider him weak and not able to stand up to Jack. And what about the others in the church who knew of this whole mess? Wouldn't they think the same thing about Bill?

"Uh . . . we've been going at this for a while now. And I don't know about the two of you, but I need a short break to visit the bathroom. Do you mind?" Bill pushed back in his chair as he prepared to stand.

"No . . . no . . . not at all. That's a good idea, actually," Jack responded.

"Yes, I could use a break myself. I'd like to get another glass of water," Alice said. "Can I get you both a glass?"

"Yes, I'd appreciate that," Jack answered.

"I can get my own, Alice," Bill said as he exited the room.

After they all returned to the room following their break, Jack spoke first. "You know, during the break I was thinking about some of the things you said, Bill."

"Really. Like what?" Bill asked.

"Mostly, I was trying to see things from your perspective. I guess I can see why you thought I was against the Highlands, and hoping to get their support shifted to the youth ministry. I have to admit, if I'd been in your shoes and had been supporting them as you have all these years—and I thought someone was trying to destroy all that in order to try some new ideas I figured were half-baked to begin with—I'd probably have reacted even more than you did. I also have to admit, I forgot along the way the times you both have supported new ideas I've brought to the committee . . . sometimes even when others were really against them. I don't remember if I ever took the time to thank you both when that happened."

Jack first looked at Alice. "So, thank you." Alice smiled in return.

Turning to Bill, Jack said, "Thanks, Bill. And forgive me for not acknowledging your support in the past—and for forgetting it along the way, too."

Bill leaned forward in his chair, and placed his forearms on the table, with his palms up. "You know something, Jack? I think that's about the first time anyone has ever thanked me for anything I've done in this church. I don't do it for any personal attention, but I have to admit, it feels good to realize somebody cares."

"Oh, we all care, Bill," Alice interjected.

"Yeah, we do. But, like me, most of us don't ever take the time to acknowledge it." Jack smiled at Bill. When he did, he noticed a softening in Bill's body language. "The truth is, you both have given a great deal of your life to this church. We younger folks don't always appreciate the sacrifice you've made here all these years."

Bill nodded knowingly and appeared ready to say something, then simply leaned back into his chair and remained quiet. He appeared to be thinking deeply about something.

A few moments passed. Jack looked at Bill and then Alice, and it was like seeing them for the first time. Maybe he was seeing them for the first time. He realized he was seeing them as the brother and sister in Christ they were to him. He realized he actually felt love for them. He felt a growing desire to get to know them better—and to work with them more effectively in responding to the Lord's leading.

"I suspect there's more each of you may want to discuss, and I'm open to whatever that might be. But I just want you both to know, again, I'm really sorry for the unChristlike way I've treated you both. I hope you can forgive me. I hope we can work things out, so we can continue to work together in the future—but this time do it as one in Christ, rather than individually."

"I'd like that, Jack," Alice replied. She then turned to Bill.

"I'd like that, too," Bill said, "but I'm not sure what to do about it from here. I mean it's all right and good what's happening here right now, but what's going to happen the next time you bring one of your mega-church ideas to the committee, and I ask you how we're going to pay for it?" Bill asked this with a smile on his face, the first full smile he'd expressed since walking into this meeting a couple hours earlier.

Alice turned toward him, alarmed, until she saw his smile and realized he was teasing—a little.

Jack chuckled, "I'm going to suggest you write a personal check."

Bill snorted, "That'll be the day." And then he joined in the laughter filling the room.

Jack turned serious. "So Bill, let me ask you a question. When I do come to the committee with an idea, how can I present it so I feel like it will get a fair hearing, and not just be dismissed out of hand, or seen as a direct threat to the Highlanders?"

"That's a good question," Bill replied. He thought for a moment. "Fact is, anybody can bring an idea to the committee, and the committee should be willing to fully discuss each one. Right?" Bill didn't wait for a response from Jack or Alice. "And it's sounding to me like the committee may even need to revisit the support we give the Highlanders." Turning to Alice, he asked, "Right, Alice?"

"As much as it pains me to consider it, yes, that would only be fair in light of what Pastor Tim was asking us to do at the last meeting." She paused. "Prayerfully, I might add."

Jack nodded.

Bill continued, "That's for sure. It appears to me we haven't been doing near enough of that . . . not together as a group anyhow. You know, a couple of those Bible references Dick asked us to read in preparing for this meeting got me thinking. I don't remember the last time we prayed as a group to ask the Lord what He wanted us to do regarding the mission work of the church. I'm not talking about the token prayer that we start each meeting with, either. I'm talking about spending some time together in prayer, listening to what the Lord may have to say to us. What do you think of that?"

"Sounds pretty radical to me, Bill. You think we're up to it?" This time it was Jack who was smiling.

"It sounds wonderful . . . exciting," Alice replied. "I'm getting goose-bumps just thinking about it. Imagine what it would be like to actually hear from the Lord and know that what we're doing came directly from Him."

"Just like in the Bible, you mean?" Bill responded.

"Yes, just like that. Imagine . . ." Alice looked off as though she were seeing something very real, but not with human eyes.

"May I return our discussion to an earlier topic, for just a moment?" Jack asked.

Alice and Bill both gave him a look that encouraged him to go on.

"Just to make sure I'm clear on something, am I to believe you both no longer assume I oppose the Highlanders and am only interested in my own youth ministry ideas?"

Bill cleared his throat. "I believed you when you explained your position on them." Bill paused a moment. "But to be honest, I guess there is a question in my mind . . . it's not that I don't trust you anymore . . . I . . . I . . . well, I guess I don't really know what I mean for sure. I guess it's just going to take some time to get past the old feelings."

"Well, I suspect we're all going to have some old feelings continuing to play while we figure out some new ways to work together," Jack replied. "I just want things to be clear between us. I want you to know: I'm not against the Highlanders personally—nor am I against continuing our support of them. But I do have to admit it has seemed to me that, in the past, reconsidering our involvement with them has been off limits. And that's all I was questioning."

"I think we understand that more clearly now. Don't we, Alice?"

"Yes. I think we have come to discover we were all assuming a great deal of one another."

Bill asked, "So I'm wondering: How do we prevent that kind of thing from occurring again? Sounds to me like it comes pretty natural to all of us."

"I don't know," Jack replied. "But I'm convinced, after visiting with Dick and Jennifer a couple times, we can learn better ways than that to communicate with one another. I know I'd prefer you guys checking things out with me any time you wonder where I'm coming from, rather than just assuming the worst."

"Me, too," Bill responded.

"So maybe that's the answer to your question," Alice added.

"What question?" Bill asked.

"What we can do to prevent these blow ups from occurring in the future," Alice responded. "We can agree that we'll no longer assume anything of one another, but instead try and clarify what we're thinking and feeling."

"Sounds good to me," Jack replied.

"Probably easier said than done, though, don't you think?" Bill added. "It's not like we have a lot of experience in being that open and direct with one another."

"That's true," Jack replied. "But I'm convinced the Lord has made us one in Him. And as parts of His body, doesn't it make sense that we would find ways to connect rather than compete with each other?"

Bill slid to the front of his chair. "So, perhaps, what we need to do is . . . ."

Alice sat silently, simply enjoying the new energy that had suddenly filled the room. Without knowing exactly when, she was now fully aware that something profoundly important and powerful had taken place. She couldn't ever remember Jack and Bill visiting as comfortably with one another as she was now witnessing. As short as an hour before, she was fearful the meeting was going to degenerate into another blowup. Now they were carrying on like best friends.

Within her spirit she prayed: *Lord Jesus, thank you so very much for this wonderful experience. Truly, I now know, not only Your peace, but, more importantly, I know You as my peace . . . our peace. Thank you, Lord, for being our peace . . . and for allowing us to experience You in this way today. May what has occurred here be but the beginning of Your miracle of peace in our hearts, as well as the very heart and spirit of our entire church family.*

As soon as she prayed these words, the thought entered her mind, and she immediately spoke it to Jack and Bill. "What about sharing this with the rest of the church?"

Jack and Bill were in the midst of brainstorming ideas about how to improve their communication, as well as the committee's, when Alice interrupted with her question. "Huh?" they both responded.

"Share what with whom?" Bill asked.

"I just had the thought that because the majority of the church knows about what took place at the meeting . . . and especially since it seems to have set off a wildfire of conflicts in the church . . ."

"Now, just wait a minute, Alice," Bill interrupted. "I don't think it's fair to pin all that's happened on us."

"I'm not, Bill," Alice replied. "But I'm also aware that there's widespread conflict and unrest in our church family. While the conditions have probably been there a long time, our little episode seems to have served as the match that ignited all the others. And our church family is hurting terribly. Wouldn't you agree?"

"Without a doubt," Jack responded.

"Of course we agree, Alice," Bill said. "You'd have to be dumber than a mud fence to not be aware of the folks who've left the church. But, again, I ask what's that got to do with us? What do you expect us to do? And what do you want to share?"

"I'm not sure just yet. But it seems to me we've experienced a miracle here today. Look at the two of you. Up until about thirty minutes ago, I don't think there was much love lost between you two. Now look at you. You act like you're long-lost friends catching up on lost time."

Bill and Jack looked at one another. They both began to laugh.

"I guess she's right," Bill commented.

"Yeah, whoda thunk?" Jack added. They all laughed together.

"So don't you both think our church family needs a miracle like what we've experienced today? At the least, don't they need to know about this miracle?"

Again, Jack and Bill looked at one another, then at Alice. Jack eventually spoke up: "I think you're raising something important, Alice. But I guess I'm like Bill, I'm not sure what should be shared, or who it should be shared with. Do we share with the whole congregation? Or should we just share with the mission committee what's taken place here today. After all, they were involved in the original situation. So I guess, at a minimum, they need to be told that things are getting resolved, so we can start working on resolving any issues that they may have connected with all this."

"Yeah," Bill added, "and if the first situation was any hint at the future, once the mission committee knows about it, the whole church will know about it in an hour or two anyhow." Jack and Bill both chuckled. Alice slowly moved her head back and forth, with a pained expression on her face.

Noticing her reaction, Jack said, "Uh . . . I guess it's really not that funny, is it?"

Alice responded in a quiet voice, "What you have observed is accurate . . . and only further points to the need to wisely decide what information we're going to share, with whom, and when. I'd also like to suggest we invite Dick in to join us. We could start by sharing our good news with him. I'm sure he'll be pleased. And we could see what ideas he has regarding where to go from here."

Jack spoke, "I think that's a great idea. What d'ya think, Bill?"

"I think it's a great idea, too," Bill responded.

Jack leaned forward, looking directly at Bill. "So . . . are we at a different place now, where we can start relating as brothers in the Lord? I know we still may have some work to do in talking out some past issues . . . but are we at a new place where we can start developing a more healthy and Christ-like relationship with one another?"

For a moment, both men studied one another. Without a word spoken, both felt a strong bonding between their spirits. Bill stood up and held out his hand, offering a handshake to Jack. A grin filled Jack's face as he stood and walked around the table. They both gripped one another's hand in a strong shake, and then bear-hugged one another, concluding with slapping each other on the back. As they separated, both men had tears in their eyes and smiles on their faces.

"Can I get in on this?" Alice asked. She stood and joined the two men, who both threw an arm around her, and then one another. "Who would have thought?" she said.

They invited Dick to join them, and excitedly told their story, each one interrupting the other to add their experience. Dick was overwhelmed with joy. He was always optimistic when God's children involved themselves in His process of making peace, as the Lord promised in Matthew 18:20 to always be present in their midst. But even Dick was surprised at the transformation begun in the lives of these three in just a few hours of open and honest sharing. Truly, the Lord had accomplished a powerful work in them this day. Dick prayed, *May this be just the beginning . . . just the beginning, Lord.*

About the Author

Rich Carroll has served as pastor of Lake Shore Community Church, Vancouver, WA, since 1979. Since 2000, Rich has directed Peace Connections Ministries, Lake Shore's outreach to their brothers and sisters in Christ who are struggling with the effects of unresolved conflict. Rich is a volunteer mediator with Community Mediation Services, Vancouver, having completed his basic certification training there in 2002. In 2003, he received certification as a Christian Mediator from Peacemaker Ministries, Inc. Rich is a member of the Washington Mediation Association, certified to mediate in the areas of Church, Family, Community, and Education. He has created an 8-hour introductory seminar entitled, "Approaching Our Conflicts In Christ," as well as a number of trainings for equipping relational peacemakers in the local church. Rich has worked as a mediator and conflict consultant with over 40 congregations, as well as a number of denominational jurisdictions.

About Peace Connections Ministries

Peace Connections Ministries, begun in 2000 by Lake Shore Community Church, Vancouver, WA, is a church-based ministry offering Christians a process of resolving issues and reconciling relationships that is Spirit-led and biblically based. Using biblical principles of relational peacemaking, Peace Connections Ministries equips Christians to respond to conflict in a manner that glorifies God, resolves issues, reconciles relationships, and reveals more deeply who Jesus is and who we are together in Him.

For more information, go to
www.peaceconnectionsministries.com

To order additional copies of this title call:
1-877-421-READ (7323)
or please visit our Web site at
www.winepressbooks.com

If you enjoyed this quality custom-published book,
drop by our Web site for more books and information.

www.winepressgroup.com
"Your partner in custom publishing."